The Disney Version

The Disney Version

THE LIFE, TIMES, ART AND COMMERCE OF
WALT DISNEY　　　　　　　　*Third Edition*
BY

RICHARD SCHICKEL

ELEPHANT PAPERBACKS
Ivan R. Dee, Publisher, Chicago

First ELEPHANT PAPERBACK edition published 1997 by Ivan R. Dee, Inc.,
1332 North Halsted Street, Chicago 60622. Manufactured in the United States
of America and printed on acid-free paper.

Library of Congress Cataloging-in-Publication Data:
Schickel, Richard.
    The Disney version : the life, times, art, and commerce of Walt
Disney / by Richard Schickel. — 3rd ed.
        p. cm.
    "Elephant paperbacks."
    Includes bibliographical references and index.
    ISBN 1-56663-158-0
    1. Disney, Walt, 1901–1966. 2. Animators—United States—
Biography. I. Title.
NC1766.U52D555 1997
791.43'092—dc21
    [B]   96-52429

Contents

Introduction to the Third Edition

IT IS HARD to believe that Walt Disney has been dead these thirty years, so ubiquitous does his name remain, so powerful is the corporation that continues to bear that name. It is just as hard for me to believe that the book about him that I began in the last year of his life, and published the year after his passing, is still alive, reissued now for the second time since its original edition went out of print.

The afterlife of *The Disney Version* is, naturally, pleasing to me. In *Enemies of Promise* the English *littérateur* Cyril Connolly set as his—any—serious writer's only worthwhile goal the creation of a book that "lasted" ten years, the while decrying the forces that make its accomplishment so difficult—especially in modern times. Indeed, when I recall the breezy confidence of the fairly young man who did not yet know how difficult writing a book could—and perhaps should—be, and remember that this one was completed with what seems to me, looking back, alarming ease, its survival for a span exceeding Connolly's ideal by a multiple of three is more than pleasing. It seems pretty close to miraculous.

For in the mid-sixties, when Richard Kluger, then an editor at Simon and Schuster, proposed that I write a book about Walt Disney and his works, it was not a self-evidently promising idea. In those days Disney was one of the great unexamined premises of American life. He was the man who had built a better mouse, and, in the postwar years, a better—if by more recent standards, quite modest—entertainment conglomerate. He had therefore prospered, just as folk wisdom decreed that any talented inventor-entrepreneur inevitably must. There was no perceivable public demand for a closer examination of his success story—most Americans were completely content with their image of Uncle Walt as a benign purveyor of family entertainment who had been justifiably rewarded for his efforts. So the morally gratifying story of his rise and triumph was blandly, endlessly repeated in the popular press, which offers almost no thoughtful portrayals of the man or probing reports on his accomplishments. Worse, tales like Disney's were deemed uninteresting by the literary-intellectual community, which did not often apply its analytical skills to his creations or think at all seriously about what effect they might be having on the tone and texture of American life. It was smart and brave of Dick to believe there might possibly be a market for something that looked at Disney and his works a little more rigorously. And, if I say so myself, it was smart and brave of me to agree with him. But we got a lot of puzzled looks and dim responses when we discussed our project with friends and colleagues.

This indifference to what became for a couple of years my ruling passion turned into a benison. I became a man with a mission. I wanted to prove the doubters wrong. And, yes, I wanted to make a little fuss at the fringe of the Disney empire. It's always fun to make rude noises in pious realms. And, besides, I thought I might gain a little notoriety by so doing—something largely unknown writers need to do.

But I never thought of *The Disney Version* as a radical critique of the man or the institution he ruled so obsessively. I'm not a radical by nature—certainly not in the careless sense that the term was used in the sixties. I was—and am—a liberal of what has become a rather outmoded sort. My ambition was social commentary—skeptical, iconoclastic, civilly "controversial"—within a critical tradition I admired. So I was somewhat startled by the strong response to the book.

By the time it was published I had become a movie reviewer and found myself banned, for a time, from Disney screening rooms. This I wore as a badge of honor. On the other hand, the employee who arranged a week-long tour of Disney operations in Los Angeles—where Walt himself proposed that I ally myself with *Reader's Digest*, whose publishing arm was thinking of doing a book about him—was fired for encouraging me. This, I thought, was a badge of shame on the company, though its behavior was perhaps predictable. Such criticism as it had previously endured had come from the cultural margins—Marxists, for example, and child psychologists, and other easily ignored sources. It had never dealt with lengthy, broad-scale criticism from a source that was both independent and mainstream. Moreover, the founder had died suddenly while the book was in preparation, and it seemed to his heirs, both corporate and familial, that something more hagiographic was in order at that moment.

The reaction from other quarters was more interesting. "About time," was the line implicitly taken by many of the book's reviewers, who were all in all quite welcoming. But the response of non-professional readers was even more heartening. I was doing some lecturing at colleges in those days, and inevitably some earnest film student would approach me after my appearance to tell me that the book had special meaning for him or her. They had all been raised on Disney's works and were now at that stage in life where, naturally, they were questioning the values—and the cultural objects—their parents, their society had pressed upon them. As grown-ups some of these same people still seek me out to praise a book that struck a questioning note at a questioning and impressionable time in their lives. Similarly, for many years I served as a sort of anti-Disney for the press, constantly asked to comment on new developments in the corporate story. Nothing I have ever written has had this continuing relevance.

Not having reread *The Disney Version* for many years, a curious thing occurred to me when I did so recently; I had begun to forget what I had actually written, and had also begun to mistake other people's readings of my work for my actual intentions and accomplishment. Looking at it now, the book seems far less an attack on Disney than either his supporters or his enemies took it to be, much more the judicious questioning of his myth and achievements that I always meant it to be. Indeed, I still feel now what I felt when I finished my work—that my portrait of Walt Disney flattered him precisely because it granted him a complexity of character and motivation that no one had previously offered. I also feel now, as I did then, that for all my criticisms, my portrayal was shot through with admiration for him and his achievements. We sprang from similar Midwestern soil and had certain inhibitions and ambitions, certain blindnesses and visions in common. In other words, I thought an authentic sympathy mingled with the various exasperations of my portrait. The publication a few years ago of a scabrous biography of Disney, a book which had him wandering the underground passageways of his studio and theme park, drunk and raving paranoia, a figure partaking it seemed to me in equal measure of King Lear and Howard Hughes, further confirmed my belief in the balance and fundamental accuracy of my portrayal.

This is not to say that I would draw it in exactly the same way now. Witnessing the long, slow decline of his company in the two decades between Walt Disney's death and the accession of the Michael Eisner–Frank Wells regime in 1984, a period in which a cautious and uninspired management overstressed one portion of Walt's legacy—his moral and cultural conservatism—at the expense of the other—his innovative enthusiasm—I came to think that I had been too critical of the young Walt. Yes, there was something all too often hard and joyless in his pursuit of his ambitions. And, yes, he was essentially an untutored man, whose taste was not without a broad vulgar streak. But when I wrote I did not sufficiently acknowledge, I think, the obstacles he had to overcome, particularly in establishing what amounted to a new movie form—the feature-length animated film. Certainly I was in those days unaware of how exceptional it was for a man operating a small, and by industry standards marginal, company to undertake such a daunting task. To put it simply, he was more entitled than I knew to his frets, frustrations, and furies. Indeed, seen from today's perspective, when Hollywood is increasingly ruled by committees of "development" executives whose chief duty is to see that nothing untoward, or singular, develops on their watch, when the same cautious climate prevails over much of American life, his doughty independence seems even more admirable.

So do those first animated features. In the years since I wrote, critical opinion about them has shifted decisively, and I believe correctly, to a much more positive view of them. When I wrote, I allowed myself to be influenced too heavily, I believe, by the folkloristic purists, who judged these films to be too warm and cuddly, not as dark and dangerous as some of their fairytale sources. That's true, of course, but I underemphasized the purely cinematic joy of these movies—their sometimes fierce comic energy set against the careful, often elegant, draftsmanship of their backgrounds. A classic standard was being established in these films, and if for a time the studio clung too closely to its conventions, was not open enough to alternative styles, it has informed and inspired a newer generation of Disney animators, providing them the base on which to build such recent delights as *Beauty and the Beast*. Some of these newer films, while retaining the pictorial beauty of the classics, have in their humorous passages an anarchic exuberance—even sometimes a nice, self-referential irony— that frequently surpasses their earlier models. One may still feel a

5

certain queasiness about some of the stories the studio chooses to make—*The Lion King*, for example, with the little animals enthusiastically worshiping the big animals for whom they are most basically fodder—but who can gainsay the technical sophistication of the imagery in these latter-day films?

Who, on the other hand, can gainsay the power of Disney's theme parks, the technology that drives them and entrances their vast audience? Apparently I could. And did in 1968. Though the book is highly critical of Disneyland (then the only operation of its kind that was up and running) and its sanitization of experience, it assuredly did not see the power of this idea. A vast industry is now engaged in replicating these parks, under many managements, all over the world—particularly, peculiarly, in the emerging nations on the far side of the Pacific Rim. And that says nothing about the competition nearer to home. Or about the proliferation of theme restaurants and hostelries scattered over landscapes both near and far. I had no idea, at the time I wrote, about the mass audience's need to have history and the wilderness and, yes, ideas tamed, turned into safe, sane, comfortably manageable venues. Nor did I see then how computerization of every kind would accelerate the creation of these parallel universes, world—or should I say worlds?—without end.

It did occur to me, a few years after the book was published, when I was having a brief run as the Anti-Disney, someone reporters could call up when they needed a cautionary comment on the lastest Disney brainstorm, that dulling effects of the Disnification of experience could ultimately have political ramifications far beyond the founder's imaginings, which I continue to believe had no hidden, or even unconscious, agenda of this sort. "When fascism comes to America," I told one interviewer, "it'll be wearing mouse ears." By which I meant that we were in danger not of amusing ourselves to death, as Neal Postman would have it, but to stupefaction. And that in that condition, we would be more easy prey for evil ideologues.

Can't solely blame Disney for leading us toward that state. Can't, however, entirely exculpate him either. He surely helped create a climate where it is increasingly difficult to breathe free. And it is surely difficult to imagine him regretting, or even realizing, the implications of what he did. However vaulting his technological imagination, his social imagination was profoundly stunted.

It is, however, possible to imagine him less than happy with the shape his company has taken in the last decade and a half. This may strike the reader as an odd notion. Since money and power were never entirely absent from Disney's calculations, his company's growth under Michael Eisner's stewardship, during which it has become the world's second largest entertainment and communications complex, owner of, among many other entities, the very television network (ABC) that Walt had in some desperation turned to for the financing he needed to create Disneyland, would tempt us to imagine the founder completely content with the afterlife of his creation.

But I'm not so sure about that. The pages that follow are full of his contempt for bankers and financiers, those cautious, temporizing men who so often looked askance at his vaulting ambitions. More than that, this book offers a portrait of a man determined to exercise day-to-day (sometimes, it seemed, minute-to-minute) control of his empire. He would have been, one imagines, alternately bored and furious at spending his life fussing over the complexities of modern, large-scale corporate finance. And one can only imagine the unhappiness of the man who virtually invented the multimedia entertainment company at his inability to exercise detailed command of Disney's many ventures into media that he probably never imagined. And that, finally, says nothing about the fact that his company, trying to remain competitive in a culture where the bleak and ambiguous tenets of postmodernism now infect our formerly cheery and morally simple popular culture, creates all kinds of works that he would surely disapprove.

It is possible that had Walt Disney lived his full span he might have chosen to stay small—keep his company a chipper mouse in

7

a cozy niche as it were—rather than venture forth on the larger, wilder seas of the modern media world. Entrepreneurs, like movie stars, have their brief, ascendant moments, and it could be that Walt Disney, for all his daring, had reached, at the age of sixty-five, when he died, an age of caution as well. About that, one can only speculate. What is beyond speculation is that he was, for good or ill—most likely an exquisitely complex blend of both—one of the most significant shaping forces in American culture in the middle third of this century, and that his ever lengthening shadow continues to shade it in curious and intriguing ways. Three decades after the fact, I still regard this book as no more than a first word on a subject about which, I suspect, there will never be a definitive last word. But, all modesty (and second thoughts) aside, I also regard it as a sharp and serious word, and I hope the reader will agree with this mature assessment, even as, perhaps, he argues with the much younger me who wrote what follows.

RICHARD SCHICKEL

Los Angeles
November 1996

Foreword

If one thing is more amazing than the warm, wonderful, heart-stopping motion pictures of Walt Disney, it is the man who made them.

What kind of man is this who has won the Medal of Freedom—highest civilian award in the United States—29 motion picture Academy Awards; four TV Emmys; scores of citations from many nations; and some 700 other awards. Who has been decorated by the French Legion of Honor and again by the Art Workers Guild of London; has received honorary degrees from Harvard, Yale and the University of Southern California; wears Mexico's Order of the Aztec Eagle; and counts his citations from patriotic, educational and professional societies and international film festivals by the hundreds?

On the surface, believe it or not, Walt Disney is a very simple man—a quiet, pleasant man that you might not look twice at on the street. But a man—in the deepest sense of the term—with a mission.

The mission is to bring happiness to millions. It first became evident in the twenties, when this lean son of the Mid-West came unheralded to Hollywood [and] began to animate his dreams . . .

—Promotion piece for *The Wonderful Worlds of Walt Disney*, 1966

THERE WERE certain words—"warm," "wonderful," "amazing," "dream," "magical"—that attached themselves to Walt Disney's name like parasites in the later years of his life. They are all debased words, words that have lost most of their critical usefulness and, indeed, the power to evoke any emotional response beyond a faint queasiness. They are hucksters' words. This book is an attempt to penetrate somewhat beyond language of this order and beyond the unthinking but all too common attitudes it represents. The attempt here is at what might be called analytic biography. The hope is to create a balanced perspective on the man, his works and the society that created him and that he, in his turn and in his special way, both reflected and influenced.

There are problems in any attempt to analyze the creators and the creations of popular culture. The most serious of these is in trying to choose which of the ill-shaped and slippery tools of understanding one wishes to apply to the task. Popular culture is an impure thing: it is commerce, it is sociology, it is sometimes art. But if the would-be analyst delves too deeply into the commercial realm, his work ends up reading like the report of a Wall Street research firm. If he indulges too heavily in the sociological mode, he finds a heavy and dubious mass of statistics and/or generalities weighing down his work. If he attempts to use the traditional language and style of literary criticism, he finds himself trying to apply fundamentally inapplicable standards to his subject, and the discussion soon degenerates into the easy moralism and the still more convenient subjectivism with which the literary community customarily discusses the art of the masses.

In the case of Walt Disney all these problems are magnified. And there are others, peculiar to his case, that further complicate matters. The most important of these is that the Disney organization has always had a very ambivalent attitude toward journalism. Though it encouraged millions of words of the stuff, it actively discouraged serious objective investigation of the man and his works. Rarely has so much been written about a public figure; rarely has so little of it been trustworthy. Therefore the sources for this book are almost all somewhat suspect, for the corporate drive has always been toward the preservation of an easily assimilated image, and for the most part, popular journalism has responded to this drive with a limp passivity that is astonishing even to one who is experienced in its ways. The magazines and newspapers, with a few honorable exceptions (see the Bibliographical Note), have preferred to go along with the view of Disney as an avuncular Horatio Alger figure, an ordinary man, perhaps even Everyman, whose career was a living demonstration that the American Dream sometimes works out in a reality stranger than fiction.

It was an attractively reassuring line to take. It made everyone—readers, writers, editors—sleep just a little more soundly to know that Walt was not only on the job but was handling it just the way they would have if they had been in his shoes. Indeed, the reportage implicitly encouraged the notion that they might well have been in his shoes if they had just had a few breaks. He seemed such an ordinary guy—well-meaning, sentimental, a lover of the cute and familiar. No intellectual, perhaps, but no con man, either. And there was just enough truth in the legend that formed over the years to make it seem very persuasive. All you had to do with it, whenever you rewrote it again, was leave out a few questions—and a few answers—about the assumptions, visions and values of the American middle class, which he both represented and served.

As a result, this book may come as a surprise to some people who turn to the lives of figures like Disney as their children turn to familiar fairy stories, in the expectation of once again seeing things come out all right in the end. I have not for one minute conceived of it as an "exposé"—the word is ludicrous in connection with someone like Disney. But it does attempt to see him coolly and objectively and within the context of our developing society. To this end, it partakes of all the disciplines previously alluded to—economics, sociology, cultural and artistic criticism—and a few others as well—psychology, for example, and history. The author does not claim to be an expert in any of these fields and, indeed, cheerfully admits to coursing through the works of many masters in all of them in search of thoughts and material that would help him come sensibly to grips with Walter E. Disney, his life and times. Generally, the material gleaned in this manner is set off from the body of the text as epigraphs heading the chapters. The idea is to indicate that all generalizations are tentative and suggestive, not final. Too many people speak with too much whimsical authority about masscult and midcult (to borrow a couple of words from one of the most whimsical of these spokesmen) for me to want to join their numbers. Here, I have wanted mainly to set forth a large body of previously uncollated information within a context that at least implies an attitude that is more critical of both Disney and his audience than was usually taken while he lived. I hope also to indicate by this examination of the life and work of one purveyor of popular culture that the subject has more—and more interesting—dimensions than many of the blithely critical attitudinizers seem to realize. Most important, I have sought—and believe I have found—in the life and work of Walt Disney a microcosm embodying a good deal of the spirit of our times, including a good many things that disquiet me as a citizen of those times and of the future they portend. In this most childlike of our mass communicators I see what is most childish and therefore most dangerous in all of us who were his fellow Americans.

Many times, as I wrote this book, people asked me why I wanted to devote almost two years of my life to the study of a man whom few writers or critics have taken seriously for more than a quarter of a century. The answer, of course, is that I undertook this work precisely because the period of Disney's greatest economic success, his greatest personal power, coincided with the decline of active interest in him in the intellectual community. As usual, the people who claim to concern themselves the most with popular culture, missed the point. When Disney ceased to make any claims as an artist they dropped him, as if only the artist is capable of influencing the shape and direction of our culture. In America, that seems to me a preposterous proposition. Our environment, our sensibilities, the very quality of both our waking and sleeping hours, are all formed largely by people with no more artistic conscience or intelligence than a cumquat. If the happy few do not study them at least as seriously as they study Andy Warhol, then they will lose their grip on the American reality and, with it, whatever chance they might have of remaking it in a more pleasing style. To me it seems clear that the destruction of our old sense of community, the irrational and unrationalized growth of our "electronic" culture, the familiar modern diseases of fragmentation and alienation, are in large measure the results of the failure of the intellectual community to deal realistically—and on the basis of solid, even practical, knowledge—with the purveyors of popular culture. If, for slightly ridiculous example, some of the easily shocked literary visitors to Disneyland in its early days had really looked at what Mr. Disney was doing there, the work of Marshall McLuhan a decade later would have been infinitely less surprising to them. But enough. The point is made. And I hope to develop it further in the pages that follow.

Though this book has the structure, and the outer appearance, of biography I would be disappointed if readers applied to it the strict, formal standards of that genre. To me, Disney was a type as well as an individual, and part of his fascination for me was that he was a type that I have known and conducted a sort of love-hate relationship with since I was a child—the midwestern go-getter. I believe many of us who were formed by that enigmatic region share certain traits, and it has been particularly interesting to me to find and point out the evidences of those traits in the Disney *oeuvre*. Some of my speculations on these matters may exceed the customs of the biographical form, as may some of my probes into mass culture. Nevertheless, I have felt compelled to proceed with them, for it is in these matters that the value of the book lies—at least for me. I therefore ask the reader to conceive of this as a volume that may be a little less than purely biographical but one that is also, at times, a little more than a biography—a study of an aspect of American culture, perhaps, or a free-form speculation on some qualities of the American mind at work or, less pretentiously, a book that, for good or ill, insists upon setting its own peculiar boundaries.

One final *caveat:* this is a study of a public man. Beyond the courtesies described in the Acknowledgments I had no cooperation from either the Disney family or the Disney organization. Therefore, the reader hoping to discover much about Walt Disney's personal life will be disappointed. In time, there undoubtedly will be an official biography, which will reveal something of his life away from the studio and the limelight. I hope there will be, and I hope the job will be entrusted to someone other than a Hollywood hack—since I firmly believe that people of Disney's power and achievement (however it is valued) are deserving of at least the same standards of scholarship that are automatically applied to the lives of obscure Civil War generals and minor novelists. Unfortunately, I have had to make do with the public record and with such oral reminiscences as I could gather in a limited time, and these, quite naturally, have tended to concentrate on the public man. They have been enough for my immediate purposes, but not enough, I know, to close the record completely.

RICHARD SCHICKEL

New York City
May 28, 1967

PART ONE

A Trial Balance

1   WALT DISNEY, 65, DIES ON COAST:
FOUNDED AN EMPIRE ON A MOUSE
                —*The New York Times*, Dec. 16, 1966

DEATH CAME at 9:35 A.M. on December 15 in St. Joseph's Hospital, directly across the street from the Disney Studio in Burbank. It appears that except for hospital personnel, including the cardiologist who had been summoned to treat the "acute circulatory collapse" that was the immediate cause of death, Disney was alone when he died. The presence of relatives or friends is unmentioned in accounts of his death. Neither the family nor the studio will elaborate on the matter, but if he died alone, it would have been characteristic of the man, for he had always been a loner, especially by Hollywood standards. Equally characteristically, he left very few loose ends untied when he died. The fiscal year of Walt Disney Productions had closed on October 1, and the balance sheet revealed grosses and profits at the highest point in its history. Moreover, the beautifully articulated machine he had constructed over some forty years, many of them frustrating and difficult ones, had, at long last, reached a state so close to perfection that even an inveterate tinkerer like Disney was hard-pressed to find ways to improve it. There were, to be sure, a couple of recreation-*cum*-real estate ventures still in the development stage, and one of them—the Mineral King winter sports center in California—was running into serious opposition from conservationist groups. In the year after he died, there arose a vague uneasiness about the ability of Disney's corporation, now headed in fact as well as in name by his brother, Roy, to continue at quite the high level of financial performance that it had attained under its founder. *Forbes*, a business fortnightly, described the studio, six months after Walt Disney's death, as being "like a fine car without an engine," and added that "the great Disney empire [was] drifting without a leader, as potential successors jockey for power." Others thought, as did Ivan Tors, a producer of TV animal stories for children (*Flipper, Daktari, et al*), that "Without Disney alive, without the personal myth of the artist who created a new form of art in the cartoon, there won't be the same attraction." In short, Disney's death created a vacuum both in the studio and in the hearts of the public that ambitious men were rushing to fill.

And yet it was hard to believe that death would prevent his machine—his beautiful, beautiful machine—from humming steadily along, clicking off profits and banalities at something like the rate it had achieved in the golden years of the early 1960s. The organization has weathered crises at least as serious as the death of its founder. To be sure, Roy Disney was not happy about the "chaos" of 1967. "I know a committee form is a lousy form in this business," he said, "but it's the best we've got until someone in the younger crowd shows he's got the stature to take over the leadership." Roy is, by his own admission, a compromiser, lacking any major creative talent, but he is also a patient and intelligent man, convinced he would do more harm than good if he attempted to run the studio by dictatorship. He also knows the strength of his company perhaps better than outsiders do. In the summer of 1967 he said: "We've never before had this much product on hand.

Walt died at the pinnacle of his producing career in every way. The big thing that's bugging American industry is planning ahead. We've got the most beautiful ten-year plan we could ask for. . . . The financial fellows think we're going to fall on our faces without Walt. Well, we're going to fool them."

He was right—up to a point. By the time Roy Disney made this statement, a production schedule had been hammered out and, to the surprise of veterans, there seemed to be some real interest around the studio in varying what had become an outmoded style. Besides, the Disneys' next of kin could reflect that the quality of the films their company produced, though important, was no longer the key to its success, since films no longer accounted for the major share of corporate income. The situation would have been considerably more perilous if Walt Disney had remained wedded to the notion of "putting over on the audience . . . something from one's own imagination," as Edmund Wilson thought he did in the late 1930s. Instead, of course, Disney placed his not inconsiderable talent in the service of what Mr. Wilson, in the same article, called the search for "an infallible formula to provoke its automatic reactions." By the time he died, he and his associates had found this formula and had managed to adapt it to every medium of communication known to man. They had even invented a new and unique medium of their very own—Disneyland. What was even better about Disney's machine, what made it superior to all its competitors, was that it had the power to *compel* one's attention to a product it particularly treasured. All its parts—movies, television, book and song publishing, merchandising, Disneyland—interlock and are mutually reciprocating. And all of them are aimed at the most vulnerable portion of the adult's psyche—his feelings for his children. If you have a child, you cannot escape a Disney character or story even if you loathe it. And if you happen to like it, you cannot guide or participate in your child's discovery of its charms. The machine's voice is so pervasive and persuasive that it forces first the child, then the

17

parent to pay it heed—and money. In essence, Disney's machine was designed to shatter the two most valuable things about childhood—its secrets and its silences—thus forcing everyone to share the same formative dreams. It has placed a Mickey Mouse hat on every little developing personality in America. As capitalism, it is a work of genius; as culture, it is mostly a horror.

2 "DISNEY'S LAND: DREAM, DIVERSIFY—AND NEVER MISS AN ANGLE"

—*The Wall Street Journal*, February 4, 1958

SOME FIGURES. In 1966 Walt Disney Productions estimated that around the world 240,000,000 people saw a Disney movie, 100,000,000 watched a Disney television show every week, 800,000,000 read a Disney book or magazine, 50,000,-000 listened or danced to Disney music or records, 80,000,000 bought Disney-licensed merchandise, 150,000,000 read a Disney comic strip, 80,000,000 saw Disney educational films at school, in church, on the job, and 6.7 million made the journey to that peculiar Mecca in Anaheim, insistently known as "Walt Disney's Magic Kingdom" in the company's press releases and more commonly referred to as Disneyland. From a state of profitability near zero in 1954 the company has progressed, over the years, to the point where its net income was $12,392,-000 on a gross of $116,543,000, which meant that the magic kingdom was very close to joining the magic circle—the 500 largest corporations in the nation—which soon it would do.

All this it had achieved by clinging very closely to the virtues of the Protestant ethic, which is a way of saying that it never went Hollywood, which is a way of saying that it was spared many of the vicissitudes that afflicted that community when, in a single year (1948) it was forced to divest itself of theaters across the nation and saw its old, reliable audience start to replace the movie habit with the television habit. Disney had some luck—the number of children between the ages of five and fourteen doubled in the period between 1940 and 1965, at which point one-third of all U.S. citizens were under fourteen—but he also made some luck. While the rest of the movie business watched in numb horror as television stole its audience,

Disney alone of the moguls—and he was not, at the time, a very big mogul—found a way to use the new medium to his advantage. With two successive shows he hosted himself—as well as the syndicated "Mickey Mouse Club" and the Zorro adventure series—TV became the keystone in a mammoth promotional arch. Each new film, not to mention Disneyland, and, implicitly, the Disney image, received the most delicious sort of publicity— that is, publicity aimed precisely at its proper audience and free of charge. For what was essentially a promotional film about the making of *20,000 Leagues Under the Sea* Disney actually received a television Emmy in 1955. There were other advantages as well. *Davy Crockett*, made as a three-part television drama, proved so successful that it was released as a feature film and generated a merchandising bonanza. Old shorts and cartoons and newer features that failed in the theaters provided acceptable, and mostly amortized, material for the television show, which also functioned much as the B pictures of Hollywood's greener days did—as a testing ground for new talents of all sorts. The show accounted for less than 8 percent of the company's gross, and since it was produced with Disney's lavish attention to detail, it did not do much more than break even. But as a loss leader for the Disney line, it was—and is—a major contributor to the studio's great leap forward. For the best part of this method of handling the studio's product was that it allowed the studio to participate in TV without surrendering control of its precious film library. As Disney's brother, Roy, who was president and chairman of the board, once said: "Since Walt and I entered this business we've never sold a single picture to anybody. We still own them all." In the spring of 1966 that amounted to 21 full-length animated features, 493 short subjects, 47 live-action features, 7 True-Life Adventure features, 330 hours of Mickey Mouse Clubs, 78 half-hour Zorro adventures and 280 filmed TV shows. At a moment when many Hollywood studios were finding that the difference between profit and loss often came from the outright sale of their old films—that is, of its history, its very corporate self—this ability of Disney's to prosper without peddling the inventory placed the studio in an enviable position. Rereleasing two or three oldies every year, the studio has averaged something like four and a half million dollars on them annually, almost all of it clear profit; in effect, the studio has automatically available to it the equivalent of the return on one new, ordinarily successful feature before it begins operation each year—and many of the Disney "classics" are doing better in the new, larger "family market" than they did when they were first released.

So it seems that from the purely commercial point of view, Disney built perhaps better than he knew when he concentrated his animated feature production on timeless tales that are incapable of becoming dated and in placing even his live-action features either in historical settings or in a never-never small town that, because it never existed in reality, can never be seriously outdated by changes in taste in furnishings or dress. His films, for the most part, are endlessly rereleasable.

These films had other uses, too. As early as 1952 Disney's Buena Vista Distribution Co. began renting 16 mm. prints of old Disney theatrical releases to schools and other organizations. That business has grown steadily through the years, and to it a variety of sidelines have been added. The firm has produced 152 35 mm. filmstrips under license by Encyclopaedia Britannica and study prints (13″x18″ poster sets on such subjects as safety and transportation for use in the elementary grades) and, lately, has experimented in educational technology with its 8 mm. single-concept film program, employing a lightweight portable projector so simple that a child can operate it. The system makes available to schools some two hundred very short films—one, two, three and four minutes in length, each dealing with a single idea—no more—that a teacher wants students to concentrate on as part of a larger study program. If the school is rich enough, it can buy dozens of the little projectors and send the films home with the child for after-hours study. Most of the tiny films are snipped from old Disney movies, particularly the nature series, while the poster prints use Disney characters and Disneyland attractions as subjects; the Disney name, of course, is prominent on all this material. Thus the studio reaps promotional benefits as well as more conventional profits and the advantages of a foothold in the growth industry of educational technology from a program that may be defined, in a variation of the old saw, as processing everything but The Mouse's squeal.

In the same period the studio slowly developed its capability in industrial film production, in which its capacity for animated and documentary film making was particularly useful. It made one-shot promotional films for American Telephone and Telegraph and the American Iron and Steel Institute, and in 1967 was making a film on family planning for the Population Council and had signed a $1.3 million contract for four 16 mm. educational shorts on health subjects to be underwritten by the Upjohn Pharmaceutical Company—the beginnings of what may be a much more ambitious program in a little remarked but potentially highly profitable field.

Finally, by pursuing an old private dream, dating back to the 1930s—the creation of an amusement park suitable for his own children—he managed to lay the groundwork for the kind of diversification that all the other film companies lust after but rarely achieve. Disneyland was not finished in time for Disney's daughters to enjoy it as children—though undoubtedly they do as mothers—but it pointed Disney toward an ancient entertainment form that had fallen on dreary, even evil, days, a form that was ripe for fresh imaginings and venturings—the amusement park, which in the variation on it Disney worked has been properly renamed "the atmospheric park." The quality of the aesthetic content of Disneyland has been endlessly debated by intellectuals. John Ciardi came away from it crying that he had seen "the shyster in the backroom of illusion, diluting his witch's brew with tap water, while all his gnomes worked fran-

tically to design gaudier and gaudier design for the mess."
Novelist Julian Halévy claimed that "the whole world, the universe, and all man's dominion over self and nature has been reduced to a sickening blend of cheap formulas packaged to sell."
Aubrey Menen, on the other hand, remarked that "the strongest desire an artist knows is to create a world of his own where everything is just as he imagines it." To Menen, Disneyland was such a creation, a true representation of Disney's truest vision and, beyond that, the kind of pleasure dome that kings and emperors used to create for their private amusement. Only Disney threw his open to the masses.

It is premature to examine these claims and counterclaims here, though it does seem fair to note that Disneyland and the newer projects it inspired claimed the largest share of Disney's psychic energy in the last decade or so of his life. It was here—and not so much in the other areas of his domain—that Disney really lived. The results of this intensive commitment were twofold. The basis of Disney's gift, from the beginning, was not as is commonly supposed a "genius" for artistic expression; if he had any genius at all it was for the exploitation of technological innovation. Thus the man who summarized the real achievement of Disneyland is not a literary intellectual at all but a city planner and developer named James Rouse, a leading figure in one of the latest manifestations of the "New Town" movement —Columbia, Maryland. Rouse put the matter very simply: "The greatest piece of urban design in the U.S. today is Disneyland. Think of its performance in relation to its purpose."

The validity of this judgment was evident to businessmen long before Rouse voiced it, and it was Disney's success in this area that simultaneously led them to him for the creation of what were, by common consent, the best exhibits of the New York World's Fair in 1964–65 and spurred Disney himself to larger related efforts. These, though they retained, as elements of the grand design, large-scale entertainment components, were more accurately seen as attempts to reexamine the customs of urban design (as in the projected "Disneyworld" development in Florida) and of recreational design (as at the projected Mineral King winter recreation area in California's Sierra range). To some degree the beginnings of these concerns were accidentally imposed upon the Disney organization. The creation of something like Disneyland requires the acquisition of the capability of handling large crowds not only efficiently (volume is everything in such an operation) but keeping them in a happy (*i.e.*, spending) frame of mind. This automatically took the company into areas of research and development on which surprisingly little intelligent thought has been expended in this country. From the engineering feats of Disneyland it is not a particularly long step to the kind of engineering required by a Mineral King project or to the creation of a small city as was originally envisioned at the Florida Disneyworld.

But there was another factor operating behind all this. That was Walt Disney's lifelong rage to order, control and keep clean any environment he inhabited. His studio, the last major such facility to be built in Hollywood during its golden age of profitability, was a model of efficient industrial organization and also a very pleasant place to work—at least as a physical environment. In July, 1966, he told a group of journalists that at least part of his recent intensive interest in city planning stemmed from his dismay at the unplanned sprawl of Los Angeles which he observed as he drove about the city. He just couldn't abide a mess, and now, at last, he had the wherewithal to try to do something about the developing national problem of the urban mess—at least as an innovator and perhaps as a creator of standards. He was heard to say that if the nation had put into the development of technologies to deal with urbanization even a fraction of what it had put into aerospace research, the problem might now be solved. As it was, he regarded urban design as the next great frontier of technology, and he wanted to be in on it.

What with the success of Disneyland and the smooth, profitable functioning of the television, music and records, merchandising and publication arms of the company, there was nothing to stop him. Indeed, the trend of his own company as well as the trend of the times urged him on. Revenue from theatrical film rental, which once accounted for 77 percent of the Disney take, had declined by 1966 to 45 percent (though its dollar volume was, of course, higher than ever). One could safely predict that film rental would decline still further as a percentage of income once the huge new element of the great Disney machine—the Florida Disneyworld—were in place and functioning, and one could predict that this state of affairs would be welcome at the company. "Now the Bankers Come to Disney" was the title *Fortune* gave its May, 1966, summary of the company's remarkable economic achievements, and the assumption is reasonable that the bankers would continue to do so. For even with the departure of the master, it seemed that the Disney Studio was well on the way toward solving the ancient Hollywood problem of achieving financial stability when the success of the basic product depends on such unpredictable factors as fads and fashions in stories and stars, the weather in the key cities when a major film is released, the ability to gain major promotional breaks for it, the ever changing whims and fancies and fantasies of the mass audience, even—perhaps in recent years, increasingly so—the attitude of critics.

These, of course, had always been matters of concern and even annoyance in the old days, but before television, when some fifty million Americans had trooped off to the movies every week not much caring what they saw, the problems had hardly been in the life-or-death category. With that kind of an audience you could safely count on making up on the straightaways what you lost on the turns so long as most of your films were kept within reasonable cost, your studio turned them out at a steady, overhead-justifying rate and you had the sure profits of the theater chains to fall back upon at all times. The years that followed the loss of the theaters (under duress of the

25

antitrust laws) and the rise of TV have been spent by Hollywood largely in the search for a new formula to replace the one that had been rendered obsolete. Many were tried. Some studios cut the number of their own productions radically—thereby cutting their overhead—and devoted most of their energies to renting facilities and equipment to independents, financing them and then releasing their products. United Artists sensibly and profitably divested itself of its studio entirely and concentrated solely on the last two functions. A few successful films like *Ben Hur* convinced others that the way and the truth lay in superproductions, in which much was staked on a very small number of films (though a few economically suspenseful ventures like *Cleopatra* and *Mutiny on the Bounty* soon convinced them otherwise). Still others believed in the small, inexpensive film of high quality, of which *Marty* was the classic example (though a few box-office failures like *The Bachelor Party* soon vitiated that faith). Nearly everyone was convinced that the handful of stars who could really draw people to the box office were worth almost anything they asked, and guarantees of one million dollars against a percentage of the gross—usually 10 percent—were by no means rare (though they often went to stars who could not deliver and whose costliness often insured the financial failure of films that, with lower-priced players, might have made money).

Nearly everyone at first reacted to television merely by praying that it would go away. A few saw in TV production a chance to use up overhead through facilities rental, but on the whole the studios were late getting into TV with shows of their own. Many compounded the first error with a second—selling sizable chunks of their film libraries to the competing medium, which improved the cash flow of the studios and kept their balance sheets looking good temporarily but placed the studios in the unenviable position of allowing their old products to compete with their new ones, often to the latter's disadvantage. The studios attempted other forms of diversification in addition to these unplanned forays into TV: they started record companies, they invested in Broadway shows, they did their best to get into merchandising in the Disney manner (though without the stable of wonderfully merchandisable characters he had built up through the years). A few even ventured into real estate, selling off the ranches where they had once shot westerns and, in one case, selling even the backlot of the main studio for real estate development or oil explorations.

But somehow none of these experiments worked really well, except as temporary expedients. Not one of the major studios escaped the last two decades without at least one major crisis; many suffered several, and a few slumped into what appeared to be a permanent state of low vitality. One major company and two minor ones went out of business entirely, and during the 1960s, six of the eight major studios suffered debilitating proxy fights as management confusion and ineptitude were reflected in lower dividend rates and spurred shrewd raiders and manipulators, a breed particularly attracted to entertainment companies, to seek control of the beleaguered companies. Not many of the raiders had any genuine interest in the production of movies; many hoped to make some quick profits—principally through the sale of film libraries to television—and get out, probably leaving the companies sicker than ever, if not dead. A few were at least as interested in the access to starlets studio ownership provided as they were in profitability. Of all the Hollywood studios only one emerged from this lengthy winter of discontent stronger than it had been. Only one advanced in status from a minor corporation to a major one, achieving financial stability at the very moment when the old-line major studios, which had once regarded it as no more than an insignificant industrial curiosity, were losing theirs. That studio was, of course, Disney's.

It was Disney's good fortune to suffer his agony earlier than the other producers. Overcommitted to feature films in the late 1930s and early 1940s, with the foreign market—particularly

vital to him—closed by the war and with an expensive new studio sucking up what capital he had, Disney had been forced to
make a public stock offering in 1940. The 155,000 six-percent
convertible shares had a par value of twenty-five dollars but
quickly tumbled to three dollars a share in the market, and only
government contracts for training and propaganda films kept
the studio functioning, its crisis hidden and the Disney name
before the public. The war work also took some of the sting out
of an extremely unpleasant strike at the studio, as a result of
which The Founder's benevolent image took its first—and possibly only—serious beating. In short, the times were bad for
Disney at precisely the moment when they were extraordinarily
good for the rest of the industry. The one good thing about the
situation—and this became clear only in retrospect—was that
the problems that were later to plague the rest of the industry
had to be met by Disney at a time when the government could
help out and when the general buoyancy of the industry could at
least keep him afloat. The result, of course, was a head start in
gathering know-how to meet the crisis that was coming—a
head start in planning for diversification first of the company's
motion picture products, then of its over-all activities. The results were spectacular.

The Disney studio had been, by Hollywood or any other
standards, a very small business from the time of its founding
in 1928 until 1954, when for the first time it finally grossed
more than $10,000,000. After that, the sales chart took a
sharply upward curve. There was one minor setback in 1960,
when *Sleeping Beauty* awakened only apathy at the box office,
but by the end of fiscal 1965 the gross income of Walt Disney
Productions, borne aloft by *Mary Poppins*' magic umbrella,
had sailed past the $100,000,000 mark (the exact figure was
$109,947,000) and by the end of fiscal '66 it was $116,543,000.
Profits, which had been no more than a couple of million at
the start of the great leap forward and which stayed low due
largely to the firm's frugal policy of using its own assets to

finance expansion whenever possible, had by the end of 1966 reached a record high of $12,392,000.

As for Disney himself, the man who only a decade before had hocked his own life insurance to finance the early stages of Disneyland, the man who had been, for most of his career, tolerated by *haute* Hollywood as an enigmatic eccentric whose presence was "good for the industry"—this man had gained what all his detractors had lost. When he died, his studio was the only one left that had no truck with the independent producers, that offered no percentage deals to stars, that made no fabulous bids for hot literary properties, that produced, with its own resources and its own full-time staff, all the motion picture products it sent out under its name. A few months before Disney died, Jack L. Warner sold his stock in the studio he had long controlled, and that left Walt Disney as The Last Mogul, the last chief of production who had to answer to no one—not to the bankers, not to the board of directors (it was dominated by his own management men, who were, in turn, dominated by him), not to the stockholders (they were happy—and anyway, one third of them were kids given a share in Mickey Mouse as an introduction to the capitalist way of life). In his domain—in "The Magic Kingdom," as his flacks insistently called it—Walter Elias Disney was the undisputed, and generally benevolent, ruler of all he surveyed.

3   *Walt Disney is one of the best compensated executives in the U.S. these days and, as he says himself, "It's about time."*
                                                    —*Fortune*, May, 1966
He was a twentieth century Cellini who supervised the mining of his own gold.
                         —Joseph Morgenstern, *Newsweek*, Dec. 23, 1966

SOME MORE FIGURES. At the time of his death Walt Disney owned 262,941 shares of stock in Walt Disney Productions. In the open market these were being traded at 69 on the day he died (they subsequently went up 9⅜ points on the expectation that the studio was a prime merger candidate), which means they were worth a little more than eighteen million dollars. In addition to these holdings, which constituted 13.4 percent of the company's outstanding shares, Disney's wife owned another 26,444 shares in the company; Diane Disney Miller, who was elected to fill her father's place on the board after he died, and her husband, Ron, owned another 43,977 shares; Roy Disney and his wife controlled 99,881 shares outright, and a corporation they had set up owned another 50,573 shares. Finally, the Disney Foundation, a charitable institution founded and funded by the Disney brothers, owned another 52,964 shares. Disney's other daughter, Sharon, and her husband owned an undisclosed amount of stock, and various Disney grandchildren held little stakes in the company as well. In all, the Disneys owned approximately 34 percent of Walt Disney Productions, and the Disney Foundation owned another 2.7 percent.

The stock was by no means the sum total of Walt Disney's estate. His basic salary since 1961 had been $182,000 a year, plus a deferred salary accrued at the rate of $2,500 per week that was to be paid to his estate at a weekly rate of $1,666.66 for about seven and a half years. In addition he had, since 1953, the right personally to purchase interest up to 25 percent in any live-action, feature-length film his company produced so long as he exercised this option prior to the start of filming. From 1961 Disney exercised this option—though only up to 10 percent—on almost all the company's films (he also extended a similar right of investment—though up to only 1 percent—to seven key executives). His interest in *Mary Poppins* alone brought him a million dollars in 1965 and, in addition, generated a capital asset estimated at another million. This money, in turn, was assigned to a family-owned company, Retlaw (which it is sometimes amusing to spell backward). The company has reaped dividends from past successes as they have been re-released, and will continue to do so, one imagines, until time itself comes to a stop.

Retlaw also had two other major functions. One was to license Walt Disney's name to Walt Disney Productions for use in merchandising agreements. Disney Productions had the right to use of the name only in its corporate title and on films and television shows in which The Founder personally participated. Retlaw had the right of choice in this matter: it could take 5 percent of any net profits derived from the business or participate in the business through investments in it up to 15 percent, or it could take 10 percent of an amount held to be the reasonable value of Walt Disney's name to Walt Disney Productions in any given situation. In a fairly typical year—1965—the company turned over to Retlaw $292,349 in royalties on deals of this sort. Retlaw's other major function was ownership of the steam railroad and the elevated monorail at Disneyland. This oddity stemmed back to the days when not everyone shared Disney's enthusiasm for the park and he found it necessary, through his own resources, to finance the railroad that circles it—and that was a part of the over-all design he as a railway buff particularly loved. The arrangement worked out so nicely that a similar one was set up when the monorail was added in 1961. The two railways grossed between two and three million annually, in the series and Retlaw paid 20 percent of the gross to Walt Disney Productions as rent for its right-of-ways and keeps the remainder for operating expenses, amortization of its $3.2 million investment in the system, and profits.

Retlaw was, in effect, the successor to the corporation the Disney family previously, held, known as WED Enterprises, Inc. (the initials, of course, are those of Walter Elias Disney). From the time of its organization in 1952 until the 1965 sale for three million dollars, of its name and its most important assets to Walt Disney Productions, it performed all the functions later handled by Retlaw. And there was one more: it served as the design, architectural and engineering arm of Disneyland. In this role it created the exhibits that bore the Disney name at the New York World's Fair of 1964–65, it was the developer of Audio-Animatronics, the system of animating three-dimensional characters that highlight many Disneyland and Disneyworld attractions and have a lovely, licensable, exploitable future, and it has created the WEDway People Mover, which is, in fact, the moving sidewalk so many have predicted and so few have actually experimented with (its first installation was in the new Tomorrowland section of Disneyland). Just how much income Retlaw produces for the Disneys in any given year is impossible to estimate, though John MacDonald of *Fortune* guessed that in 1965 Disney and Retlaw together had an income, apart from his salary and stock dividends, of more than two million dollars. With Disney's death and the ending of Retlaw's ability to participate in new film production deals, that figure, of course, deteriorated. The Disneyland railroads, however, will probably keep chugging out profits for decades to come. And Retlaw's merchandising agreement with Productions runs until 2003.

4   *It is not to Mr. Disney's discredit that, when success and fame rightly came to him, he began to expand as a person and as an ambitious business man. It was natural that he should have flourished under the warm and tinkling rain of public praise, that he should have managed to throw off his shyness, that he should have found it quite pleasant to take bows. . . . He was now moving in the area of the big producer, the Hollywood tycoon, and this was a role he managed with more pretension than with comfort and ease.*
—Bosley Crowther, *The New York Times*, Dec. 16, 1966

AMONG UNSOPHISTICATED people there was a common misapprehension that Disney continued to draw at least the important sequences in his animated films, his comic strips, his illustrated books. Although his studio often stressed in its publicity the numbers of people it employed and the beauties of their teamwork, some *very* unsophisticated people thought he did everything himself—an interesting example of the persistence of a particularly treasured illusion and of the corporation's ability to keep it alive even while denying it.

Disney himself once tried to explain his role in his company by telling a story that may well be apochryphal but is no less significant and no less quoted in company publicity for all that. "You know," he said, "I was stumped one day when a little boy asked, 'Do you draw Mickey Mouse?' I had to admit I did not draw any more. 'Then you think up all the jokes and ideas?' 'No,' I said, 'I don't do that.' Finally he looked at me and said, 'Mr. Disney, just what do you do?'

" 'Well,' I said, 'sometimes I think of myself as a little bee. I go from one area of the studio to another and gather pollen and sort of stimulate everybody.' I guess that's the job I do."

The summary is not a bad one, as far as it goes. But there were a good many more wrinkles in Disney's situation than the smoothness of this explanation would indicate. For one thing, Disney was continually, if mildly, irked because he could not draw Mickey or Donald or Pluto. He never could. Even Mickey Mouse was designed by someone else, namely Ub Iwerks, an old friend from Disney's pre-Hollywood days. Iwerks actually received screen credit for so doing on the first Mouse cartoons. In later years Disney was known to apply to his animators for hints on how to render a quick sketch of Mickey in order to oblige autograph hunters who requested it to accompany his signature. Even more embarrassingly, he could not accurately duplicate the familiar "Walt Disney" signature that appeared as a trademark on all his products. There are people who received authentically autographed Disney books and records but who thought they were fake because his hand did not match that of the trademark—a particular irony in the case of Disney, who had devoted a lifetime to publicizing his name and as we have seen, quite literally capitalizing on it.

Stories like these should not be taken to mean that Disney passed his final years living out the myth that money cannot buy happiness or that when his fortune caught up with his fame he found that all his dreams were a mockery. Far from it. Like many men who have grown rich through their own efforts, he had little use for personal display. His suits were still bought off the peg. His diet still consisted largely of the foods he had acquired a taste for in the hash houses of his youth (hamburgers, steaks and chops were staples; he especially liked chili). He drove himself to work, mostly in standard American cars, though in his last year he took to using the Jaguar that Roddy MacDowall had driven in *That Darned Cat*. He served tomato juice to visitors in his office but allowed beer to be served in the studio commissary—by no means a standard Hollywood practice—and admitted to enjoying a highball or two at the end of a workday that minimally ran twelve hours.

He traveled mainly on business and submitted to vacations with restless grouchiness. His one known extravagance was the scale model train that used to circle his home and that he conceived and then helped to build. In the early Fifties it had been his great pleasure to don a railroad engineer's cap, brandish a slender-spouted railroader's oil can and pilot grandchildren and other visitors around his yard.

The train became, over the years, the subject of a disproportionate share of Disney lore. It was as if he used it to distract attention from other areas of his private life—certainly it made excellent feature copy for popular journalism. Mrs. Disney and his daughters tried to persuade him to build the thing at the studio instead of in his yard, but he went so far as to have his lawyers draft a right-of-way contract for his family to sign giving him permission to build and maintain the train. It was a token of such seriousness of intent that they agreed to sign it, whereupon he declared that in the circumstances their verbal consent was good enough for him. He loved fussing over the train, continually adding to its supply of rolling stock, improving the grades, even digging a tunnel so that it could pass under some of his wife's flower gardens without disturbing them. Mrs. Disney once commented, "It is a wonderful hobby for him . . . it has been a fine diversion and safety valve for his nervous energy. For when he leaves the studio he can't just lock the door and forget it. He is so keyed up he has to keep going on something." She noted that a good deal of their social life in this period revolved around giving people rides on the half-mile line and that a select few were given cards designating them vice presidents of the road. She and her daughters quickly became bored with the train, but Disney did not, and he even suffered some hurt feelings over their indifference. He enjoyed —like a small boy with an electric train—planning wrecks because repairing the damage was so much fun. Once, after he bought two new engines, she heard him enthusing to George Murphy, now the Senator and then one of the toy train line's "vice presidents," "Boy, we're sure to have some wrecks now!"

The train was the only splash of color in the Disneys' quiet home life. Their friends, with the exception of Murphy, Kay Kayser, Irene Dunne and a few others, were not drawn from show business. Indeed, their daughter, Diane, became the first daughter of a motion-picture-industry family to make her debut at the Las Madrinas Ball in Los Angeles (which, in 1967, finally invited its first Jewish girl to participate). To old Angelenos the movies and the Jews were, apparently, virtually synonymous. Of the other aspects of Disney's mature home life little is known. He is recorded as having been a doting father, given to sentimental outbursts on such occasions as weddings and the birth of grandchildren, and the indulgent master of a poodle, for whom he was known to raid the ice box for cold meat. He also forbade the extermination of small pests—rabbits, squirrels and the like—that raided his wife's garden. This was, so far as one can tell, no idle image-protection on his part, but rather an expression of genuine concern for animal life. Outside the home his favorite recreation was wandering around —unrecognized, he hoped—in such places as the Farmer's Market in Los Angeles or on New York's Third Avenue, where he liked to browse the secondhand and antique shops and buy dollhouse-sized furniture. He had, Mrs. Disney reported, "no use for people who throw their weight around as celebrities, or for those who fawn over you just because you are famous."

Among countless perquisites that were available to him as the head of a prospering corporation the only one that seemed to afford him much pleasure was the company's three-plane "airline," the flagship of which was a prop-jet Grumman Gulfstream. He went everywhere on it and took an open—perhaps even childlike—pride in this particular symbolization of his status. In the months before he died, he frequently mentioned the pure jet that Walt Disney Productions had on order and that, typically, was to be a model for the next generation of executive jets—a technological leader.

But the backyard train and the plane were in contrast with the essential Disney personality. The Los Angeles *Times'* obituary editorial speculated that Disney's "real joy must have come from seeing the flash of delight sweep across a child's face and hearing his sudden laughter, at the first sight of Mickey Mouse, or Snow White or Pinocchio." Certainly the sight did not make him unhappy, but the *Times*' own biographical sketch, appearing in the same edition, carried a more nearly true statement from Disney himself on the source of his deepest satisfaction in his later years. A reporter once asked him, according to the piece, to name his most rewarding experience, and Disney's reply was blunt and brief: "The whole damn thing. The fact that I was able to build an organization and hold it . . ."

These are clearly not the words of some kindly old uncle who just loves to come to your child's birthday party and do his magic tricks and tell his jokes and find his kicks in the kiddies' laughter and applause and their parents' gratitude. Neither do they appear to bear much resemblance to anything we might expect from an artist looking back over his career. They represent, instead, the entrepreneurial spirit triumphant. They are the words of a man who has struggled hard to establish himself and his product; who has fought his way in from the fringes of his chosen industry to its center; who has gambled his own money and his own future on his own innovative inspirations and organizational intelligence and more than once has come close to losing his whole bundle. They are, most of all, the words of a man who at last is in possession of the most important piece of information a player in the only really important American game can obtain—the knowledge that he is a sure economic winner, that no matter what happens the chance of his being busted out of the game has been eliminated and that his accumulated winnings will surely survive him.

This knowledge was vouchsafed Disney only late in life, but when it was, he was fond of working variations on the theme that money was merely a fertilizer, useful only to the degree that it could make new crops of ideas and enterprises grow. This is, of course, an image that anyone brought up in the spirit of the Protestant ethic would instantly appreciate and probably applaud; it is also an image that Freud and more particularly his latter-day followers into the dark realms where the relationship between money and feces are explored, would quickly— probably too quickly—understand and explicate at dismal length. To a builder of Disney's character, though, money did in fact perform precisely the function he liked to describe, and its symbolic value was in good part just what it seemed most obviously to be—a measure of distances traveled, a way of keeping score.

Looking back, it is easy to see that Disney was neither a sold-out nor a sidetracked artist. He was a man who had obtained what he truly wanted: elevation—at least on the lower levels— to the ranks of the other great inventor-entrepreneurs of our industrial history. He was of the stuff of Ford and Edison a man who could do everything a great entrepreneur is expected to do —dream and create and hold.

5   *When he died . . . Disney was no longer simply the fundamental primitive imagist . . . but a giant corporation whose vast assembly lines produced ever slicker products to dream by. Many of them, mercifully, will be forgotten. . . .*
—*Time*, Dec. 23, 1966

DISNEY DID NOT CARE. So long as the company prospered, so long as it kept on creating fertilizer for whatever new crops he wanted to plant, he did not care. He was no longer in the art business—if he ever had been—and he was no longer the pure purveyor of a modern mythology, as many intellectuals had once thought he might be. Indeed, the least pleasant aspect of his character in the late, prosperous years was the delight he

A TRIAL BALANCE

took in conveying his contempt for art, which he often equated with obscenity.

Speaking to a magazine journalist some ten months before he died, Disney confided: "I've always had a nightmare. I dream that one of my pictures has ended up in an art theater. And I wake up shaking." He buttressed this statement with the rather broad generalization that there was entirely too much depressing and squalid material cluttering up the movie screens of the world. Somewhat defensively he added that he would "stack *Mary Poppins* against any cheap and depraved movie ever made." He proudly told interviewers about all the times he had ordered his projectionist to turn off films when they became too unpleasant for his rather squeamish taste, and admitted that he seldom sat through entire movies but rather ran them "in pieces, just to see a certain actor or actress." In short, it could fairly be said that in the last decade or so of his life he was fundamentally out of touch with the major artistic currents of his times in general and of the motion picture art in particular.

That the period of Disney's greatest economic success coincides with the period of his least interest in contemporary art tells us, perhaps, less about him than it does about American society. Despite extensive and expensive efforts to report the latest fads of the art world—pop, op, camp, psychedelic—and despite the titillated interest of many basically uncultivated people who like to create the appearance of swinging with these presumably sophisticated fads, it would appear that at heart the nation is essentially unchanged in its tastes. It may, somewhat self-consciously, sample the new artistic wares in order at least to be able to condemn them, but generally it turns with relief to the comforting banalities of television (where in truncated and debased form the great constants of our popular art—westerns, detective stories, situation comedies, true romances—abide), and when it ventures forth to the previous home of these forms —the movie house—it gives its most generous patronage to *Mary Poppins* or *The Sound of Music*. Change is surely in the air: audiences are far quicker to laugh at romances and adventures that, a decade or two earlier, they would have taken in deadly earnest. The manufacture of camp films that cue the snicker and the guffaw as carefully as an earlier generation of movie makers cued tears and tension with essentially the same material is now a staple of the industry. Since Walt Disney died, the executives, directors and writers of his studio have been foregathering weekly to see foreign films—ranging from *Georgy Girl* to *Blow-Up*—to study the techniques of the new film makers from abroad just as Disney's animators studied the techniques of the great silent film comedians: to learn what they might borrow and put to their own use. A camera angle here, a shrewd piece of editing there, will perhaps be incorporated into the studio style, which is notably conventional in its filmic techniques. But one does not expect the studio to change its heart even if it does adopt a freer style of expressing itself. Nor is there a need for it to do so. The market for broad, clean humor, for sentimentality and sweetness of outlook, for the hero easily distinguishable from the villain, for adorable animals and children—this will not diminish. Indeed, as the competition drifts away the Disney studio will undoubtedly continue to find—as it has over the last decade or so—that it is almost alone in a very rich market, a market that attracts no critical attention and very little attention from the popular press, which is preoccupied with recounting the latest outrages from the various underground and avant-garde camps. If the studio has any problem to face in maintaining its singular position, it will be one of sincerity. Walt Disney sincerely treasured the values he portrayed in his films and could scarcely credit anyone who saw art or life in more complex, less sunny terms. He was of the old American tradition that believed in keeping its frets and doubts and inner troubles to itself, that blamed its nightmares on something it must have eaten. It is hard to believe that Disney's surviving associates are all of that particular breed. They will most likely continue to give us the outer aspects of the Disney version of life, but will they be able to animate it with the same forceful belief in its honesty and accuracy that the founder did? And lacking that—the equivalent of the much-discussed "X quality" alleged to be present in the work of the great film stars —will they be able to hold their audience's attention as Disney did?

The answer will become clear only with the passage of time. But it must be noted at the outset that it is unjust to criticize Disney for being what he was. Few of Hollywood's industrial pioneers were especially noted for the breadth of their aesthetic or social vision—to put the matter mildly indeed. There is no particular reason why Disney should have been expected to be any different. Except that, as we shall see, there was a rather long moment in time when, if he did not exactly sue the artistic and intellectual communities for favor, he did not reject their heavy-breathing advances either. His personality was at once too simple and too complex for his early acceptance of their favors to be read cynically. He was not using their praise to advance the grand economic design that emerged so forcefully in the last decade of his life: it is doubtful that either he or his brother, Roy, then perceived its full dimensions. Nor should his nastily phrased suspicion toward his one-time allies be read simply as the cries of a hurt soul or of a purist who knows he has somehow gone sour but cannot admit the fact even—or especially—to himself. There may be elements of truth in both these views of the man, but neither is the whole truth. He is, in fact, best seen in a different perspective, one that reaches beyond the confines of the industry *cum* art where he made his career and into the heart of a nation, now changed and still changing, that shaped him and his type.

Walt Disney belonged to a special American breed, middle-class and often midwestern in origin. He was the sort of man who possesses and is possessed by a dream that seems to be particularly and peculiarly of this land of a time only recently past. It is a dream now much satirized but, for all that, no less

41

common among the middle-aging generation. Simply summarized it is that "it only takes one good idea . . ." In the United States one need not even complete the sentence, so clear is the implication: all you need is one winner to get started properly on the road to success.

The dream's natural place of nurture is the workshop in the attic or the basement or the garage in "Gasoline Alley" or "Out Our Way" where a man can be alone with his tools—free of the clock and the cautionary wifely voice and all the other inhibiting forces of family and society. There are several levels at which the dream operates. In some men it calls forth nothing more significant than gadgets that can solve the minor or previously unnoticed problems of organization and efficiency in closets, desks, kitchens and bathrooms and that create the infinite and humorous variety of the Sunset House and Miles Kimball catalogs. And there are the men who, possessed of a slightly higher technical skill (though not necessarily more imagination), create products of wider industrial applicability—a special gasket, say, or a variation on a standard machine tool—and actually move beyond the confines of their own backyards or the rented space in a loft downtown to a little factory of their own.

The modest successes of these people are the unwritten but often discussed footnotes in the folklore of American capitalism. The chapter headings are reserved for those who make it big—the Edisons and the Fords or, in fields closer to Disney's, Joyce Hall, who came down to Kansas City with a little money in a suitcase and the notion that greeting cards should be folded and stuffed in envelopes instead of being simple postcards, or DeWitt and Lila Wallace, who put out the first issues of *The Reader's Digest* all alone in their Greenwich Village apartment. They are the ones with the capacity to build mighty edifices on the dream without losing their proprietary interest in it. They are, most important, the ones who can endlessly replicate its essence—not with its original inspirational force but with sufficient accuracy to insure its continuing acceptability. Indeed, their aim, conscious or unconscious, must be to convert the excitement they initially generated in their audience into something less volatile, since repeated overstimulation is usually fatal to the relationship between the mass communicator and his audience. The trick, of course, is to turn the interest stirred by the original idea into a habit that is beyond the reach of criticism narrowly conceived. It is perhaps for this reason that in the last two decades there has been almost no serious criticism of Disney's work as art; most such comment has been couched almost entirely in the terms of social criticism.

For the purposes of ordinary discussion, these are certainly the most convenient terms, but they do not reveal the essence of the problem posed by mass communication. It is the business of art to expand consciousness, while it is the business of mass communications to reduce it. At best this swiftly consummated reduction is to a series of archetypes; at worst it is to a series of simplistic stereotypes. Since the eyes of the proprietors, especially after the initial act of creative inspiration is finished, are usually focused on something other than this matter of consciousness and sensibility—if indeed, they are aware of it at all —the reductive process usually proceeds erratically. This was so in the case of Disney. Particularly in the beginning, vulgarity and brilliance were inextricably mixed. If, at the end, the balance was tipped rather heavily to the side of the former, the fact remained that there was still enough of the latter present to discourage easy generalizations.

It is fair to say, however, that in the end Disney was a prisoner of his own image. In the days of his first success he was fond of telling interviewers that "we don't bother with a formula . . . I play hunches and leave psychology to others." In his last years he was still leaving psychology to others, but he was also musing out loud to interviewers in terms like these: "Awful good property . . . awful good. But I just don't think a war picture is Disney. It's not what our audience expects from us. Nope, I don't think we can do it." The machine he had created no longer served Disney; he served it, finding his personal satisfactions not in the process of artistic or quasi-artistic creation but in the process of industrial management and development. In so doing, Disney was actually serving a value that ranked, in America in general and in the background that nurtured him in particular, higher by far than an artist's values. Art to Disney's generation was justified only by the uses to which it could be put, and of these uses the social one was tolerable but not nearly so interesting—so magical—as the possibility of building a business on them or their semblance. That Disney did so was, in the popular mind, far more intriguing than any of the products he created. In the last analysis, Walt Disney's greatest creation was Walt Disney. In retrospect it is possible to see that this is precisely what he was working at for some forty years and that the ultimate satisfaction was that he died with the job completed and decorated by as many laurels as his admiring countrymen could bestow upon it. They hardly noticed that the loved object was less a man than an illusion created by a vast machinery. Even when they heard the gears clanking, as they often must have, they didn't seem to care. The trick was everything, and they would have liked to learn its secret if they could.

PART TWO

Touching Earth

---

6 *The country town is one of the great American institutions; perhaps the greatest, in the sense that it has had and continues to have a greater part than any other in shaping public sentiment and giving character to American culture. . . . The road to success has run into and through the country town.*

—Thorstein Veblen

WALTER ELIAS DISNEY was born in Chicago, December 5, 1901. His first name was taken from that of the Congregational minister who baptized him, his second was that of his father. The elder Disney traced his family back to a Burgundian officer named De Disney, who had participated in the Norman invasion of England in 1066, had settled in the conquered country and received a large estate and, as one journalistic historian gently phrased it, "lived and reared his children in a good environment and was classed among the intellectual and well-to-do of his time and age." Be that as it may, the "De" had been chipped off the family name by 1859, when Elias was born in a village in Ontario, the first of eleven children. In the 1870s the family moved to Ellis, Kansas, where they raised wheat and fattened cattle for market. At a comparatively tender age Elias went to work in the railway shops there while also learning the rudiments of carpentry. Within a decade he had made the first of the several unsuccessful moves he was to undertake in search of a competency never to be his. His first venture was in citrus growing in Florida and, apparently, he prospered at first. At any rate, he married an Ohio schoolteacher named Flora Call, who was spending a vacation in Florida, and their first two sons, Herbert and Raymond, were born in Florida. But then the frosts came, killing a crop and forcing Elias to sell out. He drifted back to the Midwest, this time to Chicago, where he worked as a carpenter on the construction of the Columbian Exposition, which opened in 1893.

It is hard to say definitely, but Elias Disney appears to fit the classic description offered by Veblen of the small operator shuttling back and forth between the land to which he was perhaps most strongly attuned emotionally and the city, which seemed to offer more economic opportunities. Essentially these types were, as the great social critic put it, "cultivators of the main chance as well as of the fertile soil," and this "intense and unbroken habituation" imbued them with a "penny-wise spirit of self-help and cupidity" that was their undoing, narrowing their vision to the point where it could encompass only momentary and paltry commercial advantages, preventing them from taking the long view and leaving their work "at the disposal of those massive vested interests that know the uses of collusive mass action. . . ." "Footloose in their attachment to the soil," they were, like the elder Disney, habitually ready "to make the shift out of husbandry into the traffic of towns even at some risk whenever the prospect of some wider margin of net gain . . . opened before their eager eyes."

The margins in Chicago, however, proved to be little wider than they had been in Florida. After the exposition was finished, Elias Disney opened a small contracting firm and ran it hand-to-mouth fashion for something more than a decade. Three more children, Roy, Walt and a younger sister, Ruth, were born in this period. In his spare time Elias served as a deacon of the

Congregational church in which Walt was baptized and over-saw construction of a new church building. Elias was a stern and frugal man, by all accounts, and never loath to use his family's muscles to further his own ends. Among Walt Disney's earliest memories was that "my mother used to go out on a construction job and hammer and saw planks with the men." Despite her aid, carpentry proved no more lucrative than orange growing, and in 1906, before Walt Disney was five, the family moved on again.

7   *I live in the country. I have no other home. I am impressed by certain things about farmers. One of them is their destructiveness. One of them is their total lack of appreciation of the beautiful—in the main.*
          —Karl Menninger, M.D., *A Psychiatrist's World*

THIS TIME ELIAS DISNEY convinced himself that his fortune lay in a forty-eight-acre farm near Marceline, Missouri, in Linn County and on the main line of the Atchison, Topeka and Santa Fe Railroad, some one hundred miles northeast of Kansas City. Even in those days a farm of this size could be no more than a hard-scrabble operation, but Elias apparently rationalized the move morally as much as he did practically. One friendly biographer of his fourth son states that Elias held strongly to the belief that "after boys reached a certain age they are best removed from the corruptive influences of a big city and subjected to the wholesome atmosphere of the country."

His eldest sons, Herbert and Raymond, objected to the move and stayed on the farm only a few months before running off —back to Chicago. According to one version of the official legend the hard calluses of farm labor ill-suited youthful hands that had recently learned to wield pool cues, but whether it was a taste for this modest depravity or a deeper kind of despair that drove them away, it appears that they were never let back into the family circle or cut in on the profits of the business their younger brothers were to start later. After their runaway, Herbert goes unmentioned in any writing about Disney, and Raymond appears only once, in an unflattering light, although it is known that Herbert became a post office clerk and Raymond, an insurance salesman.

In later life Disney was to remember the farm as a place of enchantment. In the biography of her father which Diane Disney Miller wrote in collaboration with Pete Martin, she reported that Disney could still draw a detailed mental map of the farm and that he had built a replica of the farm's red barn with its lean-tos on either side in the backyard of one of his homes. She also speculates, undoubtedly accurately, that the Main Street, U.S.A., section of Disneyland, the only section of the park through which every visitor must pass, is an expanded and idealized version of Marceline's Main Street. The symbolism is almost too perfect—the strangers forced to recapitulate Disney's formative experience before being allowed to visit his fancies and fantasies in the other areas of the Magic Kingdom.

Life on the farm was certainly more pleasant in retrospect than it had been in actuality. For Elias Disney was a hard man —a believer in physical punishment and harsh economic discipline. The children received no allowances and no playthings either. For Christmas their presents were practical items like shoes and underwear. It was Roy Disney, working at odd jobs, who supplied Walt and his sister with an occasional toy and who, as soon as Walt was big enough to try to handle it, put him on to an occasional good thing. Mrs. Miller tells a story, for example, of Roy's getting a job washing the town hearse and allowing his little brother to participate in the profits of the enterprise despite Walt's having spent most of the time playing dead inside the vehicle. The proceeds were spent at a carnival that passed through town a little later.

Difficult the Marceline years certainly were, but they were formative in several ways. In the best American tradition, they taught young Walter Disney the virtues of hard work or, if not that, at least the idea that one could stand the strain of hard labor without breaking under it. Years later Roy Disney told an interviewer that "as long as I can remember, Walt has been working. . . . He worked in the daytime and he worked at night. Walt didn't play much as a boy. He still can't catch a ball with any certainty."

The small-town life he observed undoubtedly taught Disney the spirit of "self-help and cupidity" that so marked his later business life as well as the need, as Veblen put it, to "be circumspect, acquire merit and avoid offense" that was the basis of his public image. The precariousness of the family's livelihood undoubtedly shaped his own desire not merely to succeed but to do so in a particular way—namely, to avoid surrendering any part of his autonomy to outsiders and to hold his company's stock and its decision-making power as closely as he could. The constant, hopeless indebtedness of the small American farmer is, of course, legendary, and undoubtedly there were in Marceline, besides Elias Disney plenty of cautionary examples of what constant existence in this condition can do to a man's spirit. Certainly the small land-holder's justified prejudice against bankers, the men who kept them endlessly strapped to the wheel of debt, stayed with Disney all of his days (though with his brother's guidance he did learn to live fairly comfortably with the moneymen, who were, in fact, helpful to him—in their special fashion—on several occasions). But a childhood grounding on hard economic bedrock can be invaluable to a man who spends his adult life in a highly speculative enterprise like show business, with its sudden, often shocking, ups and downs. It teaches one how much worse things can be. An often-told Disney story illustrates just this point. It seems Roy Disney one day many years later went to his brother to tell him of his deep concern for the future of their company: they were several million in debt to the Bank of America, it looked as if no more credit would be extended, the cash flow had nearly dried up, and so on and on. When Roy finished his recital, the younger Disney began to laugh—and laugh and laugh till finally his brother was infected with his hilarity. "Just imagine," Walt Disney said in effect when he could finally speak, "a couple of rubes from Kansas City being in a position to owe the Bank of America all that money."

In addition to shaping his economic style, the country town in Kansas shaped Disney's artistic and social sensibility as well. This is quite obvious in *Plane Crazy*, the first Mickey Mouse film he ever attempted. It was set in a farmyard, a setting to which Disney returned time and again in his cartoons, even though Mickey—and the rest of the characters created by Disney's animators—finally took up more or less permanent residence in a small town. A great deal of the humor in all the early Disney cartoons was of the barnyard variety, of which *Steamboat Willie*, the first Mickey Mouse cartoon to be released and the first cartoon ever to have a sound track, provided a perfect example. Its most memorable moment is a one-man band performance by The Mouse, in which he "plays" most of the familiar farm creatures as if they were instruments (the cow's udder, for instance, is turned into a bagpipe). In addition to being low, barnyard humor is often cruel, and the predicaments and punishments to which Disney's animated animals were subjected were often brutal in their initial delineation, if not in their resolutions (in cartoonland, no creature ever dies of the terrible hurts he endures). The country man, dependent on animals for sustenance and accustomed to the bloodier unpleasantries of husbandry (birth, slaughter, gross illnesses) tends naturally to be less sentimental than his urban cousin about them. This was clearly true of Disney, who may be said to have found a way of

50

"using" creatures without killing them. To the degree that he was not, from birth, inured to the more brutal realities of farm life, however, he escaped the totally indifferent attitude toward animal suffering that many farm children seem to acquire from their environment. It could be said, in fact, that Disney blended a citified sentiment about dumb creatures with this practical acceptance of the harshness and the blunt humor of the farm. His most sympathetic treatment of animals was usually reserved for undomesticated wildlife (*i.e.*, *Bambi*, and the subjects of his True-Life Adventure series), while he made the domesticated animals into clowns. He boasted, particularly in his early career, when animals formed the largest part of his subject matter, that he had only once killed a living creature, that the death was accidental and that he learned much about the need for humanitarianism from the experience. The incident occurred on the farm, and the victim was an owl that Disney tried to capture while it slept in the sun of a tree branch. The bird fought back, and the seven-year-old boy, terrified by its beating wings, threw it to the ground, where he stomped it to death. He did not recall the incident more than once in his interviews and, in fact, never acquired any very deep knowledge about animal behavior; rather, he tended, particularly in his animated work, to use them to caricature human types and behavioral patterns, not as fit objects for study or admiration in themselves. The one thing he was convinced of was, as he often said, that "every animal has a separate and distinct personality all its own," an observation that does not apply to the lower phyla and remains open to speculation—some of it semantic, revolving around the definition of the word "personality"—among naturalists, many of whom feel that Disney carried his anthropomorphism much too far in his nature films.

The drive in these films was, of course, toward a sort of multiple reductionism: wild things and wild behavior were often made comprehensible by converting them into cutenesses, mystery was explained with a joke, and terror was resolved by a musical cue or a discreet averting of the camera's eye from the natural processes. It is possible to say that the operative instinct was like the farmer's, which is ever and ever to cut away the underbrush, clear the forest and thus drive out the untamed—and therefore nonutilitarian—creatures. The tradition of the American farmer is to "take up" more land than he can work (hence the endemic condition of being "land poor") and, rather than let it stand—horror of horrors—untouched, to clear it and let it lie fallow until he can get around to it—which may be never. The survival of this instinct may be seen throughout our urban society, which abhors empty land as nature does a vacuum and rushes to fill it with something, anything, even if it is only a parking lot or a hopeful sign promising future development. In the real estate developments that so preoccupied him in his last years, Disney, the one-time farm lad, was every inch the American. Mineral King, where he proposed to build a $35-million winter and summer playground accessible to every moron who could lay hands on an automobile and a picnic lunch (the debris of which he could scatter out the window), is such a place. In its undeveloped state it is "useless"; closed to all but the hardiest most of the year behind a barrier of snow, it has been described as "a spectacular wild mountain valley, an alpine paradise of peaks, ridges and high passes." Dreadful! Bring in the all-weather road (letting the state pay its estimated $20 million cost), bring in the ski lifts and the ski lodges and the restaurants and the ice-skating rink and, for the days when the weather is bad, the bowling alley and the movie theater and, of course, the souvenir shops. Naturally, there is money in it, but there is something deeper than that at work in this national passion to "tame the land," as the cliché goes.

Karl Menninger, the Kansas psychiatrist who, by lucky accident of birth, is one of our best analysts of the midwestern, rural temperament, asks why as a people we have never really learned to love the land as it is, for itself. "What really is the nature of the soil? Is it dirt? Is civilization largely built on overcoming it, or built upon a taboo of dirt, overcoming a natural affection for it?" The question is not idle, and the career of Walt Disney is, as we shall see, much conditioned by the hatred of dirt and of the land that needs cleansing and taming and ordering and even paving over before it can be said to be in genuinely useful working order. It is certainly not unreasonable to suppose that this vision of the land—hardly a unique one and, considering how widely it was held, hardly one for which he can be criticized—began to take shape during the hard years on the farm when, whatever moments of joy Disney found there, the harshness of the life could only have emphasized the filthiness of the land. Somehow it seems appropriate that his first successful creation was a mouse, traditionally viewed as an inhabitant of unclean places and, in his natural state, often an unclean creature himself. In The Mouse, as he was conceived by Disney, all conflict that the animal's real nature might have caused was resolved by an act of creative will: reality was simply ignored. Mickey was a *clean* mouse, right from the start. All inner conflicts about the nature of the land were similarly resolved in Disney's other films: he always, and only, showed us a clean land. Indeed, the whole wide world was scrubbed clean when we saw it through his eyes. "There's enough ugliness and cynicism in the world without me adding to it," he used to say, and one understood his lack of cynicism when he made the statement.

But whatever the precise dimensions of the attitudes toward animals and the land that Disney acquired on the farm, there is no doubt that he did begin to draw in those days. One story has it that his first known work was with tar, a barrel of which, (and a brush for which,) were kept next to the barn for patching roofs and fixing drains. When he was six or seven Disney seized the brush, dipped it into the barrel and proceeded to decorate the white walls of the farm house with large and fanciful drawings of animals. He was punished for the episode, but not long afterward his Aunt Maggie presented Disney with a pad of drawing paper and a box of pencils in which he took an interest that was perhaps extraordinary. Naturally, he received no encouragement from his family, but a nearby doctor often bought his drawings with little presents.

"I recall when I was about seven," Disney said once, "the doctor had a very fine stallion which he asked me to sketch. He held the animal while I worked with my homemade easel and materials. The result was pretty terrible, but both the doctor and his wife praised the drawing highly, to my great delight."

This early encouragement apparently meant a great deal to Disney, for throughout his childhood and youth he continued to enroll in correspondence school cartooning courses and, when he was fourteen, he talked his father into letting him join a Saturday morning art class at the Kansas City Art Institute. Before that happened, however, the Disneys were to enter upon their period of deepest economic decline. In the summer of 1910 Elias Disney was forced to sell his farm, auction off his livestock and, with the proceeds, attempt to build a new life for himself and his family in Kansas City, Missouri.

8 *It takes a particular view of man's place on this earth, and of the place of childhood within man's total scheme, to invent devices for terrifying children into submission, either by magic or corporeal terror. . . . Special concepts of property (including the idea that a man can ruin his own property if he wishes) underlie the idea that it is entirely up to the discretion of an individual father when he should raise the morality of his children by beating their bodies. It is clear that the concept of children as property opens the door to those misalliances of impulsivity and compulsivity, of arbitrariness and moral logic, of brutality and haughtiness, which make men crueller . . . than creatures not fired with the divine spark.*

—Erik H. Erikson, Young Man Luther

HAVING FAILED IN agriculture at the peasant level, Elias Disney now sought once again to rejoin the other class for which he was temperamentally endowed—the *lumpen bourgeoisie*. He bought a Kansas City *Star* newspaper route of three thousand customers, for which he paid the previous route owner two dollars apiece. Elias, of course, counted on his two remaining sons, Roy and Walt, to contribute their labors to the enterprise, and so, at the age of nine, Walt Disney found himself being routed out of bed at three-thirty each morning in order to meet the *Star* delivery trucks. The other boys Elias hired to work with his sons received three dollars a week for their services. The Disney boys got nothing.

The work was brutally hard, and a couple of months before he died Disney claimed that he still had bad dreams about it. Reminiscing to a Los Angeles newsman, he said: " . . . The papers had to be stuck behind the storm doors. You couldn't just toss them on the porch. And in the winters there'd be as much as three feet of snow. I was a little guy and I'd be up to my nose in snow. I still have nightmares about it.

"What I really liked on those cold mornings was getting to the apartment buildings. I'd drop off the papers and then lie down in the warm apartment corridor and snooze a little and try to get warm. I still wake up with that on my mind.

"On nice mornings I used to come to houses with those big old porches and the kids would have left some of their toys out. I would find them and play with them there on the porch at four in the morning when it was just barely getting light. Then I'd have to tear back to the route again." Disney claimed, on another occasion, that the newsboy nightmares of his adulthood frequently centered on forgetting to leave a paper for one of his customers and having to get back and rectify the error before his father found out.

There were other rigors besides the physical and the psychological. Eager to make some money that he could keep for himself, Disney at one point talked his father into ordering fifty extra papers for him to sell on street corners. When he finished his route at six-thirty he would run home, bolt some breakfast and start hawking his own papers. The only trouble with the arrangement was that Elias insisted on taking the boy's money "for safe-keeping," and Walt never saw it again. The boy finally began ordering papers for himself, without his father's knowledge, in order to retain such small earnings as he could make. He also got a job in a candy store during the noon recess from school—and apparently kept it, too, secret from his father.

In none of the accounts of Disney's childhood is much mention made of either his mother or his younger sister. The emotional poles of his life were his father and his older brother, Roy, "one of the kindest fellows I've ever known," in Walt Disney's latter-day estimation. In this period of Walt's transition from what amounted to one American stereotype of boyhood—the barefoot farm lad—to another—the slightly ragged newsboy—Roy Disney, eight years his senior, was his confidant and mentor. "When we were kids," Disney told one of his associates many years later, "Roy and I slept in the same bed. I used to wet the bed and I've been pissing up Roy's leg ever since." In effect, Roy was the intelligent and worldly comptroller, not only of the company they formed and nurtured in later years but of Disney's personal growth. At times he was the conservative, the one who urged him to go slow, to build with care. Yet he was also, like any good surrogate father, the one who would find, when necessary, the ways and means of clearing the way for the younger man to express himself. The record is full of tensions between the brothers, but it was, for the most part, a healthy tension, of the sort that nurtures intelligent creative effort. Displayed on Roy's office wall, in later years, was the peace pipe Walt gave him to patch up one of their fights.

As for the childhood years, it is indubitable that Roy Disney offered his younger brother the clearest available vision of the possibilities of decent and humane—if rough-hewn—manhood. When Roy graduated from high school in 1911 at eighteen, he almost immediately decided to run away from home as his elder brothers had. Before he left, however, he did Walt the singular favor of telling him he did not have to stand for any more beatings from his father.

The old man's habit had been, upon the occasion of discovering a real or imagined failing, to order the boy to the basement for a strapping. According to his daughter's account, Walt had submitted to these beatings "to humor him and keep him happy"—a rather strange way of putting the matter and perhaps yet another example of the Disney inclination to reduce life's unpleasant side to casually manageable proportions. In any case, Roy advised his brother that the punishment was unjust and that he no longer had to submit to physical discipline. The boy preceded his father to the basement and waited. When Elias began to work him over with his leather strap, his son seized his hands in a grip the father could not break. They struggled briefly, and then the old man began to cry. He never again raised his hand to his son.

Two other incidents stand out in the Kansas City period. The

first is shrouded in ambiguity and is not spoken about in any of
the written accounts of Disney's childhood. It came to light in
the late forties when he fell into a political conversation with
one of his screenwriters, who was strongly oriented toward the
left. Disney inquired if the man had suffered some childhood
experience that conditioned his strong beliefs and was told that
there had been none—that he had, in fact, arrived at his political stance in his maturity and under the impress of the depression. Disney then countered with the information that his own
political conservatism was the result of a street fight. As he told
it, his family was strongly Republican in its leaning, while most
of the neighborhood was persuaded toward the Democrats. One
day on the way home from school, he was ganged up on, beaten
and forced to submit to what can be described only as a quasi-
sexual assault by some Democratic kids. He told his listener that
from that day on, he had never been able even to rationally consider the possibility of voting for anyone but a Republican.

What is odd about Disney's recital of the incident is that he
had told his daughter that his father had been a socialist who
voted consistently for Eugene Debs and had subscribed to *The
Appeal to Reason*, a well-known leftist organ. He even recalled
that among his first cartooning attempts had been a representation of a conventionalized capitalist bloated and wearing a vest
decorated with dollar signs standing in opposition to a laboring
man wearing the traditional hand-fashioned square paper hat
such as newspaper printers still make and wear. What is the
truth of the assault incident? Is it possible that Disney imagined it merely to win a debating point with his employee? It
could be, for there are variant versions of many of the important
turning points in his life in the written records of his career.
Contradicting this, however, is the fact that the drift of his reminiscences was always the same, leading to the establishment of
a mythic, if not literal, truth about his background. Is it possible that he was, in fact, beaten for upholding his father's social-

ist views? That seems a little more likely, since a Republican was hardly an exotic figure in Kansas City, while socialism might possibly have represented an intolerable eccentricity to a group of boys. In opposition to that interpretation one must recall that only a few years later Disney was perfectly willing to let his daughter discuss her grandfather's political views in a book that was serialized in *The Saturday Evening Post* and widely read. Was he, perhaps, loath to admit, in argument, that he had turned his back on a leftist heritage or that his politics were yet another repudiation of his father—an act he could never commit, possibly because of the impositions of a career devoted to upholding the virtues of family life. Even if his story were pure fantasy, it is an interesting one, expressing a need to create an intense and deep-rooted emotional justification for his political views.

Whatever the truth of this matter, there can be little doubt that among Disney's happiest moments in Kansas City were his introduction to formal art instruction and his first theatrical experiences. The former took place on Saturday mornings when he escaped his family and journeyed to the art institute for young people's classes in painting and drawing. On this one matter his father proved to be indulgent, for, as Disney later said, "he would go for anything that was educational. He was determined to improve his sons, whether they liked it or not." Art instruction, Disney liked; there seems to be no evidence that he particularly cared for anything else in the educational line. As for theater, this was a matter of amateur nights in the neighborhood movies, where he teamed with a young man named Walt Pfeiffer in an act called "The Two Walts." They won a few prizes—the largest seems to have been two dollars—and Disney won some similarly modest fees for his impersonations of Charles Chaplin when Chaplin was at the height of his first great success in the period of 1914 to 1917. Disney later tried an act in which he attempted a comic Dutch accent, flopped and retired from the spotlight until he began hosting his own television shows (although he always spoke for Mickey Mouse on his soundtracks).

The young Disney also carried away from Kansas City the memory of a showing at a special newsboys' matinee of the Marguerite Clark version of *Snow White and the Seven Dwarfs*, which was released in 1917. He traced his selection of *Snow White* as his first animated feature directly to the strong impression the silent film had made on him. Typically, it was an accident of technology more than the story line that caused the picture to catch in his mind. The film was shown in a large auditorium with a four-sided screen set up in the center and the audience grouped in a circle around it. Disney was seated, by chance, at a point where he could see two of the screens. The projectors were not perfectly sychronized, and so he had the odd experience of seeing the film twice, but with the time lapse between screenings reduced to a matter of seconds—instant *déjà vu*. He could not forget the story because he could not forget the oddity of projection.

At about this time, Disney's father again decided that opportunity was beckoning from afar. This time it was a jelly factory back in Chicago that caught his eye. He sold his newspaper route, invested the proceeds in the factory and became its chief of construction and maintenance. The move gave his son his first real taste of freedom, for he stayed behind in Kansas City to finish his school term and help the new owner of the paper route learn the business. That summer he got a job as a candy butcher on the Santa Fe Railroad, traveling mostly between Kansas City and Chicago but occasionally venturing as far afield as Pueblo, Colorado. His suppliers frequently cheated him, and he was sometimes the butt of practical jokes, as when an older candy butcher gave him a card of introduction to a hotel in Pueblo, which turned out to be a whorehouse. ("I was just a kid," Disney said later, "but I caught on. When I got through the door I broke into a run!") He loved the trains, and it was a love that stayed with him throughout his life, as his model railroad proved. A screenwriter who wrote a movie scene set in a Pullman car of roughly this vintage recalls that discussion of the scene sent Disney off into a long reminiscence about the elegance of this plush and velvet world he glimpsed for the first time in the summer of 1917 and the lasting impression it had made upon him. Disney used to delight in telling reporters of eating up all his profits by snacking on his candy and of bribing the engineers with plugs of tobacco so that he could ride in the coal car behind the locomotive and watch the countryside rushing up in front and then streaming away behind him. For a boy who had been forced to live as meanly as he had, it was obviously a golden summer—one that glowed even more brightly in memory.

When it ended he joined his family in Chicago. There he attended McKinley High School, where he did both drawing and photographs for the school paper. He also, of course, worked for his father at the jelly factory, running the bottle washer and the capper and mashing apples to make pectin. Somehow he managed to find time for further art instruction, first under a man named Carl Werntzl, then with a newspaper cartoonist named Leroy Gossett. The following summer Disney got a job in the post office, sorting and delivering mail from seven-thirty in the morning until midafternoon, then trying for extra work on the mail pick-up routes. If there was none, he would grab an elevated line gateman's cap out of his locker, ride out to a terminal of the Wilson Avenue line and stand in the shape-up for rush-hour jobs that paid forty cents an hour. "I thought it was a gold rush," he later said.

As a result of his labors Disney was able to buy a seventy-dollar camera on the installment plan, though there is no evidence that he did more than fool around with it in a boyishly inconclusive way. The tone of such reminiscences as there are of the brief second period in Chicago is predominantly one of aloneness. He seems to have had few friends—his schedule probably precluded any close attachments—and he seems to have occupied himself very much in the manner of a man waiting for something more important and interesting to happen. Girls, he once recalled, were a nuisance. "I was normal," he said, "but girls bored me. They still do. Their interests are just different."

It is possible to speculate that his relationship with his father and mother prevented the formation of the habit of trust in his fellow man. There is nowhere in his history any record of any long-standing or deep intimacy with anyone, with the exception of his brother Roy and his own wife and children. And even his immediate family seem to have been kept rigidly compartmentalized from his work, into which so much of his psychic energy was poured. He appears to have confided his troubles and his inspirations to them only rarely. Though he often exhibited a streak of gruffly sentimental generosity to old associates, there is not one to whom he ever offered more than a brief, tantalizing glimpse of the forces that formed him or of his innermost thoughts. The same is true of his relationship to the hordes of interviewers who trouped through his office in the course of an extraordinarily lengthy public career. He told dozens of anecdotes about himself—and he told them well—but they had a way of getting flattened into archetypal experiences, promoting an image of a standardly mischievous American boy of the sort who peopled his live action movies by the score. They were a screen, behind which hid a man who fundamentally—and with good psychological reason—mistrusted the human animal, rejected intimacy and discovered early that he could rely completely only upon himself. "I count my blessings," he said on numberless occasions, and surely one could say that among them, paradoxically, was his habit of distrust and his basic estrangement from people: they were qualities fundamental to his business style, enabling him to retain control of an enterprise that might easily have slipped away from a man of another sort.

During the summer of 1918 when Disney was working for

the post office, his brother Roy reappeared briefly in his life, as a recruit headed for the Great Lakes Naval Training Station outside Chicago. Walt met him at the station and was very nearly taken out to Great Lakes with him when a petty officer mistook him for one of his brother's boot camp group. Since getting away from home at about this age was very much in the family tradition, the mistake gave the youngest Disney boy an idea: why not join the Navy? He was told by recruiters that he was too young, but a friend told him he needed to be only seventeen to join the Red Cross Ambulance Corps. He was a few months shy of that age, and in any case, his father refused to sign his application for a passport. But his mother intervened, saying that she preferred knowing where her son was going to having him run off blindly as his elder brothers had. She signed the application and then turned her back as Disney jiggered the true birth date she had felt compelled to write in.

Disney passed the rest of the war at a staging area in Sound Beach, Connecticut, where, as he recalled it, the service was not much fun. Though the drivers were not officially soldiers, they did have military discipline, complete with a guardhouse which, he claimed, he frequently occupied as a result of "clowning." The group was disgusted when the armistice was signed before any of them got a chance to get overseas. There was, however, still a need for truck drivers in Europe in the period immediately after the guns ceased firing, and Disney was one of fifty drivers in his group who were chosen for this duty—he claimed his was the last name on the list read out in camp—and sent to France after all.

It was, apparently, good duty. He drove all sorts of vehicles, including five-ton trucks, and he spent a good deal of time on the road, free of close supervision, delivering relief supplies all over France. He had to face a board of inquiry one time when a truck he was driving broke down, his assistant got drunk instead of reporting the incident to headquarters as he was supposed to, and the exhausted Disney fell asleep in a nearby shack at precisely the time help finally arrived and towed the vehicle away without him. Disney later claimed it would have been a dreadful disgrace to be kicked out of the Red Cross. "If you couldn't make it in that easy-going outfit," he said, "you were considered hopeless."

In due course all was forgiven and he was assigned as a driver to a canteen at Neufchateau. It was there, with time on his hands, that he made his first real money as an artist. As he recalled it he painted a cowboy on the canteen truck, producing a mild sensation and causing his local bosses to put him to work drawing signs for the canteen. Then he painted a replica of the Croix de Guerre on his leather jacket, soon he was duplicating the decoration for everyone in his outfit at ten francs per job. All this activity brought him to the attention of a con man known in the Disney annals only as The Georgia Cracker. He was doing a nice little business selling German "snipers' helmets" to young American replacements then streaming through Neufchateau to relieve combat troops from their occupation and garrison duties in Germany. The Cracker had acquired a supply of new German helmets into which he carefully shot a bullet apiece, adding just the right touch of authenticity to the item, which was a great favorite with the recruits. He now asked Disney to paint them with phony camouflage colors to add to their realism, after which he banged them up with rocks and rubbed them in the dirt to complete the illusion of battle wear. Again, Disney received ten francs apiece for his work, and it was welcome, particularly since he was getting nothing but rejection slips from such back-home humor magazines as *Life* and *Judge*, to whom he started sending cartoons at this time.

What with his art earnings and his savings from his pay envelope and the proceeds from one particularly good night at the poker table—he won something like three hundred dollars—Disney was able to return home in 1919 with a small grubstake. His father had a job waiting for him in the jelly factory—a steady twenty-five dollars a week—but Disney had made up his mind to have a go at commercial art. His father was against the idea, and presumably to escape his ongoing opposition, perhaps to avoid the competition he might encounter in Chicago, Walt decided to leave most of his capital in his mother's safekeeping and head back to the familiar ground of Kansas City. He had nothing more definite in mind than attempting to get a job as an apprentice artist on what was then regarded as the greatest of the midwestern newspapers, the Kansas City *Star*.

PART THREE

K.C. to L.A.

9 *The atmosphere of . . . the prosperous Midwestern city, as a whole, after all, was primarily one of literate optimism.*
   —Charles Fenton, *The Apprenticeship of Ernest Hemingway*

The personalities involved were not always mean, hypocritical, evasive, fearful individuals; frequently they were afflicted with a kind of frustrated pride, more often by an excessive narrowness of cultural experience, a lack of the opportunity to educate themselves.
   —Frederick J. Hoffman, *The Twenties*

THE POPULATION OF Kansas City almost doubled in the first two decades of the twentieth century, rising from 163,-752 in 1900 to 324,410 in 1920. Situated at the junction of the Kansas and the Missouri rivers, it had been a trading and distribution center since the middle of the nineteenth century, when it had also served as the starting point for wagons setting out on both the Santa Fe and Oregon trails. By the beginning of this century it was a place of booming enterprise, with its stockyard, its grain market, its heady interest in real estate. As much as any American city of the time, it was a place where the go-getter, the hustler, the man who was on the rise, could find a congenial atmosphere in which to test his salesmanship and the quality of his commercial vision; in Veblen's terms it was the country town grown up, the principal trading center for a vast and vastly prosperous agricultural region. Yet the city had about it an open and spacious quality that, perhaps, reflected a style and mood generated by the surrounding prairies. In any case, there was—and is—a generosity to the design and layout of Kansas City that contrasts vividly with that of the more constricted-seeming midwestern metropolises farther east. It was one of the first American cities, for example, to incorporate a great deal of open land within its boundaries for development as parks, and it therefore remains one of the few cities to meet what experts regard as the minimum standard for recreational space—one acre for every three hundred inhabitants. It is not and never has been a city particularly noted for its interest in the high culture—among its major contributions to the modern American way of life is the shopping center, the first of which was located there in the 1920s—and its leading citizens have traditionally been modest to a fault when it comes to civic dogooding, but it is, in general, a handsome and pleasant place. "Who in Europe, or in America for that matter, knows that Kansas City is one of the loveliest cities on Earth," André Maurois once asked, probably thinking particularly of the Country Club and Mission Hills residential districts that were built around the shopping center in the 1920s and where, as one journalist recently put it, "among the imitation Tudor houses there are running brooks, broad boulevards embroidered with statuary and country clubs as pretty as a Hollywood set."

Behind these façades, things were not always so pleasant. For instance, Roy Wilkins, present head of the NAACP, came to Kansas City in the same period as Disney and, working on a Negro newspaper there, discovered, as he recalls, the first deep racial prejudice he had ever encountered (he had lived previously in Minnesota). Downtown, where the Prendergast machine held sway, building toward that free-swinging period

K.C. TO L.A.

of its total dominance in the late 1920s and early 1930s, venality and corruption were becoming a standard part of the business style. In a few years former convicts would be able to find a place on the police force, the uniforms of the waitresses in one of the more popular clubs consisted of nothing more than a pair of shoes, and the city, in general, had a regional reputation second only to Chicago's for sinfulness. The present Mayor, Ilus Davis, recalled recently that the downtown atmosphere was "corrosive." "We had 104 unsolved murders in a twelve-month period. It got so they didn't even report it in the paper. There were slot machines in every drugstore. It was a near complete breakdown of society." The nice people turned their back on this corruption, doing business with the machine when they had to and never seriously opposing it. About all that came out of that era was a school of jazz, to which the city lent its name and of which Bix Biederbecke was the most famous practitioner. It is interesting that this, one of the few significant footnotes Kansas City has contributed to our cultural history, was nurtured by the city's criminal element.

In addition to jazz, Kansas City had another claim to glory—the Kansas City *Star*, which promptly turned down Disney's application for work as an artist and even as an office boy. The paper was indeed a paragon among the provincial journals of the time. Less than two years before Disney's return to Kansas City, its city room had been serving as one of the principal training grounds for the young Ernest Hemingway (who curiously enough shared with Disney, though at a much more intense level, Chicago, Kansas City and the Ambulance Corps as formative backgrounds). Through it had passed, and continued to pass, some of the great reportorial and executive names of the new style of journalism then developing. The *Star*, in fact, contributed institutionally to that development—the lean, terse prose its legendary style book demanded of reporters becoming something of a model for other newspapers striving to shuck off the leisurely, excessively ornamented and overly liter-

69

ary style that had afflicted American journalism during the latter portion of the nineteenth century and the early years of the twentieth. The *Star* did not have a terribly wide-ranging world view, and its owners and managers were constitutionally incapable of seeing life in a particularly sardonic or satirical way. To temper the style he absorbed in its service Hemingway "required," according to Fenton, "a sustained encounter with provocatively deceitful situations" not obtainable in Kansas City.

What was true of him was undoubtedly even more true of the town's less-gifted citizens. Kansas City appears to have been a good place to come from. Its spirit was more open, perhaps even a shade more sophisticated, than that of the other regional metropolises of the Midwest. A young man could find friendly encouragement for his ambitions there, even, as Hemingway did, some solid hints about how to proceed toward their practical realization. What was missing from its atmosphere is what is often missing from cities of its type even today—a sense of life's more dangerous and tragic undertones, its more fantastic overtones and, most of all, an opportunity to sense the patterns, philosophic and poetic, that an artist can sometimes apprehend in the seemingly random events of the passing days and weeks.

The American Midwest is a highly practical place. Its habit is to ask how much, how big, how far, and, sometimes, simply how. It rarely asks why. The bluff and hearty manner it affects is not a conscious pose: it believes in its own friendliness and good spirits—and it is as surprised as anyone when clues to its hidden, darker side escape and intrude upon the carefully slow and easy surface it genuinely prefers for its habitat. It may or may not be afraid of the depths, particularly the personal ones, that intellectuals and easterners and Europeans (terms which are, among the folk of the region, virtually synonymous), but it certainly dislikes them, finding them depressing to contemplate and the work of explicating them of dubious practical value.

For a young man of developing artistic potential, then, Kansas City offered two possibilities. If he knew where to look for them and had some interest in exploiting them, he could find a short stay there quite educational: it was not so closed and so narrow an environment as it may look to some who have never experienced such a place. If, however, the young man had neither the background nor the temperament to seek in its environs the intellectually or artistically shaping experience, then the town had a natural tendency to send him in quite a different direction. It seems fair to say that Disney, unlike the conveniently comparable Hemingway, lacked the necessary preparation to make good use of such opportunities as Kansas City could indeed offer the young artist. Hemingway, for example, was the scion of a comfortable and literate middle-class professional family; Disney was the son of a man whose principal preoccupation was a search for the peripheral chance, and there is no evidence that there was anyone in his family to supply either a softening or a broadening of that mean and narrow sensibility. Success, economically defined, was the one universally agreed-upon goal of his young manhood, and the lack of it clearly soured his father and turned him into a potent negative example.

As a practical matter, the difference between Disney and Hemingway can be simply put: the writer's father had enough influence to obtain, through friends, a place for his son on the *Star;* Elias Disney did not.

Although neither Hemingway nor Disney pursued formal education beyond high school, there were differences in their opportunities here, too. The former at least received his diploma, and he had the good fortune to obtain it from a suburban public school system that prided itself on its quality. Disney, on the other hand, received a catch-as-catch-can schooling in several undistinguished places and did so while devoting his spare time to neither reading nor sports nor imagination-stretching idleness. He had to work after school and on vacations in order to contribute to the family economy. The upshot is clear: one man's imagination was free to grow as it might;

the other's was early forced into the most practical and least-elevated channels. One man was able to use the not inconsequential resources of Kansas City as a place to begin the exploration of a much wider world; the other, although he moved through it almost as quickly, was never able to grow intellectually or emotionally beyond it. Hemingway was influenced by Kansas City, as he was by many youthful experiences. Disney was easily absorbed by it and its values. The quality of his sensibility, of his fancies and fantasies, even the means of his later success and the measures he applied to it, remained the most practical and the most obvious ones he observed in Kansas City in particular and the Midwest in general.

One thinks of Disney's Americanism, of the kind of clean, moral, simple and innocent stories he most often chose to present on the screen, of the right-wing politics of his later years, of his broad, gag-oriented sense of humor, containing no elements of social or self-satire, as entirely typical of the tastes of the region that formed him. The geographic center of the nation is also, broadly speaking, the most passionately American of the American regions. Life on the prairies seems to nurture an intense, if innocent, ethnocentricity. The Cheyenne Indians, who previously wandered the plains states and claimed the territory for their own, were in the habit of referring to themselves as "the human beings" and denying similar recognition to strangers.

As a result, within a few years the Midwest would become, as Frederick J. Hoffman put it, "a metaphor of abuse" and, for a time, it would indeed seem that "the progress of the American had . . . been reversed" with the bright young men and women—in particular the would-be artists—fleeing from the banality, the decadent puritanism, the suppression of life, the fear of death and the hypocrisy that seemed to infect both the small towns and the larger cities of the midlands, and heading east, if not all the way to Europe, in search of freedom, sophistication, style, culture and moral maturity. This view of the life of the region and its meaning is certainly no longer news, and though what was once a living metaphor to an entire literary generation has now become an unthinking stereotype, it still contains a modicum of truth. The young man who, like Disney, chose to stay in the region and who, when he finally decided to move, went still farther west instead of back east, was making an unconscious choice of sides in the decade's great confrontation between philistinism and art. There is a clue in this choice to the aesthetic he would eventually embrace—a clue available even before his career presented him the opportunity to make that choice in any significant way.

In short, Disney was not an exceptional young man, and his discontent was not with the system but with the failure of his family to rise within it. There is no record of what he thought of the literary expatriates, but one imagines his being puzzled by them. He was, without knowing it, on his way to proving anew the truth of a statement by Lewis Mumford, that prescient man, made in the very year Disney finally abandoned Kansas City and headed to the new outpost of midwesternism, Los Angeles. "The truth of the matter is that almost all our literature and art is produced by the public, by people, that is to say, whose education, whose mental bias, whose intellectual discipline, does not differ by so much as the contents of a spelling book from the great body of readers who enjoy their work." This was to be the source of Disney's strength and of his weakness, and his unthinking ability to make the right choice for himself at this time is not to be lightly dismissed. All those who found real power in the new world of mass communications showed a similar sense of identification with the new masses. It would have required a young man tuned and tempered in a very special way—a way quite different from Disney's—to seek out and absorb the lesson, say, of cultural relativity in Kansas City or Chicago. An exceptionally exceptional young man.

Such criticism of the cultural climate of the region as the foregoing may imply should be tempered, however, with an appreciation of the virtues Disney could find there in his apprenticeship. Against the satiric vision of that time and place we have inherited from the Sinclair Lewises and H. L. Menckens, we should balance—more often than we usually do—the remarks of a figure like Eric Hoffer. "Imagine an American writing about America and not mentioning kindness," he said recently, "not mentioning the boundless capacity for working together, not mentioning the unprecedented diffusion of social, political as well as technological skills . . . not mentioning the breathtaking potentialities which lurk in the commonest American." All of these considerable truths about himself and his kind were made manifest to Disney in Kansas City. There, for the first time he glimpsed his own potentials and the potentials of a new and by no means highly regarded medium of communications, and in that unlikely place, he discovered people who could help him begin to realize both. That he glimpsed a commercial gift in the first instance and a commercial potential in the second is not completely surprising. He had, after all, never aspired to be anything loftier than a cartoonist, and such training as he had was as a *commercial* artist. In addition, his father was opposing his plan to try art as a career, and Disney probably felt that he had to demonstrate to the old man that he could make a living as an artist, perhaps even become what he had always wanted to be—an independent entrepreneur, beholden to no one.

In short, the history of Disney's three-year sojourn in Kansas City—not a struggle for artistic expression but rather a struggle for commercial stability—suggests that it was fatuous ever to see him as a man who prostituted an artist's potential on the altar of commerce (one has only to try to imagine him in a Left Bank garret). The miracle is rather the opposite—that there was enough force in his pen, and in those that he hired, to be mistaken for so long as an honest primitive.

The joke, really, is on the intellectuals, who for so many

years mistook him for their own. He was an energetic man, and it is possible that, swayed by their excellent opinion, he may have, for a time, tried to live up to their image of him, but it is almost certainly more accurate to surmise that Walter Elias Disney finally became what he apparently wanted to be from the start—a wildly successful entrepreneur of art or, more properly, its simulacrum. Indeed, it begins to seem, given his family and his geographic background, that he had very little choice in the matter. Certainly in 1919, he had none. At that point, and throughout most of the 1920s, Walt Disney was running so hard just to stay alive and ahead of the bill collectors that he had no time to reflect on the niceties of art versus commerce. His major problems were (a) to eat and (b) to stay free, free as his father never had been.

10 *Gotta hustle*
   —George F. Babbitt

DISNEY'S FIRST JOB in Kansas City paid only fifty dollars a month and it lasted for only about six weeks, but it was very educational. He was an apprentice in a commercial art studio doing work mostly for one of the town's advertising agencies. He got the job by showing, as samples, the cartoons he had done in France, and then only after he worked for the studio without salary for a week. There was nothing exalted about the job—he did rough pencil layouts of ads dealing with farm supplies, for the most part—but he liked the atmosphere, and he learned some valuable tricks of the trade.

"When you go to art school you work for perfection," he was to say later. "But in a commercial art shop you cut things out, and paste things over, and scratch around with a razor blade. I'd never done any of those things in art school. Those are time-saving tricks."

The other valuable thing that happened to Disney in this brief period was his meeting with Ub Iwerks, who worked in the studio specializing in lettering and in air brush work. He was undoubtedly Disney's superior in the techniques of their common craft, and more important in the long run, he was a man endlessly fascinated by the technical problems of motion picture production and played a key role in developing many of the devices and techniques that later gave the Disney product the technical edge it consistently maintained over its competition.

Iwerks told an associate later that the first time he ever saw Disney, Walt was seated at his drawing board, practicing variations on his signature, an activity often associated with willful attempts to resolve the identity crises of adolescence (and Disney, not quite eighteen, was still an adolescent, by any means of reckoning). Surely this first experience of turning what had been a knack into a profession was a significant moment for Disney and one in which the creation of a suitably mature and impressive signature was a symbolically correct, if faintly comic, gesture.

Disney's job in the art shop did not last. The Christmas rush for advertising material petered out toward the end of November, and he passed most of December once again in the employ of the post office department. At night he worked up a somewhat more sophisticated set of art samples employing the slickeries and trickeries he had acquired in his first job. Just after Christmas, Disney and Iwerks went into business for themselves.

They acquired free desk space in the office of a publication called *The Restaurant News*, the owner of which also paid them intermittent fees of around ten dollars for doing illustrative line cuts and occasionally talked his advertisers into buying their services. Disney appears to have provided such capital as the partnership needed—for drawing boards, desks, an air brush and a tank of air—out of the five hundred dollars his mother was holding for him. In the great family tradition she naturally inquired precisely what he intended to do with the money before she released it to him, and he was forced to write her, with some asperity, that he was about to follow another great family tradition and set up in business for himself and that, in any case, the money *was* his.

At any rate, the partnership was a modest success from the start. In their first month the young men took in $135, slightly more than their combined previous salaries. A few weeks later, however, they saw in a classified ad that an artist was needed at a concern called the Kansas City Film Ad Company. Disney who was then, as always, a good salesman despite his occasional moodiness, answered the ad, evidently hoping to get the firm to take on both Iwerks and himself. There was room for only one artist, however, and since the salary was $40 a week, there was no question that it would represent a substantial rise for whoever seized the opportunity. Iwerks deferred to Disney in the matter—taking their business for himself and letting his partner take the higher-salaried job. In theory it was an equitable arrangement since the business gross, undivided between two men, came close to equaling the salary Disney would earn. Unfortunately, Iwerks had none of Disney's sales talent, and over the next couple of months the business dried up.

Meantime, however, Disney had found his métier. Kansas City Film Ad was, in its little way, in the animated cartoon business, turning out crude one-minute advertisements—silent and in black and white, of course—for showing on local theater screens. It used one of the oldest and crudest techniques of animation—in effect, paper dolls, cut-out figures whose arms and legs worked on dowels and could thus be moved infinitesimally as each frame of film was shot, giving the illusion of movement. The technique, of course, has none of the flexibility or subtlety of drawn animation, but the state of the art in those days was quite primitive, even beyond the confines of Kansas City. Indeed, it is fair to say, as one veteran animator, recently did in recalling the era, that "nobody was doing good work in those days—everybody was doing the same kind of thing."

Nevertheless, it was a naturally attractive business to many young commercial artists of the time, for the field seemed to be—though actually it was not—wide open for innovation, far more so than many of the other areas for which their talents were suited. Disney was no exception—he was genuinely fascinated by the work and its problems—and, within a couple of months, Iwerks joined him at Kansas City Film Ad. Together they devised sundry improvements on the cut-out animation technique, hiding the joints of their figures to give them more fluid movement and making sure that they were placed accurately so that such bendings and twistings as the figures were subjected to were closer to nature.

There was no time for experiment on the job, however, and Disney soon talked his boss into letting him borrow a camera to play with in his garage in his spare time. He worked up a sample reel of local jokes and announcements, apparently something like a satirical newsreel, which he sold to the Newman Theater in Kansas City. It was called The Newman Laugh-O-Gram, and its successors ran on a regular basis at the theater, with a by-line credit for Disney on it. He also did special work for the theater—one short celebrated the theater's anniversary with movie stars popping out of a cake, another featured a little professor who announced he had a sure cure for people who read titles out loud—a Rube Goldberg invention that caused the offender's seat to disappear and sent him down a chute and out into the street. It was not very high-level stuff, obviously, and Disney, when asked to name a price for his Laugh-O-Grams, had forgotten to calculate a profit margin into his figure. As a result, he was doing his basic moonlighting at cost.

However, in the pricing of his other jobs he was able to compensate somewhat for this oversight, and he was soon doing well enough to return his borrowed camera to his daytime employers and buy one of his own. Shortly thereafter he felt he was ready to leave Kansas City Film Ad and launch a full-time production company of his own. He retained Laugh-O-Gram as his corporate name, somehow rounded up working capital in the surprisingly affluent neighborhood of fifteen thousand dollars, moved out of the garage where he had been working and engaged a group of helpers. These he paid nothing, promising them only the opportunity to learn and, perhaps, a share of future profits. This was the beginning of the basic relationship with employees that he was to develop more formally in Hollywood later on, where an elaborate apprentice system supplied his studio with young talent at low prices. It was not a wholly exploitative system—the opportunity to learn was genuine—but the system was ultimately a factor in creating the extraordinary bitterness that attended the great strike at the Disney studios in 1940. His first assistants were soon making salaries because Laugh-O-Gram quickly sold a series of seven animated fairy tales, each seven minutes in length; among the subjects were *Puss 'n' Boots* and *Little Red Riding Hood*.

Motion picture distribution in those days was a free-booting enterprise (it still is to a surprising degree, especially among the small independents), and though Disney's representative in New York was getting the prints around, somehow his share of the grosses was not getting back to Disney in Kansas City. Rather quickly he was forced to let his staff go, and shortly thereafter he was forced to abandon his apartment and live in the Laugh-O-Gram offices, sleeping on a pile of pillows. The experience was only the first of several bad ones with the people and firms who distributed his films through the years, and each of them reinforced his essential suspicion of outsiders—an attitude that the native midwesterner has to guard against anyway —and it surely reinforced the passion with which he invested

79

all his efforts, in later years, to control his own economic destiny.

In the years prior to 1923, when he left Kansas City for good, Disney was forced to a wide variety of desperate expedients to keep alive in his profession. Whenever he needed a haircut, he traded cartoons to a barber, who displayed them in his shop window. He used his camera, his only asset and one to which he managed to cling right up to the end, to take little movies of babies for their parents to project in their living room. And he served as stringer for such newsreel companies as Selznick, Pathe and Universal. Whenever an assignment came his way, he would hire a flivver, paste a press sticker on the windshield and head for the event—often some natural disaster—he was supposed to cover. The usual request was for one hundred feet of film, for which he was paid a dollar a foot if it was acceptable. If it was not, the newsreel firms sent him an amount of unexposed film equal to what he had shot.

One of his principal sources of support in those days was his brother Roy, who for a time was at a veterans' hospital in Tucson, then at one in Los Angeles, recovering from tuberculosis. He periodically dispatched a blank check to his younger brother with instructions to fill it out in any amount up to thirty dollars. Disney customarily went the limit. His other major source of aid was two brothers who ran a Greek restaurant that occupied the ground floor of the building in which Disney had his studio. He had credit there up to a limit of sixty dollars, and as he recalled, he was usually close to it, with the use of his brother's checks going mainly to keep the restaurant owners appeased. At one point, at least, they cut off his credit, and Disney was forced onto a diet of dry bread and beans he scrounged from an abandoned photographic studio next door. A couple of days later one of the Greeks happened to wander in as Disney was downing one of these meals, took pity on him and invited him downstairs for something more substantial. Disney's daughter Diane, once asked him if he didn't regard this as the low point of his life, only to have him deny that it was any such thing. "No, it wasn't bad," he is reported to have said. "I love beans" —a statement his later dietary habits tended to prove.

In the lean years after the failure of Laugh-O-Gram, Disney actually managed to produce two animated films. One was an educational effort, designed to teach children the advantages of dental hygiene. It was called *Tommy Tucker's Tooth* and was underwritten, in the amount of five hundred dollars, by a Doctor Thomas McCrum, who later sold it to the Deener Dental Institute, a local clinic. When McCrum called Disney to tell him that the money was available and to invite him over to work out details, Disney was forced to tell him that he couldn't leave his studio to meet him. His only pair of shoes had fallen apart, were in a shoe store in his building (he had padded back to his studio in his stocking feet after leaving them for repair) and that he needed $1.50 to retrieve them. The dentist came to him.

Far more significant to Disney's future was another film he had made as a last effort to salvage Laugh-O-Gram. It was called *Alice in Cartoonland*, and it was a twist on what was then a popular animated cartoon series, *Out of the Inkwell*, created by Max Fleischer, who was to gain somewhat more fame later with his *Betty Boop* series. Fleischer's characters, in the earlier effort, literally popped out of an inkwell or up off a drawing board to perform their little bits of crude comedy against real or seemingly real backgrounds. Disney's notion was to place a live actor—in the first instance a child who did some modeling at the Kansas City Film Ad Company—into a cartoon. She was never seen except against drawn backgrounds, and everyone she associated with was a drawn figure. (The trick was simply accomplished: she was photographed only against white backgrounds, and the drawings were made on white backgrounds; the two films were then integrated in the printing process.)

Disney claimed that he secured an agreement from his creditors, when he went bankrupt, allowing him to keep a print of the film as a sample of his work, but whether anything as formal as a legal agreement actually existed, or was necessary, is unclear. The fact is that even the proceeds of *Tommy Tucker's Tooth* and of his other free-lance activities did not come close to covering Disney's debts when it became clear to him that his future in Kansas City was limited and that he would have to repair to the West Coast if he wanted to make good in the movies. He finally had to sell his camera—at a profit—to finance his trip west, then went around to his creditors, asking them if they would accept a partial settlement in order for him to make a fresh start. Most of them refused his offer, telling him that he would need the money for a grubstake and to repay them later, when he could afford it. "They were wonderful people," he said, recalling the period.

In later years Disney invited the barber with whom he had bartered drawings for haircuts to come to the Coast for a visit at his expense. He also lent quite a bit of money, after his great success with Mickey Mouse, to one of the restaurateurs who had carried him in the lean days. Indeed, he drew a little lesson in folk economics from the experience. The man wrote to him, sometime in the 1930s, asking for a thousand dollars to help re-establish the restaurant business after he had spent some time as an automobile dealer. Disney advanced him the money. A little while later he wrote again, this time for five hundred dollars to buy an air conditioner for the place. Again the money was advanced. The next time the man applied for funds—to buy out a partner—Disney turned him down. The point was, as Disney phrased it, "that the $60 worth of food [he] let me have on credit cost me $1500." It should be added, however, that Disney, for all his latter-day moralism about lending, had been a habitual borrower and raised a critical $250 he needed in his early days by writing for a loan from the organist of a Kansas City theater for whom he had done animated sequences of music and lyrics to flash on the screen during the community singing that used to be such a familiar part of moviegoing. He also borrowed money from the Kansas City girl whom Roy Disney ultimately married and who had also helped out with free meals during the days of his bankruptcy, and at one point he got $60 from his brother Raymond, then working as a bank teller in Kansas City—a loan that was to have some consequences for both of them.

All of this is significant only to demonstrate how much Disney was a product, however unwillingly, of the climate of small enterprise well beneath the attention of banks and bankers. It is, of course, a world of suspiciousness relieved by sudden, often inexplicable, generosity, a world where the basic salesmanship must be done on the friends one turns to for backing, where the rules insist that debts incurred in this way are debts of honor, but where one must be ever wary of the con man willing to violate them. It is a world of people lured on by tales of others like themselves who became millionaires on the basis of a small investment in some inventor's dream and of people made cautious by the equally prevalent tales of promoters who skipped town with everybody's hard-earned savings. Nowhere is the fulcrum on which we balance our dream of wealth against our nightmare of insecurity more precariously—or more poignantly—balanced, for this is a world of borrowers who can't afford to lose yet can scarcely bear to go on as they are. One does not pass through this world, especially after a childhood like Disney's, unscarred. His future economic style—frugality in day-to-day matters, willingness to plunge on his own ideas, distrust of the outsider who might somehow take it all away from him—was surely an acting out, on a large scale, of the truths he had learned in Kansas City.

11   *Arthur Koestler suggests that there is in the revolutionary "some defective quality" which keeps him from growing up. The indications are, however, that the present trend toward juvenile behavior has been gathering force for over a century and has affected people who cannot be classed as revolutionaries. . . . the American go-getter, though he has no quarrel with the status quo, is as much a perpetual juvenile as any revolutionary.*
          —Eric Hoffer, *The Temper of Our Times*

HOFFER'S THEORY OF the juvenile nature, which he sees as a mass phenomenon and as a principal factor in the creation of the temper of our times, suggests that we are not at the beginning of an era of radical change but well along in a transformation that began with the industrial revolution at the end of the eighteenth century. The urbanization of the millions who were scooped up off the land and set to work tending the new machines has been, in his view, the central fact not only of our own historical moment but that of our fathers and grandfathers as well. It may be said to account for the gropings of Elias Disney as much as it did his son's. It is not that the machines are, in themselves, dehumanizing but that the changes they bring to every area of human existence have a vastly upsetting effect, forcing uprooted millions to seek new identities in a world that appears no longer to offer them traditionally reassuring values. The result is a human type who, as Hoffer says, is "juvenile, primitive and plastic," for the juvenile is "the archetypal man in transition" and whenever we are subjected to drastic change, we recapitulate to some degree the adolescent's passage from childhood to manhood, a process that "results in some degree of primitivization." *En masse* this means we attempt to seek identity by resort to mass movements, nationalism, charismatic leaders, medicine men and, of course, the kind of nostalgia for a carefully falsified past which Walt Disney, among others, was later to trade in so successfully.

One warm July day young Disney, twenty-one years old, already an experienced, if failed, go-getter, waited on the platform at the Kansas City station to board the Santa Fe's California Limited. If ever there has been an archetypal man in transition, it was he. He wore a checked coat and a well-worn pair of pants that did not match the coat. In his imitation-leather suitcase there were a couple of pairs of socks, a couple of pairs of underwear, an extra shirt and some drawing material. In his pocket he had, so goes the official legend, forty dollars, all that was left from the sale of his camera. "But his head was packed with ideas," his daughter writes. "Someway, somehow, when he got to Hollywood, he'd get to the top of the movie heap."

He had no realistic reason to believe he would be any more successful on the Coast than he had been in the Midwest. Indeed, he had no precise notion of what he wanted to do once he got there, beyond that standard dream of glory, "breaking into the movies." By any reasonable method of judgment he was no more than a journeyman at any of the motion picture crafts in which he had dabbled, and he had none of the interest in self-expression or cultural and social observation that usually drives and sustains any artist worthy of the name. He had, to be sure, accidentally found a congenial medium in which to exercise whatever talents he might have, but at this stage the motion picture was to him what real estate was to George Babbitt—a means to some ill-defined, but economically rewarding end. It was by no stretch of the imagination an end in itself. He saw the movies only as a living, not as a life. There is no way of knowing how or what he thought of himself or, indeed, if he made any attempt to find in himself a unique quality. In retrospect the three years in Kansas City seem to have been a last chance for him as an artist. Had they been less harassed and desperate, it is possible—just barely possible—that he might have been able to integrate into a unique artistic personality the ego so badly shredded in his loveless, rootless childhood. Instead, he adopted, with very little need of modification, a prevalent mass style—that of the go-getter—and then he got out to get.

That Walt Disney remained perpetually the juvenile that he was chronologically when he came to Kansas City for the second time and still was psychologically when he left it for good, turned out to be no bar to his economic success. Quite the contrary. It enabled him instinctively to purvey to his audiences precisely what they wanted—perhaps needed—in a way that few others so consistently managed. That he seemed to remain psychologically preoccupied with his own isolation and therefore be cut off from most forms of social intimacy was no problem, either. At first he played the part of the primitive artist allowing "the professors" to explain his own work to him and then scoffing boyishly at the explanations. It was a most satisfactory public relations device, tiding him over until he could fashion the more avuncular but still homespun public style of his later years. There were plenty of public relations men to help him with it, and, of course, the mass media were only too happy to conspire in the maintenance of this image. Their readers and viewers liked it, for it was untroubling; the proprietors of the media liked it because Disney was such a reassuringly clean and decent mogul—and Protestant, as few other moguls were. He could be used to blunt a lot of generalized moral and religiously prejudiced criticism about mass communications.

But all this was in the future. The young Walt Disney might have been a rube, a cornball, a hick, on anybody's scale of sophistication, but he was something else as well. "History is made," says Eric Hoffer, "by men who have the restlessness, impressionability, credulity, capacity for make-believe, ruthlessness and self-righteousness of children. It is made by men who set their hearts on toys."

PART FOUR

Back to the Drawing Board

---

12 *Know ye that at the right hand of the Indies there is an island named california, very close to . . . the Terrestrial Paradise. . . . The island everywhere abounds with gold and precious stones. . . .*
—Ordóñez de Montalvo, Las Sergas de Esplandian (1510)

All too many of us Americans who took part in the conquest of the empty continent, when we finally got to Los Angeles, found we had put the emptiness inside.
—George W. Pierson, The Humanities and Moral Men

INSIDE. Where it was safely hidden, even from oneself, particularly if oneself was very, very busy. You might not notice it for years and others might never notice it at all, especially in Los Angeles, where there were so many important things going on.

Out of the chaos of many small competitors, the large studio system was beginning to evolve, a business was becoming an industry—"*The* Industry," as it is still reverently referred to on ceremonious occasions. In 1923, a few months before Disney arrived, another young man named Irving Thalberg, less than three years older than Disney, left Universal to join a one-time junk dealer named Louis B. Mayer as his chief of production at the small Metro Studios. Within a year they would merge with the Goldwyn Studio, under the aegis of Loew's, Inc., to form the firm that would quickly become the biggest of the sausage factories, Metro-Goldwyn-Mayer. Famous Players-Lasky had sometime before absorbed Triangle, which had itself been a merger of three of Hollywood's leading creative forces—D. W. Griffith, William Ince and Mack Sennett—to form Paramount, which numbered among its assets the strongest theater chain of the time. Griffith had meantime—and unhappily—joined with Douglas Fairbanks, Mary Pickford and Charles Chaplin to form United Artists in 1919. In the years that followed, other combinations of producers, and of producers and theater chains, were effected. The result was a recapitulation of a process that had been going on elsewhere in American industry for some time—a reduction in the number of independent production units but with each of the remaining units becoming larger and at least potentially more efficient and more stable than they had been separately. Disney, when he finally arrived in Hollywood, felt that he was almost a decade too late to do what a slightly older group of pioneers had done—set up shop completely on their own. It would be something like a quarter of a century later, for example, before he had his own distribution corporation and was free of the percentages of the gross which the larger companies exacted from him—as well as from other independents—for getting their work into theaters.

The changes being wrought in the industry were not solely economic. However quaintly a silent film from the middle of the 1920s may flicker before modern eyes, the fact remains that in the years between 1919 and 1923, they had begun to lose their innocence. Erich von Stroheim had, for example, begun to make the series of films (*Blind Husbands, The Devil's Passkey, Foolish Wives*) that Lewis Jacobs was to characterize as "melodramas of lust" in all its forms. "Executed with a hard unrelenting honesty, they were by turns sordid, scathing, mocking, ironic," and they "brought to the screen an individuality, a maturity, and a meaning not to be found in the pictures of the DeMilles, the Inces. . . ." In the very summer that Walt Disney arrived in Hollywood, von Stroheim, his cast and crew, were toiling in the incredible heat of Death Valley to complete the shooting of his blighted masterpiece, *Greed*, in which for the first time he was to direct his mordant gaze upon an America that, as J. K. Galbraith has put it, was "displaying an inordinate desire to get rich quickly with a minimum of physical effort."

DeMille himself had turned to sex comedies that were very racy by pre-war standards, and his famous bathtub scenes were already becoming a legend. The very names of the stars who were born in the post-World War I era—Valentino, Gloria Swanson, Clara Bow—evoke for us today a faintly comic image of an industry both reflecting and helping to create a new American atmosphere. The year 1923 was fairly typical of the period. Pola Negri (whose last screen appearance was in Disney's 1964 film, *The Moonspinners*) was driving men to ruin, insanity or suicide in *Mad Love*, released in March of the year, then suffering most deliciously, a few months later, for her transgressions in *The Cheat*, about which *Time* magazine, founded that same year, commented: "The spectacle of a hot iron sinking into the white contours of [her] shoulder should be 50¢ worth to anybody." At that, it was no more sadistic than Lon Chaney's writhing under the lash in *The Hunchback of Notre Dame*, which appeared the same month.

In short, film content was changing, trying to grow more sophisticated. Many of the great names of the movies' early days —men who had been at the pinnacle of the industry only five or six years before—were suddenly racing to catch up with the new mood. D. W. Griffith, to whom, as Charles Chaplin said, "the whole industry owes its experience," simply could not make the transition. His 1923 release, *One Exciting Night*, was deemed jumbled and pointless and failed; it was neither the first nor the last of his increasingly desperate attempts to respond to the new spirit of the times. William S. Hart, "the greatest cowboy that ever faced a camera," had been forced into retirement two years earlier and now emerged to find that, although the critics still liked him in *Wild Bill Hickok*, the public was indifferent to his realistic vision of the West. They wanted a more romantic, less gritty version of their pioneer heritage. Even Buster Keaton, who was perhaps the greatest of the silent comedians, ran into trouble with his first long film, *The Three Ages*, in which he had difficulty in sustaining his comic line for an hour and a half.

Of the great early established names, only a few emerged from the year unscathed. Douglas Fairbanks had abandoned the attempt to deal with the contemporary scene several years earlier and in 1923 released one of his most successful historical romances, the marvelously athletic *Robin Hood*. His new bride, Mary Pickford, emerged from a brief retirement with a new image: she stopped trying to be America's Sweetheart Forever in this transitional year and, her famous golden curls tucked on top of her head, appeared in *Rosita* as a Spanish street singer who rises to the nobility. Even Chaplin changed. His first release of 1923 was *The Pilgrim*, and in it his "Little Fellow," the beloved tramp, appeared as an escaping convict turned minister ("custard piety," one critic called it). Chaplin did not even appear in his second 1923 effort, *A Woman of Paris*, which starred the leading lady of his shorter, earlier comedies, Edna Purviance, and dealt with a Parisian mistress whose tinseled world comes tumbling down when the youth she used to love suddenly reenters her life. For her director it represented a considerable shift from his usual mode.

No one knew quite what to make of it all. Intelligent commentators declared that there was still something awfully naïve about the new cinematic sophistication, that by and large the spirit of *True Romance* had won out over the spirit of romantic truth. "Breathes there a man with a brain so dead that he has not repudiated those curly co-eds, those red-blooded 'Society folk' with midnight bathing parties, those flat-footed vampires?" *Time* inquired with the iconoclastic exuberance of its youth. Even so, the cry of the censor was heard in the land, and Will Hays, the Indiana politician who was hired in 1921 to cleanse the blot placed on the industry's banner by the Fatty Arbuckle scandal, and who, with his high collars and *pince nez*, was the personification of midwestern rectitude, was hard put to keep up with the demands for moral purity that the older America was making on the movies.

In this period he got very little help from his new constituents. After two hung juries, Arbuckle had just suffered through his third trial for the manslaughter death of a bit player named Virginia Rappe, who had been his companion during a wild San Francisco party in 1921; director William Desmond Taylor was murdered in 1923, and two well-known actresses, June Taylor and Mary Miles Minter, were unpleasantly linked with his free-wheeling life, though not with his death. And clean-cut Wallace Reid, an important leading man who had been revealed to be a drug addict, died in 1923 in the hospital where he was attempting to find a cure. Hays and the industry leaders drew up a blacklist of personalities whose morals might cause them future difficulties, DeMille wrapped a soothing Biblical cloak around the industry by releasing *The Ten Commandments* (which nevertheless contained a very satisfactory orgy sequence), and there was a general effort to tone down Hollywood's excesses both on screen and off. Adolph Zukor gave out an interview in which he said, "Hollywood is a very quiet place. A *very* quiet place. No drinking—very little smoking. And as for the evenings . . . they're practically inaudible. No sound at all but the popping of the California poppies."

Others were less bland about the situation in Hollywood. In the wake of the Reid tragedy, Miss Elinor Glyn, the English novelist who coined the word "It" as an expression of the ultimate in libidinal energy and who was almost single-handedly responsible for the cycle of Ruritanian romances so much a feature of this period, was asked what would happen next in the sorely tried film colony, and she sagely replied: "Whatever will bring in the most money will happen." As for the intellectuals, some of whom were beginning to sound as if they would like to like the movies, they were disappointed. It might seem to one journal of opinion that "almost every hamlet has a good film every week," but Joseph Wood Krutch spoke for the majority when he declared that "the inanities blessed by Mr. Hays are more genuinely corrupting than any pornography."

It is impossible to say what, if anything, Walt Disney thought of all this when he arrived in Los Angeles. Since, like many Americans who were essentially technological innovators, his social imagination was rather underdeveloped and since he faced such a difficult battle for survival, it is likely that it all seemed rather remote to him. Emotionally he was as far away from the heights where these alarums and excursions were taking place as he had been back in Kansas City. Indeed, the small circle into which he moved was one of emigres from the midlands—rootless, envious, nostalgic, intellectually and emotionally juvenile—like those who, since the 1920s, have been the source of Southern California's reputation for crankish, cultish excess. It is likely that if he thought about the morality of the movies and the industry that made them, he was vaguely disapproving. All his life he remained essentially alienated from the industry's power structure and unwilling to join it either socially or in its endless, frantic searches for the formulae of box-office success. To borrow Isaiah Berlin's famous metaphor, the industry's leaders were the foxes who knew many things and he was a hedgehog who knew one important thing.

They were quick men with the peddler's instinct to vary his

stock and his spiel the minute he senses a slight restlessness in the crowd and the smallest clue to their next whim. They were, many of them, children of the ghetto—colorful, volatile, emotional and, if not what one would call cultivated, then in love with the game and cheerfully cynical about its rules and its outcome. If they had a flaw it lay, not in the ignorance and the occasional brutality and trickery of their business style, which provided so much good copy for journalists and other malcontents through the years. In retrospect, there was something refreshing about all that chicanery in the context of a nation that has always been rather too pious about the role (and rule) of business.

No, their problem was that they were still immigrants—even those who had been born here. They did not have, bred in their bones, the culture of the American majority; they always had to go out and look for it—a quest that frequently left them a half-step behind its shifts in mood, and rarely more than a half-step ahead of it. They nearly always came out ahead, because the art of survival *was* bred in their bones, but they were nervous men, and that is what made them adopt the more obvious manners of the autocrat—their style in dealing with underlings, their enormous homes, cars and offices, the retinue of ubiquitous sycophants.

Disney, the hedgehog, had no such insecurities. He knew what he knew about Protestant, middle-class, midwestern America, and he knew that what he liked, it liked. He needed no public opinion polls (though he used them, in later years, because they were so reassuringly scientific), few sycophants (he had them, but that was more their problem than his) and, above all, no atmosphere of excessive materialism to reassure himself about the value of his own opinions or work. The determined informality of his manner was no affectation, at least at first, though at the end, when he was a multimillionaire, it was a trifle disconcerting, in the same way it is to see pictures of Nelson Rockefeller chomping on a hot dog. It was this in-bred sureness of his audience (which was merely himself multi-plied) that led to his ultimate success and led people to misunderstand him as one kind of genius when he was actually a genius of quite another sort.

What is most significant about the atmosphere of Hollywood in the 1920s as it relates specifically to Disney's history is that in this period the town acquired its reputation for wickedness among Disney's class and kind, a reputation that has never been completely expunged. We have observed that the industry was at expensive pains to cleanse its reputation, and it is precisely in this area that Disney was most useful to the lords of celluloid creation. Whenever the voices of the moralists grew too shrill, Disney could always be pointed out as a purveyor of clean, uplifting family entertainment and he could be counted upon, too, for statesmanlike comments on the need to maintain a climate of moral excellence and the pleasure he took in contributing to it. These, too, were apparently quite sincere in their motivation.

As a result of this natural cleanliness of outlook, he was responsible in some measure for the demise of the one great contribution Hollywood made, without knowing it, to our cultural heritage. This was, of course, the short comedy. The great comedians—Chaplin, Keaton, Harry Langdon, Harold Lloyd, Laurel and Hardy—were beloved by both the plain people and by those intellectuals who were paying attention. And with good reason. They had developed to a precise and subtle degree the art of physical comedy, often known, imprecisely, as "slapstick." But despite the high regard in which many held their work, there was a countercurrent. James Agee, in his autobiographical novel, *A Death in the Family*, has the mother of a small boy object to Chaplin as "that horrid little man. . . . He's so *nasty* . . . so *vulgar!* With his nasty little cane; hooking up skirts and things, and that nasty little walk!" In 1923, a magazine noted that "our good old uncles and funny old aunts" demurred from the view that Chaplin and the rest represented art. "They said that when one comedian dropped a lighted cigar down another comedian's trousers it was not art. And for their part they couldn't see anything funny in one man hitting another in the seat of what they termed 'pants.' In their day [it] was a disciplinary objective; they refused to admit the right of Charles Chaplin to make it simply the butt of a jest." Disney, when he borrowed the balletic movements and timing of the silent comics but changed the actors from human to animal form in his cartoons and removed the sexual references from the great routines, effectively disposed of many of their objections. What had been nasty as a form of human behavior became acceptably adorable as obviously fictive animal behavior.

Disney was even useful, as a silent example, to the maniac fringe who insisted that control of the movies was vested in the international Jewish conspiracy. One had merely to wave in his direction to indicate that the *goyim* were not barred from success in this field. There was a certain irony in this, since Disney appears to have shared, in mild form, some of the anti-Semitism that was common to his generation and place of origin. His studio was notably lacking in Jewish employees, and at least once he presented a fairly vicious caricature of the Jew on screen.

In 1923, whatever his fantasies of the future, Disney's practical, immediate ambitions appeared modest enough. He made no attempt, on first arriving in California, to set up in business for himself. He did not even turn first to animation in his search for work. He reasoned that the studios, now beginning generally to work on the rationalized, production-line basis that Thomas Ince had pioneered a few years earlier, would need plenty of directors and that there might be a considerable turnover in the field. He therefore presented himself to the man at Universal who had been handling his newsreel submissions and got from him a visitor's pass to the studio. He then proceeded to hang around the lot, trying to pick up tips on directing and also trying to discover where, if anywhere, opportunities might lie. After a couple of weeks he scaled his ambitions down somewhat, but even at the lower levels of Universal, there were no jobs for him.

He was at least halfway convinced that he was too late, by perhaps six years, to break into animation, but since that was the only area in which he had any prior experience, he rented a battered camera, made an animation stand out of scrap lumber and set up a studio in the garage of his Uncle Robert Disney's home, where he was staying (room and board was five dollars a week). He was still getting occasional small loans from brother Roy, who was by now in a veterans' hospital in Sawtelle, California, where he was drawing eighty-five dollars a month in disability pay from the government. The only hope Walt Disney had—and it seemed a faint one—was his old *Alice in Cartoonland* sample, which the Lloyds Film Storage Company was attempting to sell to distributors in New York. He certainly could not afford to wait any longer for action on it. Nor did it appear that a lengthy siege of the employment offices of the other studios would be a much better gamble than trying to set up his own business again. There are, he later philosophized, two kinds of people. "The first kind are licked if they can't get a job. The second kind feel they can always do *something*, even if jobs are scarce." He was definitely one of the latter types.

Even so, he cannot have felt very hopeful as he set up shop again. He was acutely aware of the successes Paul Terry had achieved with his two series, *Aesop's Fables* and *Farmer Al Falfa*, as well as Pat Sullivan's crude but effective *Felix the Cat*, not to mention the work of such prominent pioneers as Raoul Barre and Fleischer. Then, too, a number of the popular comic strips of the day, among them *Mutt and Jeff* and even George Herriman's *Krazy Kat* (which proved to be as literally inimitable in animation as it was figuratively so on the page), were getting considerable attention from the producers, who then, as now, were mightily inclined toward products on which the audience was possibly presold. Disney later commented that he felt that the field, neither large nor profitable, was overcrowded, even though its growth, in the decade since its birth, had been far slower than that of the rest of the movie industry.

13 *"Energy is eternal delight."*
   —William Blake

IT IS CUSTOMARY to begin most histories of animation—indeed, of the movies in general—with a reference to the Lascaux cave paintings or, at the very least and latest, to the pictographs of Egypt or the decorations on some Greek vases which, if spun in the hand, imparted the illusion that a figure, drawn in the various attitudes of movement, was actually moving. All of these art objects, as well as many others, like the Bayeux tapestry, are claimed by historians seeking to attribute to the movies, a suitably long cultural pedigree, though these objects may be more accurately said to have represented the wish for the ability to make pictures move rather than the actual accomplishment of the deed.

In fact, animation may reasonably claim a longer history than the movies themselves, which had to wait upon the invention of photography. Man has been drawing since prehistoric times, and the principle of persistence of vision, on which all illusions of motion are based, was known to Ptolemy. Thus animation of a sort was used commercially for the first time as early as the sixteenth and seventeenth centuries, when publishers brought out books—often pornographic in nature—containing little figures that seemed to move when the pages were rapidly riffled. It was not until 1825, however, that the first toy based on the principle of persistence of vision was developed. In that year Dr. John Ayrton Paris demonstrated a simple little gadget known as the Thaumatrope, which was nothing more than a cardboard disc with a string on either side, so that it might be twirled between thumb and finger. There was an image on each side of the disc, and when the disc was rotated, these drawings would seem to combine; thus a child might be able to observe a bird that seemed to pop into a cage or a rider jumping onto his horse. In 1832 Professor J. A. F. Plateau of Brussels came forth with something he called the Phenakistoscope, which may be regarded as the first mechanical animation device. It was no more than a notched wheel mounted on a handle. If you held it up to a mirror and peered through the notches the figures painted on the reverse side seemed to move as you observed them in the mirror. Two years later virtually the same device was independently conceived by Simon Ritter von Stampfer of Vienna, who called his version the Stroboscope. Actually, both men had been preceded by W. G. Horner of Bristol, England, who perfected, as early as 1834, a somewhat more sophisticated toy he called the Zoetrope. It was a slot-pierced drum, revolving on a pivot. You placed a flat disc in the bottom of the drum and a paper band around the sides. On each disc were painted figures in various stages of a movement. By peering into the slot and rotating the drum, a very satisfactory illusion of motion was obtained. Horner's gadget did not reach the market until 1867, and in a decade it was improved upon by Professor Emile Reynaud of Paris, who did away with the slots and notches all the preceding devices had utilized. His Praxinoscope had a series of mirrors in the center of the drum, and you kept your eye on them while rotating the outer disc, where the band of carefully drawn figures was placed. He even devised, a few years later, a method of projecting his moving figures onto an enchanting little table-top stage.

Neither he nor his various competitors, who called their gadgets by such names as "the wheel of life" and the "wheel of the devil," would ever master large-scale theatrical projection. The line of inventive work that led up to the virtually simultaneous invention of the movies by the Lumière brothers in

France and by William Kennedy Dickson, working for Edison in the United States, stemmed directly from still photography and proceeded through George Eastman's vital creation of flexible celluloid film and thence to the Kinetoscope, which was a true movie in its creation but not in its presentation, because it could be viewed, like a peep show, only by a single person. At last came the Vitascope, which Edison marketed in 1893, and the Cinematograph of the Lumières. But all these men were wedded to the photographic reproduction of movement and had little interest in animation, which no one seems to have thought of as a possibility for the new medium.

It was not until 1905 that J. Stuart Blackton, a one-time artist for the New York *World* and later a producer for Edison, attempted an animated film. It was called *Humorous Phases of Funny Faces* and consisted of, among other actions, a man rolling his eyes and blowing smoke rings. In the flood of short films emanating from the studios in those days it was largely ignored as interest focused on the first story films following in the wake of the hugely successful *The Great Train Robbery*, produced in 1903. A number of other artists did attempt animated films, but none was particularly successful until Winsor McCay, creator of the exquisitely drawn Little Nemo comic strip, animated *Nemo*, did a little film about a mosquito, and then made his great breakthrough with *Gertie the Dinosaur*. *Gertie* was conceived as part of a Vaudeville act. Her image was projected on a screen, and she seemed to respond to commands McCay issued from the stage. The big climax of the routine was her catching and eating an apple that McCay appeared to toss to her (but actually palmed).

After *Gertie* (whose other wondrous trick was to seem to drink a whole lake dry and then spit it all out—a simple matter of reversing the film) the animation market began to open somewhat. John R. Bray had a success with his *Col. Heeza Liar in Africa*, a 1913 satire on Teddy Roosevelt's big-game hunting expedition, and developed it into a series. At about the same time, Earl Hurd, who worked for Bray, provided the infant industry with a technological breakthrough to match the one McCay had had achieved with audiences. Until Hurd appeared, it had been necessary to draw, *in toto*, each frame of the film—a tedious and expensive business that effectively prohibited films of any length and, indeed, any sophistication of animation. Hurd developed the idea of doing his animations on celluloid and photographing them against a background that needed to be changed only when the scene changed. This eliminated a great deal of redrawing and concentrated the artist's attention on the principal problem of the cartoon, which is movement. The cells, as they quickly came to be called, presented a fairly serious fire hazard at first, when nitrate celluloid was used as the basic material, but with the introduction of acetate safety film, this problem was soon eliminated. Even though the early animators frequently saw their work literally go up in a puff of smoke, the development of the cell technique was essential to getting the business moving in even the low gear that pertained throughout the second and third decades of this century.

There was a great deal wrong with the animated film business at the time Disney decided to go back into it. Some of the trouble was artistic, some was financial. To be sure, a couple of the basic conventions of the animated cartoon had already been adopted. The repeal of the law of gravity had occurred in Raoul Barre's atelier as early as 1917. He was then producing the *Mutt and Jeff* series and one of his teams was doing an Alpine sequence in which Mutt was to be shown leaning against a guard rail with a steep drop below. A careless cameraman forgot to place the cell containing the rail before his camera, and so the character appeared, in the rushes, to be leaning on thin air. Barre, who was French and formal, was not amused, but his American gagmen laughed to see such a sight. Before long cartoon characters were walking on air, on the ceilings, anywhere they might get a laugh, and, of course, the basic device is still much used today. Similarly, the emphasis on anthropomorphizing animals was discovered early, especially in the work of Paul Terry. Because they are rounder- and softer-looking than clothed humans, they were thought to be easier to animate and caricature; they were not bound by realism the way their competitors—live human actors—were, and audiences could easily feel simultaneously affectionate and superior to them. Finally, the uses of cruelty without consequences were discovered. A cartoon character could take a great fall, break into a dozen pieces and be put together again, no harm done, with a few strokes of an animator's pen, thus conventionalizing and therefore deemotionalizing sadism.

Still, despite this establishment of the basic aesthetic of the industry, the animated cartoons, five minutes or so in length, constituted no more than a curious appendage to a curious industry. Drawing remained crude and hasty, the technique of animation reflected no more than a suggestion of the skills that were to come, while the plot lines were generally no more than a string of gags. There was no attempt to develop character in the course of the little films, and there was a fairly firm belief that only animals were suitable as characters, since their spontaneity and physical characteristics made them almost automatic caricatures when they were placed in human postures and predicaments. Finally, the lack of color and sound was never the advantage in animation that it occasionally was in some silent films, and both ingredients were nearly always more sorely missed in the cartoons than in feature films. Lacking color, the animators were working without one of the graphic artist's basic resources. Without sound, they lacked the dramatist's basic tool. And lacking the artistry of some of the actors and directors who worked in features, as well as the wealth of the major studios, cartoons had nothing with which to compensate for these disadvantages. In particular, the need for titles to tell jokes and explain the action was a serious disadvantage and slowed down the comic movement.

But it was the economic situation of the animators that was

perhaps the most distressing aspect of their fledgling art. The days were past when Paul Terry received just $405 outright, with no possibility of additional royalties, for his first cartoon, *Little Herman*, which he had done entirely by himself over a period of several months. But they were not much past. The going rate for an ordinary cartoon was around $1,500, and though a shop with a series of proved popularity might get somewhat more, there was still no participations in the grosses of the films. What was worse, the theater chains preferred to buy their short subjects in blocks (a situation that continues today) and so had no interest in the odd film of more than routine interest. What they wanted were series about which they could say that if you had seen one you had seen them all, thus obviating the need for screening the product carefully or even thinking much about it. As for the distributors, they were interested only in keeping costs and troubles at a minimum. Quality, experiment, any innovation that might run up the cost per foot of the shorts, these were in no way pleasing to them.

That any young man was willing to attempt such a business must remain as a permanent tribute to his stubbornness. That Disney, alone of all the men who went into animation was able to emerge from it a full-fledged tycoon (several made a bit of money out of it eventually) must stand as a tribute to organizational abilities of a very high order.

14   *The young man walks fast by himself through the crowd
. . . blood tingles with wants; mind is a beehive of hopes buzz-
ing and stinging. . . .*

*The young man walks by himself, fast but not fast enough,
far but not far enough. . . .*

No job, no woman, no house, no city.

—John Dos Passos, *U.S.A.*

DISNEY'S FIRST MOVE, once he had made up his mind to
go into business for himself again, was to renovate his old
Laugh-O-Gram idea—a series of topical joke anthologies—and
try to peddle it to the local theaters. He began hanging around
the offices of Alexander Pantages, who controlled a chain of
West Coast movie houses, and finally got a junior executive to
listen to his idea. The man informed Disney that Mr. Pantages
would not be interested in the series. But unknown to both, the
boss overheard the conversation from his office and called out,
"How do you know I wouldn't?" He then appeared, listened to
Disney's pitch and told him to make up a sample reel.

Disney got to work. Since he had no choice but to do all the
work himself, he kept it very simple—using white stick figures
on a black background and no more than a suggestion of backgrounds—a tree, a sliver of a moon in the sky, a simple horizon
line. Pantages seemed to like the sample—which utilized over-
printed titles to tell its jokes—and it is said that he was on the
point of closing a deal when word arrived from the East that a
distributor named Charles Mintz was willing to pay Disney
fifteen hundred dollars apiece for a series of *Alice in Cartoonland* subjects.

The offer placed Disney in a predicament. He had what
looked to be a sure thing with Pantages, and his brother who
had helped to finance the sample reel out of his modest govern-

103

ment stipend was reluctant to pull out of it for what seemed a more chancy venture. In addition, it was clear to Roy that they would need capital from an outside source if they were to undertake a series of the longer (nine hundred feet) and more technically difficult *Alice* reels. Their discussion on this occasion set the pattern for many discussions that were to follow as the Disney enterprise grew, with Walt pressing for the expansive project, Roy at first resisting him and then giving in and somehow finding the ways and means of financing it.

Their needs for *Alice* were small—five hundred dollars in order to make their first reel—but their resources were equally modest. Indeed, about the only person to whom they could turn was their Uncle Robert, who was essentially as unyielding a type as their father. Disney had had an argument with him on his first day in Los Angeles when the older man had asked him if he had come through Topeka on his way west and had been told that the train bypassed the city. Uncle Robert insisted that *all* Santa Fe trains ran through Topeka, and the argument was not resolved until his wife checked with the railroad and found out that indeed Disney's train had entirely missed Topeka. The uncle thereupon nursed a grudge for several weeks.

Now, when the brothers applied to him for a short-term loan to tide them over until the distributor paid for their first reel, he refused, claiming that "Walter doesn't pay his debts." Quizzed on the point, he replied that he knew Disney had never repaid his sixty dollar debt to his brother Raymond in Kansas City. It seems that after that loan had been made, Roy Disney had the idea of getting his brothers to chip in and buy their mother a vacuum cleaner and wrote to Walt asking for a contribution and also asking him to solicit one from Raymond. The latter replied that Walt could make a contribution to the Christmas fund in his name, deducting it from the amount Walt already owed to him. Characteristically, Walt did no such thing. He simply wrote Ray out of the whole transaction and split the cost of the machine with Roy. There is no record that he ever paid Raymond back, either; the incident was apparently the final split between them. Now it very nearly cost him his big chance. But Roy smoothed things out; they got their money from Uncle Robert, and Disney rented a tiny office nearby, enabling him to move out of his garage workshop. Roy had to dig up another $250 to finish the first *Alice*, but somehow it was done, and in short order they received their first fee from New York—representing a 100 percent profit on the $750 invested. Uncle Robert was paid back immediately, and he, too, now disappears from the Disney story.

The first *Alice* films were only about one-third pure animation. The rest of the footage was made up of Alice playing with her pals, who were neighborhood kids Disney recruited for fees of about fifty cents apiece. Uncle Robert's police dog was also featured in their activities. Only Alice was actually integrated with the cartoons, usually in dream sequences or in stories that she seemed to make up and tell her playmates. About the only thing the pictures had going for them was their inexpensiveness to the distributor and the gimmick, quite crudely done, of mixing a live actor in the same frames with cartoon characters.

Still, no one was getting rich on them. Disney's drive for technical perfection, one of the most important elements in his career, manifested itself early. He did all the animation himself, of course, functioned as director and cameraman on the live sequences and even constructed the sets single-handed. Even so, costs mounted as he put more money into the settings and paid a little more to his child actors (at their demand). Finally, he was forced to hire a cameraman, because Roy was never able to master the steady rhythm required to crank the old-fashioned, hand-powered silent movie camera. He tended either to overcrank, which slowed down motion as it appeared later on the screen, or to undercrank, which caused motion to appear jumpy and unnaturally speedy. The best executive decision he made in this period, however, was to send to Kansas City for Ub Iwerks, who could draw. .

By the time Iwerks reached the West Coast the Disney brothers had managed to turn out a half-dozen *Alice* subjects, but they were barely making enough to live on comfortably, since Walt insisted on instantly plowing each month's modest profits back into their next release. They borrowed money— from the organist back in Kansas City for whom Disney had done his animated song sheets and from Edna Francis, the girl whom Roy would eventually marry and from whom Walt had got an occasional free meal in Kansas City. (Walt, incidentally, sent the letter asking for her loan without his brother's knowledge and then had to talk him into accepting it when it arrived.) The brothers lived with great frugality, sharing a small apartment, where Roy did the cooking and beans again were the mainstay of their diet. When they went out to eat, they tended to buy a single tray of food in a cafeteria and then split its contents.

But neither personal discipline nor an earnest attempt to improve their product could change the fact that the *Alice* series was not doing well in the theaters. Indeed, after the sixth one had been released, Charles Mintz appeared on the West Coast and attempted to obtain a release from the contract. The Disneys were close to seeing his point and agreeing to the cancellation. The one thing that caused them to resist his blandishments was the fact that *Alice* Number Seven was already in the can, and they wanted at least to get a return on that investment. By this time Iwerks was on the job, and his skill at the animation board and the know-how gathered through trial and error over Disney's first half-year of work combined to produce their first solid commercial success. Mintz kept the *Alice* contract in force and then renewed it twice more, with slight raises in the price paid to the Disneys.

It is difficult to imagine just what anyone saw in the *Alice* films. Even compared to the low grade maintained by their competitors, the Disney pictures were feeble. Alice was nice and she was conventionally pretty, but she had no real character beyond a certain willingness to try anything and therefore get into "situations." The animals that accompanied her were, at best, sketchily drawn and lacked the strong element of caricature, in both features and movement, that is the mark of good animation; indeed, most of the time their definition was so weak that nothing could be seen except the broadest outline of their shapes and movements. The Disneys, even quite well on in their career with *Alice*, had still not learned how to find ways for the animation camera to approximate the flexibility of the live-action camera. There were no close-ups, no odd angles, few variations in the camera's basic point of view, which was well back from its subjects and observed them head-on. Since backgrounds were still being kept to a minimum, the over-all impression one gains on seeing an *Alice* film today is of tiny figures cavorting in a white void. Typically, its jokes look as if they had already been stale at the time Disney and his helpers originally made use of them, and so the films have the rude, crude, flat air of the old comic strips about them. Finally, there is none of the fast-paced rhythm, none of the careful construction of a gag line, building, building, building to an inevitable, and inevitably hilarious, climax as the silent comedians were so brilliantly doing at this time and that Disney's organization was itself to master within a very few years. In short, *Alice in Cartoonland* was, by and large, a limp, dull and cliché-ridden enterprise. All you could really say for it was that it was a fairly ordinary comic strip set in motion and somewhat enlivened by a photographic trick. It seems worthwhile to note that Disney owed his survival, at least in part, to this trick of blending live and animated action, just as he owed each leap forward during the rest of his career to his ability to seize upon similar technological advances and exploit them while his rivals were still fearfully contemplating their possible drawbacks.

Disney later claimed that when he arrived in Los Angeles he had worked out a program for himself, calling for him not to get married until he was at least twenty-five years old and had ten thousand dollars saved—certainly a very sensible program for a go-getter and one often advised and even practiced by the breed. However, the natural expansion of his little studio, once the *Alice* series was established, turned out to be the instrument that spoiled his plan. He asked a young woman in the office if she knew of anyone who might be added to the staff, and she suggested a girl named Lillian Bounds, who lived near enough to the studio so that she could walk to work and thus avoid paying carfare. It was a worthwhile saving, since Disney could pay her only fifteen dollars per week, a fact she failed to establish when she was hired. She was newly arrived in town from Lewiston, Idaho, where she had attended business college, and was living with her sister and brother-in-law while getting established. Legend has it that the girl who told her about the job did so only on condition that she promised not to marry the boss, upon whom she had fixed her own eye. Another legend, often told by Disney himself, was that he fell so far behind in salary payments that he had no option but to marry Miss Bounds.

In any case, it is clear that they had one of those poverty-stricken, faintly comic romances that were later to become something of a staple in Disney's live-action films. The Disney brothers at this point were paying themselves salaries of just thirty-five dollars a week and putting the rest back into the studio. Walt Disney was putting a fair share of his wages into the maintenance of a Ford roadster, since a car was already a necessity in Los Angeles. It was also useful in advancing romance. Because they all frequently worked nights, Disney had fallen into the habit of taking Miss Bounds and the friend who had got her the job at the studio home in his car and "when he started dropping the other girl off first so he could talk to me," the future Mrs. Disney knew he was interested, she later recalled to a reporter. One night when they were working alone at the office, Disney suddenly interrupted dictation to plant a firm but slightly surprising kiss on her lips. The only thing holding their relationship back was that Disney still didn't have a suit.

"We would sit outside the house in the jalopy because Walt had nothing but his old sweater and trousers and he wouldn't go in the house," Mrs. Disney said. "Finally one evening he gulped: 'If I get a new suit—will you let me come in and call on your family?' " She said she thought that would be fine, and he forthwith acquired the clothes by appealing to his brother, who declared that both of them needed suits and even indulged his sibling to the extent of letting him buy one for forty dollars, five dollars more than the top limit they had previously agreed upon. Disney, so that story goes, was so pleased by the purchase that very nearly the first thing he said upon finally being presented to his future in-laws was "How do you like my new suit?"

One of Mrs. Disney's memories of this period is of a night when she and her sister were visiting friends, and her fiancé, with a rare night free from both work and romance, decided to drop in at a movie. "A cartoon short by a competitor was advertised outside, but suddenly, as he sat in the darkened theater, his own picture came on. Walt was so excited he rushed down to the manager's office. The manager, misunderstanding, began to apologize for not showing the advertised film. Walt hurried over to my sister's house to break the exciting news, but we weren't home yet. Then he tried to find Roy, but he was out too. Finally he went home alone." The reason for Disney's excitement was that he had never had a chance to see one of his pictures actually playing in a theater. Mrs. Disney wrote, many years later, "Every time we pass a theater where one of his films is advertised on the marquee I can't help but think of that night."

On the one occasion when Disney discussed his marriage publicly he was determinedly unromantic and unsentimental about it. He thought his future bride was a good listener and that she would provide him with "companionship," he said. He claimed that what really decided him was that his brother had asked Edna Francis to come out from Kansas City and marry him and that it was obvious that he, Walt, would "need a new roommate." His manner of proposing was as utilitarian as his attitude toward the enterprise. He and Lillian had been planning to purchase a new car together, but one night he simply said to her, "Which do you think we should pay for first, the car or the ring?" She replied that the ring was uppermost in her mind and that settled the matter. With their customary frugality the Disney brothers located a cut-rate jewelry merchant in an upstairs backroom somewhere, and Disney passed over some thirty-five dollar rings and, after some haggling with both his brother and the merchant, settled on a seventy dollar diamond set with sapphires. Roy and Edna Disney were married in the spring of 1925 in Los Angeles, Walt and Lillian Disney in July of the same year in Lewiston, in the parlor of her brother, who was the town's fire chief. Their wedding night was spent on a train heading toward Seattle, where they planned to board a steamer for a leisurely trip back to Los Angeles. Disney, alas, developed a toothache and spent the night sitting up with a Pullman porter, helping him polish shoes.

Back in Los Angeles the young couple settled first in a tiny apartment, then purchased a prefabricated house in the tudor style. It cost seven thousand dollars and was located in the Silver Lake district, which lies between Hollywood and Los Angeles and was then a fashionable middle-class area. The house was convenient to Hyperion Avenue, where Disney had acquired a store and converted it into the nucleus of his first large-scale studio. Before it would begin to grow into the almost legendary establishment it became for an entire generation of young animators, however, Disney was to endure—and learn from—a failure of striking bitterness.

By 1927 it was becoming clear to Mintz that the *Alice* series had run its course, and he dispatched his brother-in-law, George Winkler, to Los Angeles to encourage Disney to create something to replace it. He and his little team came up with an idea for a series featuring a rabbit, and his name was selected by throwing all the suggestions into a hat and inviting the distributor to pick one blind. The name he drew was "Oswald," and thus was *Oswald the Rabbit* born.

He was an advance over *Alice*, but he was not exactly *Mickey Mouse* or even a *Bugs Bunny*. He was round and rather cuddly though reasonably naturalistic in design. He owed as much to the tradition of the *Peter Rabbit* series as anything. That is to say he was innocently mischievous and rather more childlike in manner than the furry and feathery anthropomorphs that were to come after him, both from the Disney studio and its competitors. By this time the price on the Disney product had reached $2,250 a reel. *Oswald*, much more sophisticated in technique than *Alice*, was instantly more successful than the earlier series had ever been.

The only thing the Disneys could not understand was the almost monthly visit they received from George Winkler. He customarily brought them their check and received from them their latest film and the art for the lobby poster, which the studio also did. The visit represented a job of no importance, and even in the nepotistic movie business, messenger work seemed beneath the dignity of the most incompetent in-law. The Disneys soon discovered the meaning of Winkler's visits.

Full of confidence, taking his wife along for the ride, Disney entrained for New York in 1927 to renegotiate his contract with Mintz (who, by this time, was releasing the films through the facilities of Universal Pictures). There was still six months to run on the original *Oswald* contract, and Disney planned to ask only for a modest raise in fees—to twenty-five hundred dollars a film. He was instead asked to take a cut back to eighteen hundred. He refused—and then found out the reason for Winkler's trips. He had been instructed to ingratiate himself with as many of Disney's small staff as he could, hinting to them that there might be raises if they were willing to leave Disney at the right moment. He told Disney that he must sign or risk losing some of his key people—and *Oswald*, too, since he was copyrighted in the Mintz firm's name (a common practice in the animation industry then, one probably borrowed from newspaper cartooning, where the practice insures the life of a popular character after his creator's death or desertion). Disney fought back. He allegedly told Mintz that if the four men Winkler had been able to recruit would leave him they would undoubtedly leave Mintz just as readily. He also told him that they would be no real loss to him—that he would be able to replace them easily. In this, he was right. Animation was still a relatively unsophisticated art, and a reasonably competent and well-trained commercial artist could be trained to the work fairly easily. It was not until later that the techniques of animation advanced to the point where a long apprenticeship—as much as fifteen years, according to some artists—was necessary to create a full-fledged animator, and it was the Disney studio that evolved both the techniques and the training program for the young men who needed to master them.

Even so, Disney later recalled that he actually felt none of the confidence about his own future that he expressed to Mintz, and he was apparently deeply hurt, as he always was, by his employees' willingness to leave him. Even in later years, when his employees left for better cause than this, he still read ingratitude and personal disloyalty in their decamping. In point of fact, his first deserters got their come-uppance. Within a year the veteran animator Walter Lantz had replaced them on the *Oswald* series.

This incident further deepened Disney's natural distrust of the people with whom he was forced to do business. In the future he was always exceedingly careful to control all rights in his creations. Indeed, even when he began buying literary property from writers outside his organization, as feature-length animation and live-action feature projects virtually forced him to do, he did everything in his power to make the original story and characters his own. Part of this was accidental: his well-geared merchandising organization, with its many "versions" of original stories like *Bambi* and *Mary Poppins* (designed to catch all age groups) and with its intensive program of licensing dolls, toys and games based on the subjects, had a natural tendency to blanket the original. But part of it was anything but accidental. Disney naturally got credit above the title and in far larger type than the original author, who could not get a contract from the organization without agreeing to submit his creations to the merchandising process. Even worse, they, their spouses and even their children traditionally had to sign a release preventing them from ever making any future claims of any sort against the Disney organization for the material sold. When writer Cynthia Lindsay referred to Disney as "the well-known author of *Alice in Wonderland*, the *Complete Works* of William Shakespeare, and the *Encyclopaedia Britannica*," she was not unfairly summarizing popular opinion of the authorship of the works his studio had taken over.

In short, Disney learned an important lesson in New York in 1927, though he was certainly not aware of how right he was when, before boarding the train for California, he sent a wire to his brother that read: "Everything O.K. Coming home." He thought he was merely trying to prevent Roy from worrying during the several days they would be out of touch while Walt was traveling west, but he was in fact predicting their future—and rather modestly at that.

PART FIVE

Bringing Forth
The Mouse

15 *The age demanded an image*
Of its accelerated grimace,
Something for the modern stage,
Not, at any rate, an Attic grace;

Not, not certainly, the obscure reveries
Of the inward gaze;
Better mendacities
Than the classics in paraphrase!
                          —Ezra Pound, *Hugh Selwyn Mauberley*

THERE ARE UNCOUNTED versions of the birth of Mickey Mouse, for Disney, his flacks and hacks, could never resist the temptation to improve upon the basic yarn. This much seems to be true: that the idea to use a rodent as the principal character for a cartoon series came to Disney on the train carrying him back from his discouraging meeting with Mintz in New York. The most flavorsome telling of the tale appeared under Disney's own byline in an English publication called *The Windsor Magazine* in 1934 (though it is doubtful that he did more than glance at the draft his publicity department prepared for him).

The key section begins with his boarding the train, with no new contract and no discernible future.

"But was I downhearted?" he inquires. "Not a bit! I was happy at heart. For out of the trouble and confusion stood a mocking, merry little figure. Vague and indefinite at first. But it grew and grew and grew. And finally arrived—a mouse. A romping, rollicking little mouse.

"The idea completely engulfed me. The wheels turned to the tune of it. '*Chug, chug, mouse, chug, chug, mouse*' the train seemed to say. The whistle screeched it. '*A m-m-mowa-ouse,*' it wailed.

"By the time my train had reached the Middle West I had dressed my dream mouse in a pair of red velvet pants with two huge pearl buttons, had composed the first scenario and was all set."

It is well known that the name Disney first gave his creation was Mortimer Mouse—borrowed, it is said, from that of a pet mouse he kept in his Kansas City studio. Disney himself never claimed this, though he frequently confessed "a special feeling" for mice and readily admitted that he had kept a fairly large family of field mice in his Kansas City offices. Originally he had heard their rustlings in his waste paper basket, but characteristically, he refused to let them have the run of the place. Instead, he built cages for them, captured them and allowed one of them, who seemed especially bright, the occasional freedom of his drawing board. He even undertook a modest training course for the little fellow, drawing a circle on a large piece of drawing paper and then tapping him lightly on the nose with a pencil each time he attempted to scamper over the line. Before long he had trained him to stay within the circle, though he would venture right up to the line and at mischievous speed, at that. When it came time to leave Kansas City, Disney set all of his mice free "in the best neighborhood I could find," as he later put it. Of his parting with his special pet, Disney said that he "walked away feeling like a cur. When I looked back he was still sitting there, watching me with a sad, disappointed look in his eyes."

There are two versions of the renaming of the cartoon mouse. In the more common one Mrs. Disney is reported to have found Mortimer too pretentious and insisted on a less formal-sounding title for the little chap; some say she suggested the name Mickey, others that Disney named his new character and she approved it during the course of their long train ride back to California. Yet another story is far more prosaic; it is simply that one of the first distributors Disney approached with his new idea liked it but not the name and that it was his objection that caused Disney to rename his creation.

In any case, it is certain that immediately after he returned from New York, Disney set his little studio to work on a cartoon that had a mouse as its principal figure even as the studio was fulfilling the last demands of his contract with Mintz. "He had to be simple," Disney later said, in discussing the details of The Mouse's creation. "We had to push out 700 feet of film every two weeks [actually, the production schedule was slightly less frantic than this], so we couldn't have a character who was tough to draw.

"His head was a circle with an oblong circle for a snout. The ears were also circles so they could be drawn the same, no matter how he turned his head.

"His body was like a pear and he had a long tail. His legs were pipestems and we stuck them in big shoes [also circular in appearance] to give him the look of a kid wearing his father's shoes.

"We didn't want him to have mouse hands, because he was supposed to be more human. So we gave him gloves. Five fingers looked like too much on such a little figure, so we took one away. That was just one less finger to animate.

"To provide a little detail, we gave him the two-button pants. There was no mouse hair or any other frills that would slow down animation."

117

In short, The Mouse was very much a product of the then-current conventions of animation, which held that angular figures were well nigh impossible to animate successfully and that clearly articulated joints were also too difficult to manage, at least at the speed of drawing demanded by the economics of the industry. Hence the odd appearance of so many old cartoons when we glimpse them today on the programs our children watch on television—the thick round bodies contrasting so oddly with the rubbery limbs of the characters. In a few years, thanks largely to the leadership of the Disney studio, these conventions were abandoned, but whatever advantages their adoption provided economically was offset, as Disney later said, because they "made it tougher for the cartoonists to give him character."

Indeed, it is possible that The Mouse would have had a life no longer than many of his competitors if a technological revolution had not intervened and presented Disney with an opportunity that was particularly suited to his gifts and interests and that he seized with an alacrity shared by few in Hollywood. *Plane Crazy*, in which both Mickey and Minnie Mouse made their first appearance, was on the drawing boards—in a silent version, of course—on October 6, 1927, when Warner Brothers premiered *The Jazz Singer*, the movie that broke the industry's resistance to sound. A practical sound system had, in fact, been available as early as 1923, when inventor Lee DeForest toured the lecture circuit showing sound movies of prominent vaudeville acts; since he was working outside the customary commercial channels, the industry could safely ignore him. It also managed to ignore a series of short films, featuring the voices of famous opera singers, the movietone newsreels of William Fox, who achieved the first sound-film box office success with his coverage of Lindbergh's transatlantic solo flight, and even Warner Brothers' *Don Juan*, which had a musical score and sound effects and even a little introductory speech by Will Hays hailing the new technological miracle. Warners' at that time was a studio desperately trying to stave off bankruptcy, and the success of *Don Juan* led them to extend their experiments by filming some of the sequences in *The Jazz Singer* with sound film, making it the first film to integrate sound with the story. Only a modicum of the dialogue was recorded, but all the musical sequences were, and the result was a sensation. Warners' immediately added similar sequences to three other movies the studio then had in production and laid plans for an *all*-talking picture. The rest of the industry formally agreed to fight the "Warner Vitaphone Peril," but by the spring of 1928, opposition had collapsed and all the studios were rushing into production with sound pictures. There was nothing dignified or even very intelligent about the transition period. It was, indeed, a hysterical scramble in which Walt Disney and his problems, never in the forefront of anyone's mind, were almost entirely lost from view.

At this point the previous frugality of the Disney Brothers paid off. Between them they had somewhere between $25,000 and $30,000 in personal assets, and their studio, though not wildly successful, could afford to go ahead with its first three Mickey Mouse films even though they had no contract for them. or any real idea of who might be persuaded to distribute them. In addition, they were in somewhat the same position as the nearly bankrupt Warner Brothers had been: they had nothing to lose by experimenting with sound; their investment in unreleased product was negligible; they had no investment in actors whose vocal qualities might not be suitable to the microphone, and in the animated cartoon they had a medium ideally adapted to sound. The early sound camera was virtually immobilized in the soundproof "blimp" necessary to prevent its whirrings from being picked up by the microphone. Disney, of course, had no such problem with the camera. The animation was shot silently as always, and sound was added later. This meant that his little films retained their ability to move while all about them were losing theirs. Just as important was the control he could exercise over the relationship between pictures and sound. They could be perfectly integrated simply by matching the musical rhythm to the rhythm of the drawn characters' movements. (Later on, the planning of music and movement would be carefully integrated from the earliest moment of production as the influence of an idea in one area flowed to the other. Far from being a simple accompaniment, the music became in the Disney studio product an almost equal partner with the visual imagery, the sound effects and the dialogue in creating the total effect of the film.)

True to his taste and talent for technological innovation, Disney hesitated only briefly before plunging into sound-film production. After *Plane Crazy*, he shot a second Mickey Mouse, *Gallopin' Gaucho*, silently, but in his third Mickey Mouse, *Steamboat Willie*, he began to experiment with sound.

His chief assistants were Ub Iwerks, in these early days getting a "drawn by" credit on the title card of each film, and a young man named Wilfred Jackson, a newly employed animator at the studio who liked to play the harmonica in his spare time. The picture was plotted to the tick of a metronome, which set rhythms for both Jackson, who played standard, public-domain tunes on his mouth organ, and Iwerks, who got from the metronome a sense of the rhythms he would have to use in his animations. The calculation of the ratio of drawings to bars of music was thus arrived at far more simply than it would be only a few years later. To color the sound track further, Disney rounded up tin pans, slide whistles, ocarinas, cowbells, nightclub noisemakers and a washboard. When the animation was finished, the co-workers invited their wives to come over to see something new one evening, then ducked behind the screen and played their "score" live, through a sound system Iwerks concocted out of an old microphone and the loudspeaker of a home radio. In later years Disney recalled that the ladies had been vaguely complimentary about their efforts but had not allowed their husbands' novelty to distract them from what they considered the main business of the evening—girl talk about babies, menus, hairdressers and so on. The story, like so many of Disney's reminiscences, seems a little too patly similar to situation comedy, but, on the other hand, the performance was probably not terribly impressive at this early stage.

By early September, 1928, however, he felt he was ready to head for New York again in search, first of all, of someone to put his perfected score on a sound track and, second of all, of a distributor. By this time Disney and his co-workers had on paper their complete score, down to the last rattle of a cowbell, and had devised a system by which a conductor could keep his beat precisely on the tempo of the film. Sound speed was standardized at ninety feet of film per minute, or twenty-four frames per second. The musical tempo was two beats per second, or one every twelve frames. On the work print Disney took with him, a slash of India ink had been drawn at every twelfth frame, causing a white flash to appear on screen every half-second. All a conductor had to do was key his beats to the flash, and in theory, if he never missed a flash, he would reach the end of his strange-looking score at precisely the moment the film ended.

But first Disney had to find someone willing to record his sound track, and then he had to find a conductor willing to sacrifice the most important variable at his command—tempo—to a gang of musically illiterate cartoonists. Neither was easy to find. The best sound system was controlled by RCA, and though the company was perfectly willing to take Disney's work, it was unwilling to follow his score. Its technicians had already added tracks to some old silent cartoons and were convinced, apparently, that close synchronization between music and sound effects and the action on the screen was, if not impossible, then certainly not worth the effort. Disney knew otherwise and refused to relinquish his precious piece of film to them. They, on the other hand, were not about to let a twenty-seven-year-old stranger tell them their business.

Disney then started on the rounds of those entrepreneurs who

121

owned outlaw sound equipment—that is, recording devices either not covered by the patents controlled by RCA or its chief rival, Western Electric, or which those giants had not moved against in the courts. Here, again, history was repeating itself, for the first silent cameras and projectors had been controlled by Edison and licensed only to producers and theaters that belonged to his so-called "trust." His invention had been so attractive that long before he gave up the fight to enforce his rights, the trust had been effectively broken by a number of competitors too vast to bring them all to book. The situation never grew quite so unreasonable in the sound business, for both the quality of the patented systems and the power of the firms that controlled them were such that it was to everyone's advantage to rationalize the market. But it was impossible in those early days to control everyone, and Disney had no real difficulty in locating someone to take on his recording chores. The trouble was that the man he found was a semilegendary figure named Pat Powers, who had learned the movie business—and his code of ethics—in the freebooting days before World War I. It is said, perhaps apocryphally, that Powers, who at one time distributed Carl Laemmle's Universal Pictures, actually resorted to throwing his books out the window (he was on the twelfth floor) rather than let Laemmle take a look at them at a moment when the producer got to wondering where his profits had gone. It is also said that Powers had the foresight to have a man waiting in the street below to retrieve the books and make a getaway with them. Disney was to be victimized by the casual unseemliness of this style during his association with Powers, but he appears to have known what he was getting into, and Powers did have a sound system he was willing to put in Disney's service—the "Powers Cinephone."

Powers was amenable to allowing Disney to supervise the recording session and engaged a conductor, Carl Edwardi, who led the band at New York's Capitol Theater, rounded up the musicians and handled all the details—which included a price of $210 per hour for the thirty members of the orchestra, plus fees for the four men who were to handle sound effects and for the technicians. The first session went badly. The bass player's low notes kept blowing tubes, and Disney himself, doing, as he was always to do, the Mickey Mouse voice, blew a tube when he coughed into an open mike. Worst of all, Edwardi flatly refused to key his beat to the flashes on the screen, no doubt reasoning that a man of his reputation ought to be able to conduct, unaided by mechanics, a score consisting of "Yankee Doodle," "Dixie," "The Girl I Left Behind Me," "Annie Laurie," "Auld Lang Syne" and so on. After three hours and some $1200 in costs they still had nothing usable on the track, and Powers, who had promised to pay all excess costs should Edwardi not live up to his reputation, declared that his offer had not included the musicians' salaries—it was to cover only the cost of the sound equipment and the film. Disney had no option but to wire his brother for more money, and to raise it, Roy Disney sold, among other things, Walt's Moon Cabrolet, an automobile with red and green running lights of which Disney was particularly fond. At the next session Edwardi agreed to try following the flashes on the screen, Disney cut the orchestra almost in half (dispensing with the bothersome string bass among other instruments), dismissed two of the sound effects men and took over some of their functions himself. This time, everything worked out as planned, and within days Disney was making the rounds of the New York distributors, trying to get someone to handle *Steamboat Willie* for him.

It was a disappointing business. In the crisis atmosphere of that year a man with a cartoon short subject, even one with an artful sound track on it, did not have high priority. The tendency was to stall Disney and then to look at his product, if at all, only after screening more commercially promising projects. Disney recalled peeping out through projection booth windows, trying to gauge reaction in the screening rooms, on those rare occasions when his work was given a showing. He also recalled getting his best laughs from the projectionists next to him.

But at one of these screenings a figure, if anything, more legendary than Powers happened to be present, and it was he who sensed the possible exploitation value of Disney's film. His name was Harry Reichenbach, and as a press agent he had previously promoted an utterly ordinary piece of *kitsch* called *September Morn* into a scandal of international proportions. At this time he was managing the Colony Theater in New York, and he asked permission to book *Steamboat Willie* as an added attraction. Disney was hesitant, fearing that with the New York cream skimmed off, he would have an even more difficult time in persuading a national distributor to take the film. Reichenbach argued, however, that this was a special film demanding special treatment. Unless extraordinary attention such as he was prepared to engineer was focused on it, the little picture would simply be lost in the flood of new sound films. He offered Disney a two-week run beginning September 19, 1928, and Disney talked him into paying five hundred dollars a week for the privilege.

The strategy worked. Reichenbach got the press to attend and write stories about his added attraction, and Disney spend a good deal of time at the Colony listening to the laughter of audiences responding to the first genuinely artful use of the new technology of sound film. After the run at the Colony, *Willie* moved to the S. L. Rothafel's two-year-old Roxy Theater. Now the distributors started coming to Disney, asking him what he wanted to do and what they could do to help him. They got only part of the answer they were hoping for: Yes, he did want to go on making Mickey Mouse cartoons; no, he did not want to sell them the films outright. The loss of *Oswald the Rabbit* was still fresh in his mind. This time, he insisted that he retain complete control of his product. Again, it appeared that he had reached an impasse.

It was Pat Powers who rescued him. He was looking for markets and promotion for his Cinephone device, and he sensed in the Mouse exactly the sort of gimmick he needed. In return for 10 percent of the gross Powers offered to distribute the Mickey Mouse films through the system of independent or "state's-rights" bookers. It was one of the simplest, and oldest, methods of film distribution, and indeed, some of the major figures in the movie industry got their start in the state's-rights business, which still exists in truncated form. What happened was that an independent distributor bought the right to distribute an independent film in a given territory and then, taking a percentage of the gross for his trouble, peddled the films thus acquired to theaters in the district, which generally comprised several states. The advantage was obvious: a salesman for an operator like Powers could easily canvass the relatively few state's-rights bookers in several territories efficiently and frequently and sell more film more quickly than he could if he had to approach each theater owner separately. Of the several disadvantages, the most obvious was that the system took three sizable slices off the top of the gross—one each for the theater owner, the state's-rights man and the national distributor—before any profit dribbled back to the original producer. Worse, the state's-rights distributors usually did not have access to the very best theatrical outlets, many of which were owned outright by the large production and distribution companies, many more of which were locked into more or less exclusive agreements with the major firms under the block booking system. This system demanded that the theaters take large packages of indifferent films in order to obtain the opportunity to show the ones that contained major stars and, of course, offered the greatest potential profit. These people simply did not have the time or the inclination to handle independent films. Finally, with film and money changing hands so often, there were many opportunities all along the line to hide profits without much fear of subsequent audits. (This problem has risen again to plague a new

125

generation of independent producers who must release their pictures through established distribution firms and must depend on their word about the grosses against which their percentage is figured.)

Despite all these disadvantages, Disney had no real choice if he wished to retain control of his product: he had to release on a state's-rights basis or not at all. He was asking no more than customary terms—a five-thousand-dollar advance for each negative print furnished a would-be distributor and a 60–40 split of profits, the larger figure going to the distributor once the advance was paid back. But still there were no other takers, and one gathers that the Powers offer was not only financially attractive but gratefully received by a man tired of worrying over money and deals at a moment when he sensed that he had, for the first time, a real hit, one on which he might build a future of incalculable brightness. The main thing, at this point, was to exploit his sudden advantage, to get more films into the works and before the public. Disney behaved in this period much like a man anxious to leave the details until later, a man who knew that large immediate returns were less important to him than immediate production on as large a scale as he could manage. He seemed to sense that it was this that would establish the value of his name and thus improve his bargaining position in later rounds.

So he closed with Powers and got to work, while still in New York, on the creation of scores for his two unreleased silent Mickey Mouses, *Plane Crazy* and *Gallopin' Gaucho*, as well as for a brand-new vehicle for the Mouse, *The Opry House*. Again he turned to Kansas City for talent he could rely on: the faithful theater organist who had previously lent him money was brought east to score the films. By the time he left the city early in 1929, Disney had a package of four films ready for release. Their cumulative impact when they went into national distribution was simply tremendous, so much so that Disney was emboldened to attempt an animated short without Mickey or Minnie but one that, however primitive it may seem to a modern audience, nevertheless represents an extremely important advance for the animated cartoon.

That picture, of course, was *The Skeleton Dance*, the first in the famous series of *Silly Symphonies*. In *The Opry House* Disney had already moved beyond "Turkey in the Straw"; the musical feature of the film was a Rachmaninoff Prelude. Now he decided to do a sort of "Danse Macabre," which would ultimately include some quotations from Grieg's "March of the Dwarfs" (from the *Peer Gynt* Suite) among other bits and pieces of serious music. Obviously this was not suitable material for Mickey and his gang, whose activities were firmly located against an American small town and country background. Disney would have to break with the most firmly held of all the conventions of animation—the use of animals as the principal characters.

It is difficult to say just what was driving Disney culturally at this time. Although he had studied the violin briefly as a boy, he had no real musical knowledge or, indeed, standards, as his cheerful chopping and bowdlerizing of music testifies, not only in *The Skeleton Dance* but in all his later work, not excluding his mightiest effort at uplift, *Fantasia*. Indeed, when he was working on *Fantasia* he so felt his lack of musical training that he subscribed to a box at the Hollywood Bowl concerts, where, he recalled to a co-worker, he invariably fell asleep, lulled by the music and the warmth of the polo coat he liked to wrap around himself in those days. One suspects that his desire to bring serious music into an area where it had not previously penetrated was based on several considerations. First there was a commercially intelligent desire to differentiate his work from that of competitors who showed neither the ability nor the ambition to move beyond their low origins. Then there was the technical challenge that complex music presented to the animator. As early as 1925 he had made a little short in which a cartoon character seemed to conduct a theater's live orchestra from the screen. He also had toyed with the notion of supplying musical cue sheets to theater musicians so his silent shorts could be properly accompanied. There was also, perhaps, that vaguely defined, yet keenly felt, lust for "the finer things" that was so common among people of his *lumpen bourgeoisie* background. His father, after all, "would go for anything that was educational," and Disney himself proved throughout his career that he was chipped off much the same block (though his ideas of what was educational and what was not were often eccentric). Finally, and perhaps most important, there was his own shrewd sense of what, precisely, was the basis of his new success.

To understand this, one must take a closer look at Mickey Mouse. There is no more useful tool for this purpose than the print of the silent version of *Plane Crazy* owned by the Museum of Modern Art in New York. The film is not a bad piece of animation when judged against the standards of its time. Particularly in the anthropomorphizing of inanimate objects, like the airplane in which Mickey takes Minnie up for a ride, it is quite good. The machine, like others that followed it, actually registers emotions: it strains forward in anticipation of action, cowers when it sees obstacles looming ahead, and so on. The construction of the story, too, is superior to that found in most competing cartoons. It is, like most silent comedies, live or animated, nothing more or less than a string of physically perilous disasters, each more absurd and more dangerous than the last but all stemming from a perfectly reasonable premise—the natural desire of a young swain to prove his masculine mastery by taking his girl friend for a ride in an airplane he has designed and constructed. Some of the gags along the way are crude: a dachshund, for instance, is wound up tight, like the rubber bands boys use to drive their model planes, and serves as the power plant for Mickey's plane. And none of the nuances of gesture and expression that the great silent comics had developed in the course of shaping their art were within the range of Disney's animators. But the naturalness and inevitability with which the temporary and ill-conceived solution to one problem of flight leads to another are extremely clever. When, finally, the tension generated by the possibility of the ultimate disaster is resolved innocuously (Minnie parachutes to safety with a great display of patched bloomers, Mickey successfully makes a forced landing), it is clear that one has been in the presence of a work in which talent and intelligence, however crude, have been manifested.

One also observes that Disney and his people made shrewd use of satire by giving Mickey's hair a Lindberghian ruffle when he stands in his plane taking bows for his achievements. And one is impressed, too, by the fact that, faced with the need to create a truly original cartoon—under particularly trying circumstances at that—Disney had the wit to draw upon his own background for subject matter. There was, of course, his remembrance of the mice in his Kansas City workshop, but more important were his drawing upon the world of the barnyard for background and the spirit of the independent tinkerer-inventor for the film's psychological motivation.

But having observed all this, one is still bound to believe that The Mouse, as originally conceived and silently presented, was a very shaky basis for the empire that was to come. As *Time* observed in its acute biographical sketch of Mickey (December 27, 1954), "he was a skinny little squeaker with matchstick legs, shoe button eyes and a long, pointy nose. His teeth were sharp and fierce when he laughed, more like a real mouse's than they are today. . . ." Mickey's disposition matched his appearance. He was quick and cocky and cruel, at best a fresh and bratty kid, at worst a diminutive and sadistic monster, like most of the other inhabitants of that primitive theater of cruelty that was the animated cartoon. Five minutes with The Mouse, however diverting, were quite enough. His amazing—indeed, impossible—voyagings, in various guises were often amusing enough in their broad conception, and they supported some excellent comic situations, but the truth is that at the outset it was the witty, constantly surprising use of sound to punctuate the

129

stories and the technical genius of the animation—and its visual orchestration—from which the best laughs derived.

This is nowhere more obvious than in *Steamboat Willie*. In it The Mouse has, if anything, regressed as a character; he represents nothing more than the spirit of pure, amoral and very boyish mischief. Employed as an assistant to the villainous Peg-Leg Pete, he takes it upon himself to rescue Minnie, who appears to be the river boat's sole passenger, from Pete's lustful advances. In the course of the ensuing chase the mice find themselves in the boat's hold, where domestic animals are being kept. A goat nibbles some sheet music, Minnie cranks his tail as if it were the handle of a street organ and out of his mouth comes "Turkey in the Straw." There then ensues a formidable concert—in which a cow's teeth are played as if they were a xylophone, a nursing sow is converted into a bagpipe and so on, in a marvelously inventive and rapidly paced medley. The gags are not very subtle ones, and indeed, there is something a little shocking about the ferocity with which Mickey squeezes, bangs, twists and tweaks the anatomy of the assembled creatures in his mania for music. But even today the cumulative effect of the sequence is catchy; in 1928 it must have been truly stunning.

What happened in *Steamboat Willie* was both a rediscovery and a discovery. The rediscovery lay in the effects of animation on an audience. As Professor Erwin Panofsky says in his justly famous essay, "Style and Medium in the Motion Pictures," "the primordial basis of the enjoyment of moving pictures was not an objective interest in specific subject matter, much less an aesthetic interest in the formal presentation of subject matter, but the sheer delight in the fact that things seemed to move, no matter what things they were." Throughout the 1920s animators were extending the range of movement the camera could record; they made inanimate objects move, they made animals move like humans (and, sometimes, humans move like animals), they gave visual expression to emotion through contortionistic (and therefore caricaturistic) movement of every sort of creature. Now Disney was forced by the rhythmic patterns of music to orchestrate this movement more carefully. Instead of being a series of random effects, the cartoon achieved through music more solid structure than it had been possible to acquire from an unadorned story line. The audience was therefore able to rediscover some of the joy in observing pure movement that had first attracted it to film—a sense of delight that, with the exception of the work of the silent comedians, it had been increasingly denied as movies grew more literary in orientation throughout the twenties.

As for Disney's discovery, it is very simply expressed: he saw that sound was not merely an addition to the movies but a force that would fundamentally transform them. The silent film, as Panofsky points out, was never truly silent: the humblest neighborhood theater employed a pianist to underscore its shifting moods. It was then rather more like a ballet than any of the other traditional art forms. Most people supposed that with the addition of sound the film would come to be, perhaps even should be, more like a stage play. What Disney sensed was that it was about to become a totally new form, one in which, as Panofsky put it, "what we hear remains, for good or worse, inextricably fused with that which we see; the sound, articulate or not, cannot express any more than is expressed, at the same time, by visible movement. . . ." In short, and in less elevated terms, Disney was the first movie maker to resolve the aesthetically disruptive fight between sight and sound through the simple method of fusion, making them absolutely "coexpressible," with neither one dominant nor carrying more than its fair share of the film's weight. To put it even more crudely—and rather as one imagines many of his first audiences might have put it—"he made things come out right." The animal concert in *Steamboat Willie* presages those wonderfully intricate animation sequences that were to be the high points of his studio's work in years to come—a rendition of "The William Tell Overture" continuing aloft in a twister in the Mickey Mouse short *The Band Concert* (1935); the house-cleaning sequence in *Snow White;* the ballet of the hippopotamuses (to "The Dance of the Hours") in *Fantasia*, for example. All are infinitely more sophisticated than Mickey's musical interlude in *Willie*. But their fundamental appeal is the same: "they come out right." And it is perhaps not inappropriate to note that their fascination, both terrifying and thrilling, is not unlike the kind one derives from observing a brilliantly engineered assembly line functioning at its best.

It would be preposterous to assume that Disney knew, philosophically, where he was going in *Steamboat Willie*. He, too, simply liked things to come out right. But he knew better than his distributors where the basic appeal of his films lay. They were convinced that Mickey Mouse was, like the characters who had preceded him as the leading figures in cartoon series, an exploitable personality, a "star" of a sort. Disney went along with them—though for reasons of his own, to be explored later —but grasped that it was technique, not personality, that was bringing the people in (at least in the first year or two). We shall return later to his attempts to overcome the problem of The Mouse's fundamentally cruel character (by turning him first into a straight man, then a supporting player and finally by simply utilizing him as a corporate symbol). Even though within months Mickey Mouse cartoons were getting billing on marquees, an almost unprecedented commercial tribute for a short subject, Disney was determined not to be Mouse-trapped. Whether he was consciously aware of The Mouse's basic weakness for the long economic pull, whether he was impelled by a genuine desire to broaden his experiments or to upgrade his medium and his culture, or whether it was a combination of these and other factors that drew him on, it is difficult to say. What is known for certain is that in May of 1929—with The Mouse series barely under way—he had *The Skeleton Dance* ready for release. He sent the print off to Powers, who rejected it, telling

Disney to stick to mice. Disney then took it to a friend who ran one of the theaters in the United Artists Los Angeles chain and got him to show *Dance* to a morning audience. One of the man's assistants sat with Disney during the screening and when it was over, told him he could not possibly recommend it for regular showings, even though most of the customers seemed to like it. Disney's companion claimed it was simply too gruesome.

Still Disney pressed on. He tracked a film salesman all the way to a pool hall because the man was alleged to be influential with Fred Miller, owner-manager of the Carthay Circle Theater, one of the most prestigious houses in Los Angeles. The man actually managed to get *The Skeleton Dance* to Miller, who took a fancy to it, showed it and collected an excellent set of notices. Back the film went to Powers, this time accompanied by its West Coast reviews and with the advice to get it seen by Roxy personally. The famous showman also liked it, put it into the Roxy Theater and found himself with such a successful short on his hands that he held it over through several changes of features.

The Skeleton Dance has no story and no characters at all. It is set in a graveyard in the smallest hours of the night, when the skeletons emerge from their graves and vaults, dance together for a few minutes and then, with the coming of dawn, climb back into their resting places. It is such an innocently conceived movie that it is hard to imagine its frightening any child, and the connections of Gothic and grotesque art, to which Disney was frequently attracted, must have seemed quite advanced to an audience that rarely saw such iconography at the movies.

Its dividends for Disney were not to be counted merely in box-office terms. Indeed, after a year of work and twenty-one completed films, Disney economically had very little to show for his efforts. What it did was add another string to his bow, forming the basis for a series of films in which, free of the artistic conventions and story lines imposed on him by Mickey and his "gang," he could experiment with techniques, and whether he planned on this or not, he could begin building his reputation with the intellectual community. He even had one or two very large financial successes with The Silly Symphonies, though at first his distributors insisted on a very strange billing: "Mickey Mouse presents a Walt Disney Silly Symphony."

Meantime, it was becoming clear to Disney that his deal with Powers was not working out at all as he had hoped it would. Throughout this year of extraordinarily hard labor, he and his brother had been unable to get a full financial report from their man in New York. Instead, Powers sent them checks for three or four thousand dollars, enough to keep going, but nothing like what the Disneys felt they should be getting if the Mickey series was the success everyone was convinced it was. Even more disturbing was the rumor that Powers was about to try to make off with Ub Iwerks. Powers had been led to believe, not totally erroneously, that Iwerks was the real talent at the Disney studio and that if he could be lured away and set him up in his own shop, he might be in much the same position Disney himself was now in—that is, as a producer with a possibly unlimited future. In any case he hoped to use the threat of hiring Iwerks as a way of bringing Disney to satisfactory terms on a new contract.

Disney and his wife again entrained for New York, this time taking along Gunther Lessing, an attorney who was to become a powerful force within the Disney organization (a persistent story identifies Lessing as a one-time aide of the Mexican bandit Pancho Villa, a tale that gained both wide circulation and credence among the Disney strikers in 1940 when Lessing undertook the role of management's most unyielding negotiator and spokesman). In Powers, they found a man who had outsmarted himself. He had not expected The Mouse to be the great success that he was. Planning to use Disney's creation as no more than a loss leader in the promotion of his sound system, Powers had neglected to make a tight contract with Disney. It ran for only one year, with no renewal options. From the moment he realized that Mickey Mouse was far more valuable than his Cinephone, he had been trying to squeeze Disney. It was this attempt to bind Walt to him with extralegal ties that had led to his pursuit of Iwerks and to his withholding, throughout the year, of the full amounts due Disney on his contract.

Now Powers' strategy became clear. He greeted Disney by showing him a telegram from his Los Angeles representative indicating that Iwerks had now signed a contract with Powers to produce a cartoon series of his own. He also informed Disney that he could not examine his books to determine what money was due him unless he agreed to a new contract, although, of course, he was free to undertake a costly, time-consuming court fight for a fair accounting. On the other hand, Powers did not wish to appear unreasonable. His true aim, after all, was not to drive Disney to the wall but to continue to participate in an extremely profitable arrangement with the young producer. If Disney agreed to sign the new contract, he would not only receive the sums due him for his last year's labor, but Powers would tear up his contract with Iwerks and agree to pay Disney $2,500 a week in the future.

Disney asked for a little time to think things over, and he later recalled that it was not until he was walking back to his hotel that the full magnitude of the $2,500-a-week offer struck him. It was more money than anyone had ever mentioned to him before, and he remembered muttering the figure aloud, to the wonderment of various passersby. The impressiveness of the sum was undoubtedly a mistake on the part of Powers, as indeed was his whole strategy, since it was based on a fundamental misreading of his man. The $2,500 had the effect of confirming Disney's own estimation of the value of what he was doing. It also indicated to him that he was not without bargaining strength himself.

Before he had left home his brother had told him that he must obtain an immediate cash advance from Powers in order to keep the studio operating, and so, when he returned to the

135

distributor for further discussions, he casually mentioned the need for cash. Anxious to indicate his good will, Powers drew a check for $5,000, and Disney stalled him until it cleared. Then he broke off negotiations with Powers.

He made no attempt to retain Iwerks, who, with Powers' backing, set up his own shop and, for a while, produced a series called *Flip the Frog*. It did not catch on, perhaps because he lacked the one talent everyone who ever worked for him agrees that Disney possessed in abundance—that of a story editor. He certainly lacked the Disney brothers' ability to control costs on the one hand and to master the fast-talking financial world beyond the studio door. Within a few years Iwerks was back at work for Disney, where he supervised special effects on many of the studio's major productions and was instrumental in developing improved animation technique as well as the multiplane camera, on which he had actually begun experimentation during his brief independent fling. He won two Academy Awards for his technical achievements. He remained at the studio until his death in 1971, and in his late years, besides working with Hitchcock on *The Birds* figured prominently in the development of an improved matte process that made possible not only the technically perfect blending of animation and live action in *Mary Poppins* but also its brilliant illusions of flight and the sequence that was the film's highpoint, the dance over the rooftops of London. Personally, Disney's relationship with Iwerks always remained on a business-only basis. Witnesses report Disney carefully looked the other way when passing Iwerks on the lot or, at best, spoke to him in monosyllables. Iwerk's technical genius was valuable enough to Disney for him to tolerate his presence, but he never could forgive his long-ago moment of disloyalty.

PART SIX

Everyone Grows Up

---

16 *And every week, every day, more workers joined the procession of despair. The shadows deepened in the dark cold rooms, with the father angry and helpless and ashamed, the distraught children too often hungry or sick, and the mother, so resolute by day, so often, when the room was finally still, lying awake in bed at night, softly crying.*
—Arthur M. Schlesinger, Jr. *The Crisis of the Old Order*

I encountered nothing in 15,000 miles of travel that disgusted and appalled me so much as this American addiction to make-believe. Apparently, not even empty bellies can cure it. Of all the facts I dug up, none seemed so significant or so dangerous as the overwhelming fact of our lazy, irresponsible, adolescent inability to face the truth or tell it."
—James Rorty, *Where Life is Better* (1936)

OBVIOUSLY THE BUSINESS to be in was the illusion business. At least at first. Buoyed by the novelty of sound films and by the need of its audience for inexpensive escape, the American movie industry maintained its general prosperity until 1933, slumped briefly, recovered (eighty million admissions were purchased in 1936), joined the rest of the economy in the 1938 recession and thereafter matched the rest of the nation's business cycle until the postwar period, when, as noted, it failed to participate fully in the general boom. It cannot be said that the Disney studio performed exceptionally well from a business analyst's point of view during the industry's period of retained prosperity, 1930 to 1933. By their very nature it is difficult to make a great deal of money on short subjects, especially animated cartoons. The shorts share an underdeveloped land on the margin of the industry, and the only hope of continuing success with them is to achieve efficient, large-volume production at low unit cost and with rapid turnover. Animated films have the additional problem of being more costly to produce than live-action films of the same length. Disney's strategy, given this situation, was to sacrifice any hope of large immediate profits and strive only to keep operating while building up diversified sources of income and a reputation for quality production. This, he hoped, might sustain a break-out from shorts into feature production, where real profits and genuine stability lay, if they lay anywhere in so chancy a business as the movies. In pursuit of this goal it was necessary for the studio to attack simultaneously on several fronts—the economic, the technological and the aesthetic—and it had to be prepared for a long struggle.

Economically, Disney's first need, in 1930, was for a new distributor. He went first to Metro-Goldwyn-Mayer, which had no major cartoons series of its own and was interested. M-G-M decided, however, to turn Disney down for fear of deepening its already substantial reputation for mercilessness, the inevitable concomitant of its rapid growth to first place in size among the studios. It simply did not want to be in a position where it might look like a bully stealing a property from a small operator like Powers.

Harry Cohn, the president of Columbia Pictures, had no such qualms. He was a little guy himself, but even if he had not been, he was not a man to hesitate when Frank Capra, the decade's leading comedy director, praised Disney's work and indicated that his studio's product was available for distribution. This time Disney had no trouble striking a bargain that allowed him to retain ownership of his films and the independence of his studio. The trouble was that his drive for an improved product continued to push costs up. At the time he signed with Columbia a Disney short cost $5,400 to produce. By late 1931 he was spending $13,500 on each little film and doing no better than breaking even on them.

He was also beginning to break down, emotionally. Each film he turned out barely paid for the next one, and the problems presented by his leading character were also extremely frustrating. The Mouse more or less fitted the description of him, written three years later by no less a literary figure than E. M. Forster, who found Mickey "energetic without being elevated" and added, "No one has ever been softened after seeing Mickey or has wanted to give away an extra glass of water to the poor. He is never sentimental, indeed there is a scandalous element in him which I find most restful." The trouble was that some people were scandalized without refreshment by Mickey's style. It was also true that although people wanted to identify with him—and many succeeded—it was not possible to make his alter ego into the universal hero Disney seems to have wanted him to become. His popularity, as Gilbert Seldes said in 1932, had "some of the elements of a fad, where it joins the kewpie and the Teddy Bear" and that, obviously, was not good enough for Disney. Mickey had to become both more verbal and somewhat softer in manner if he was to satisfy Disney—and if he was to be transformed from his fad status into the kind of symbol that can ride above any shift in the wind of fashion. By the time Forster wrote, this process was already well under way.

It seemed to disturb Disney, almost as if it were his own personality that was being tampered with. It also presented him with purely aesthetic decisions that were painful to him. Lik-

able as Mickey was becoming, his new sweet self was as difficult to use as the core of a film as his old sharp self had been. He
was still not funny in and of himself: he was merely unfunny in
a different, though perhaps more generally appealing, way.
This humorlessness as well as his naïveté and his enthusiasm
for projects were perhaps the first traits he inherited from Disney, who insisted that he had a sense of humor, put down those
who lacked it, but was never the author of a genuinely funny
remark that anyone ever recorded.

Thus Disney apparently saw as early as 1931 that, despite
strenuous efforts to avoid it, he was, as he later said, "trapped
with the mouse . . . stuck with the character." Mickey
"couldn't do certain things—they would be out of character.
And Mickey was on a pedestal—I would get letters if he did
something wrong. I got worried about relying on a character
like the mouse—you wear it out, you run dry." The answer for
him was diversification. "We got Pluto and the duck. The duck
could blow his top. Then I tied Pluto and Donald together.
The stupid things Pluto would do, along with the duck, gave us
an outlet for our gags."

The process of developing new characters, however, was
slow. As of 1931, Disney had in addition to Mickey and Minnie
only the villainous Peg-Leg, a couple of rubber-limb and circle
combinations known as Clarabelle Cow and Horace Horsecol-
lar, who were serviceable but not memorable and who were, in
any case, the products of a style of animation Disney wanted to
move beyond. It is true that a prototypical Pluto had appeared
as one of a pair of bloodhounds chasing Mickey in *The Chain
Gang* in 1930 and that he had appeared again alone with The
Mouse in *The Picnic*. He was known only as "Rover" in that
picture, however, and his useful presence did not make itself
felt until he acquired his one, true name and the beginnings of
his marvelously eager, innocent and therefore troublemaking
identity late in 1931. Goofy did not make his first appearance—
as an extra in a crowd scene in *Mickey's Revue*—until 1932,

and he, too, had another name at first—Dippy Dawg. The Duck did not arrive until 1934, when he had one line of dialogue ("Who—me? Oh, no! I got a bellyache!") in *The Wise Little Hen*. His genesis is, however, interesting. It seems Disney heard Clarence Nash, who has always done Donald's voice, on a local radio show, reciting "Mary Had a Little Lamb" as a girl duck. He discovered that Nash was employed by a local dairy to put on shows for schools, hired him away and then tried to create a character to match his duck voice. It was not until some forgotten genius changed the duck's sex and temperament that Nash found his métier. The other members of the stable (or "gang," as Disney's people preferred to call it)— Chip and Dale, the team of comic chipmunks, Daisy Duck, Donold's inamorata, and his three nephews Huey, Louie and Dewey —all came along several years later than the duck.

Which is to say diversification of characters—the creation of new stars, if you will—required most of a decade and therefore was not the immediate answer that Disney required to his problems. The same may be said of his attempts to diversify stylistically. He clung steadfastly to the Silly Symphonies idea, about half of which were original material, the other half based on traditional folk material (with a heavy reliance on Aesop). But until *The Three Little Pigs* became his biggest short-subject success in 1933–34, the series did not make a large, direct contribution to his financial progress. If anything, it did the reverse.

The temporary solution to the problem of keeping Mickey fresh and amusing was to move him out of the sticks and into cosmopolitan environments and roles. The locales of his adventures throughout the 1930s ranged from the South Seas to the Alps to the deserts of Africa. He was, at various times, a gaucho, teamster, explorer, swimmer, cowboy, fireman, convict, pioneer, taxi driver, castaway, fisherman, cyclist, Arab, football player, inventor, jockey, storekeeper, camper, sailor, Gulliver, boxer, exterminator, skater, polo player, circus performer, plumber, chemist, magician, hunter, detective, clock cleaner, Hawaiian, carpenter, driver, trapper, whaler, tailor and Sorcerer's Apprentice. In short, he was Everyman and the Renaissance Man combined, a mouse who not only behaved like a man but dreamed dreams of mastery like all men. His distinction was that he got the chance to act them out. As Forster said, "Mickey's great moments are moments of heroism, and when he carries Minnie out of the harem as a pot-plant or rescues her as she falls in foam . . . he reaches heights impossible for the *entrepreneur*."

Unfortunately, it was as an entrepreneur that he finally found his more or less permanent identity. By the middle of the 1930s he more and more frequently appeared as the manager and organizer of various events—often variety shows and concerts (where at least he got the chance to conduct)—and one cannot help but suspect that this was a reflection of Disney's strong identification with The Mouse. By then Disney himself was occupied principally as the manager, organizer and coordinator of an organization that had grown from a handful of people to a complex of some 750 employees when *Snow White* was in full production in 1937. Here there was still opportunity for mastery but hardly for the heroism implicit in the life of the pioneer Disney had been. The Mouse was by this time rounder, sleeker (and far more humanoid in design). And like his creator he was also more sober, sensible and suburban in outlook—better organized. His "gang" was carrying the whole comic load.

But in 1931 all this was still in the future, and though Disney undoubtedly perceived something of the direction in which he wanted to go, he certainly did not see it in any detail. All he knew was that he wanted more and he wanted it better, and he was driving himself in the time-honored tradition of the American success ethic. He recalled later that he often took his wife out for dinner, then suggested dropping in to the studio to do a few minutes' work. She would stretch out on a couch in his office and fall asleep, and he would plunge on at his job, losing track of time until he glanced at his watch and found that it was after one in the morning. When he woke his wife and she asked what time it was he would tell her it was only ten-thirty. He claimed she never discovered his trick. She spent a fair share of her time trying to keep dinners warm when he worked late at the office. On one especially forgetful evening he stayed far, far into the night and she grew quite irritated, though as she later said, she could never stay mad at him very long. "I think the apology that time was a hatbox tied with a red ribbon. But don't think there was anything as prosaic as a hat in it! It held a chow puppy, with another red ribbon around its neck."

Still, he was beginning to pay the price. "I kept expecting more from my artists than they were giving me, and all I did all day long was pound, pound, pound," he said later. "Costs were going up. Somehow, each new picture we finished cost more to make than we figured it would earn; so I cracked up . . . I became irritable . . . and I couldn't sleep. I got to the point where I couldn't talk over the telephone because I'd begin to cry. . . ."

Finally, he consulted a doctor, who recommended a long trip. Disney and his wife set forth on an eastbound train, not precisely certain of their destination but with some vague hope of realizing his boyhood dream of taking a steamer trip down the Mississippi. None was available and the idea was abandoned (though the relationship between the wish and the fulfillment it had already received in *Steamboat Willie* is clear and emphasizes again how heavily Disney drew on his own background for material and how direct and simple was the process of transforming it into story material). Instead of taking the river trip, they proceeded to Washington, D. C., where Disney tried to arrange a meeting with General Pershing, who Disney thought was "everything a man should be." A press agent asked if he would accept an interview with President Hoover instead, but Disney declined, settling for an autographed copy of Pershing's

143

memoirs. After a few days he and his wife boarded a train for Key West, took a ship to Havana, where they spent a week, then took another ship for a leisurely cruise to Calfornia via the Panama Canal. On his return Disney immediately plunged into an intensive experiment with athletics. He worked out at an athletic club and tried boxing, wrestling and golf. But "when he tried sports he worked so hard at them that he only got more tense," Mrs. Disney later recalled. Instead of playing golf "like a normal person, he got up at four-thirty in the morning to get it out of the way before he had to be at the studio," she said. "He talked about the dew on the grass and the sunrise until I decided to take up golf with him. But we never went far. Walt would fly into such a rage when he missed a stroke that I got helplessly hysterical watching him." Disney finally settled on horseback riding as an ideal, non-competitive athletic endeavor, hurrying back from the studio each night to join his wife for a twilight ride in the hills near their home. It had a salutary effect on the Disneys—they credited it with curing a temporary inability to conceive children—and it led Walt Disney to his one major ostentation of the period which was polo. Ultimately he had a string of twenty ponies, a reputation as a poor rider but an occasionally inspired competitor and a one-goal rating that he attributed to his paying a very large bill at the Riviera Country Club, where the Hollywood horsy set played. His interest in horses also led him to make an investment in The Hollywood Park, a racetrack that quadrupled in value while he held on to the investment.

17 *Work is our sanity, our self respect, our salvation. So far from being a curse, work is the greatest blessing.*

—Henry Ford

Walt has always operated on the theory of making today pay off tomorrow.

—Roy O. Disney

THERE WAS ALWAYS something obsessive about Walt Disney's personality. His single-minded concentration on his career, his possessiveness about his business, his unwillingness to share its management with any outsiders, his singular identification with The Mouse, the paternalism and the parsimony that marked his dealings with employees—all these qualities now began to be noted as the organization started growing and Disney necessarily grew more remote. He became something of a sneak in his own studio, prowling the corridors at night and on weekends, trying to get a glimpse of story ideas and sketches before his writers and editors were ready to show them (and forcing them to elaborate stratagems to hide their work until it was ready). He took a similar interest in the physical plant itself, leaving notes for the maintenance people when he discovered, for example, a burned-out light bulb or an overflowing trash can. In later years he even patroled the vast reaches of Disneyland on the same errand, leaving instructions on sheets of blue note paper that he alone in the organization used. In short, he carried the search for perfection to absurd lengths, and although he never again suffered a collapse like the one of 1931, he never learned to let up on his people either.

He also acquired, at about this time, an obsession with death, which was so marked that even his daughter commented upon it in her study of her father, although she reduced it to a minor eccentricity. She claims it began at a party where a fortune-teller predicted he would not live beyond his thirty-fifth birthday, a prediction that plagued him even after he sailed past that date in excellent health. He felt that he had, at best, been granted only a reprieve. For the rest of his life he avoided funerals and when forced to attend them, fell into long, brooding depressions. He even avoided would-be biographers, commenting to more than one acquaintance that "biographies are only written about dead people." He apparently feared that not only would such studies pry into business and personal secrets (he made little distinction between the two), but they might have the effect of reversing the usual order of things and somehow *cause* his demise. While he lived, no book about him or his studio appeared unless he approved the contents, which meant that they all heavily stressed neutral, technological matters and said little about the master except to praise his creative genius. When one writer had his request for official sanction for his work turned down and threatened to go ahead without his help, Disney quickly arranged his daughter's collaboration with Pete Martin on *The Saturday Evening Post* biographical series that appeared in 1957.

In 1932, however, with his "nerves" under good control, his obsessions had their uses. For example, his rage for order. At first Disney and his co-workers had continued the traditional practice of their competitors—simply making up a story as they went along, adding and subtracting gags in a helter-skelter fashion and hoping the whole thing would hang together when it was finished. Quite early, however, Disney decided that stories ought to be at least outlined at a preliminary meeting. These often took place in the dining room of his own home, at night, with a film can containing candy as the table's centerpiece. By 1931, however, the inefficiency and the lack of control implicit in this system became annoying to Disney and he created a story department, staffing it with those animators who had shown the greatest gift at concocting useful plot lines. He thus firmly and forever separated word men from picture people in the early, creative stages of a production, though they all came together frequently as work proceeded. For a time he continued the night-time meetings but only to "gag" a preset story line. A two-page outline of it would be circulated throughout the studio along with a note, one of which, dated 1932, went as follows:

> A swell story to gag—
> Especially the fight sequence where all four characters are chasing the old cat all over the back yard trying to rescue the little helpless canary.
> So let's all hop to it and have some good belly laughs ready by
>
> Tuesday Night—June 14th
>
> Thanks,
> Walt

Even this limited informality was soon to be abandoned, however, for it lacked a method by which the most important element of a cartoon, its visual humor, could be observed, criticized, improved. The answer was the story board, which was nothing more elaborate than a series of sketches of the key moments of an action sequence pinned up in the order of their occurrence. On its face this seems a minor innovation. But a way of seeing a cartoon prior to the beginning of the expensive animation process was actually a quite significant step toward the solution of a problem that had nagged animation from its beginnings.

Disney credited the invention to Webb Smith, a one-time newspaper cartoonist who began his career with Disney as an animator, then switched to the story department when it was formed. Smith's other just claim to fame is as the creator of the most highly regarded of all Pluto's adventures—his accidental encounter with a sheet of very sticky flypaper and his gorgeously orchestrated efforts to extricate himself from its dread clutches. It was an almost perfect piece of visual humor. In any case, Smith had retained his habit of sketching out gag sequences instead of writing them down. These he generally spread all over the floor of his office, an unsightly and sometimes confusing business that he one day abandoned in favor of pinning his sketches on the walls. At first, it is said, Disney was furious at the notion: he claimed that the holes left by the pins would ruin the walls, which he had just spent a good deal to redecorate. But the conflict between his rage for artistic order and his rage for tidy housekeeping was resolved when quantities of corkboard were ordered (they had the virtue of being portable, too), and Smith's idea quickly became an established —even ritualistic—part of the studio's planning procedure. It was a key innovation in the process of rationalizing the chaos of cartoon creation—a process that was one of Disney's principal preoccupations throughout the Thirties. Indeed, storyboarding passed from the Disney studio to many others as live-action directors found it most useful in keeping track of tricky plots and in visualizing camera angles and decor in advance of shooting.

Far more significant than the storyboard, however, was Disney's partial conversion to color production late in 1931 and the signing of his first genuinely profitable releasing contract with United Artists in 1932. Color processes had been skulking around the edge of the movie business almost as long as sound systems had been before they were generally adopted. As early as 1929 Technicolor had marketed a two-color process that was used for novelty effects but, at its best, had been unreal because of its inability to provide the film maker with a full tonal palette to work with and that, at its worst, had been downright garish. In 1932, however, Technicolor created a three-color process which, though imperfect, represented a major breakthrough. "That was what we were waiting for," Disney later said. "When I saw those three colors all on one film, I wanted to cheer."

At the time he had a Silly Symphony called *Flowers and*

148

Trees in production, and he immediately decided to scrap its completed footage—almost half the film—and reshoot the whole thing in color. Roy Disney was appalled, not just at the waste of perfectly releasable film, but at the whole notion of going into color production, which added more than ten thousand dollars to the cost of each short. As guardian of the books, he had the unpleasant task of pointing out the risks involved in each of his brother's embraces of a new technology, and this was neither the first nor the last such squabble he was to have with his brother. His frugal soul was so upset by the *Flowers and Trees* situation that he actually went around the studio trying to enlist allies in the effort to talk his brother out of his folly. He did not succeed. Disney sold it, on the basis of a one-minute sample, to Sid Grauman, proprietor of Grauman's Chinese Theater, who was looking for something suitably uplifting to play with the world premiere engagement of Irving Thalberg's high-toned production of Eugene O'Neill's *Strange Interlude*. Disney rushed the production to gain this prestigious booking. The picture did very well at the box office and became the first Disney production to win an Academy Award, as the best cartoon of 1931. At the same time, Disney also received a special award for the creation of Mickey Mouse.

Flowers and Trees was one of those heavily arty Silly Symphonies that age ungracefully. It is the story of a romance between a boy tree and a girl tree, which is almost sundered by a wicked, stumpy growth who in his maddened pursuit of the girl —it *does* sound ridiculous—manages to set fire to the forest, a conflagration that is dampened only by the combined efforts of all the resident botanical growths. Again, it was the technological novelty of the film, not its intrinsic artistic quality, that sold it. And it must be admitted that the color, though its tones tended toward gray, was effective to a degree only slightly below the level of quality that Technicolor would ultimately achieve.

Best of all, from the standpoint of the studio's future development, its early interest in the new color process—and the promotional value of its popular film—established it in a highly favored position with Technicolor. This was formalized in an agreement under which Technicolor gave Disney the exclusive right to its three-color process for cartoon production until the spring of 1935, forcing his competitors to make do with the two-color process or to resort to the inferior Cinecolor process. It was, in those days, a tremendous competitive edge, and it made the Silly Symphonies, the only films in which Disney used color until 1934, fully as attractive to exhibitors as the Mickey Mouse series.

By 1932 Disney was close to becoming, if not big business, then a major factor in his field. In that year, seeking to improve on his soon-to-expire Columbia contract, he turned down an advance of $15,000 per short from Universal's Carl Laemmle, who told Disney that he was making a grievous error in spending as much as he did on his films, which had risen in production costs from $5,400 in 1929 to $13,500 by this time. Disney finally got the sort of deal he wanted from United Artists, which gave him 60 percent of the gross on each film—a complete reversal, it will be noted, of his earlier splits with producers—and his advances were raised to more than $20,000 a film. Under this contract, which ran until 1937, Disney was obliged to turn out twenty shorts a year: they were the only nonfeature productions UA distributed. On a typical color film the economics went something like this: Disney spent about $27,500 to produce each of them, added another $17,500 for prints and another $5,000 for advertising, shipping, taxes, foreign duties and other miscellaneous costs, bringing the total expense of a short to $50,000. He expected each picture to gross about $80,000 in its first year of release, $40,000 in its second. After UA's distribution fee was deducted, his receipts in the first year amounted to about $48,000, which meant he did not begin to take a profit until the second year. Then he might expect to receive profits of $22,000 (remember that starting the second year of each film he would typically still be $2,000 behind on that film). Once this cycle was functioning fully, Disney was spending about one million dollars on current production and taking in about $440,000 above that figure in profits on the United Artists arrangement. To this he could add about $20,000 on receipts from older films still being handled by Columbia and income from a third source—merchandising—that we will deal with later. In all, it was estimated that by 1934 he was taking in $660,000 a year in profit, most of which he was pouring back into the studio. Even so, it is clear that he had accomplished something of an economic miracle, for it must be remembered that the years of this stupendous growth in profitability were the years during which the rest of the country was wallowing in the deepest trough of the depression.

Nor should it be imagined that Disney's rewards during the years of the UA contract were purely economic. That studio, of course, was controlled by Charles Chaplin (Disney's boyhood idol), Mary Pickford and Douglas Fairbanks, and Disney later recalled that "I was a protégé of Mary, Doug and Charlie" and remembered his satisfaction when Chaplin invited him over to study United Artists' books; he also recalled the far deeper satisfaction he received after abandoning the UA arrangement and scoring his huge financial success with *Snow White:* "Then Charlie came over and studied *our* books."

18 *I build my house of stones.*
I build my house of bricks.
I have no chance to sing and dance,
For work and play don't mix.
Who's Afraid of the Big Bad Wolf, the big bad wolf?
—American popular song, 1932

DISNEY WAS TRAVELING in one of the better Hollywood
circles now. Behind him were the days spent at the mercy of the
New York fly-by-nights and the ignominy of being handled by
Harry Cohn's Columbia Pictures, then little more than the most
prosperous house on Hollywood's Poverty Row. United Artists
was then, though not the most profitable studio in Hollywood,
certainly the one with the most class, and it had an independence of mind in its management that Disney found welcome.

Disney always enjoyed showing people around his studio and
explaining to them exactly how the exotic process of creating an
animated film proceeded (eventually he made one film about it,
The Reluctant Dragon, and several TV shows). So one day in
1933 he invited Mary Pickford to tour the Spanish-style studio
on Hyperion Avenue (its walls were stucco and it surrounded a
grassy courtyard, and only a giant replica of Mickey Mouse atop
the main building marred the serene effect). He arranged for
Miss Pickford to meet Frank Churchill, one of his composers,
Ted Sears, a story man, and Pinto Colvig, whose duties included providing the voice for Goofy. "Why don't you do that
'pig' thing for Mary?" Disney casually inquired. Whereupon
they played for her (on, respectively, the piano, the violin and
the ocarina) a little tune Churchill had written for which Sears
had supplied some simple lyrical couplets. Little Mary loved it
and told Disney, "If you don't make this cartoon about the pigs,
I'll never speak to you again."

152

She need not have feared. *The Three Little Pigs* was indeed finished, and the song Disney's helpers sang for the visiting celebrity—"Who's Afraid of the Big Bad Wolf"—became the first musical hit ever to come out of an animated cartoon. The picture became the second Disney product to win an Academy Award (indeed, in the period of 1932 to 1942, Disney only twice failed to win an Oscar for the best cartoon of the year). The picture grossed $125,000 in the first year of its release, twice that before its run was finished, and Disney claimed it did not really take off until it reached the neighborhood houses, where the plain people congregated. Then it became so popular that Disney and Technicolor could not supply enough prints to the clamoring theaters, which resorted to the ancient practice of "bicycling" prints. That is, one of them would rent it and then, while it was not being shown, get it over to other theaters in the neighborhood so their patrons could glimpse it too. Naturally this cut rental costs—and cut Disney's profits somewhat—but resort to the antique practice, much favored by exhibitors before the industry was well rationalized, reflected the incredible demand for the little film more than it did a general reversion to former ethics.

Summarizing the year's films on the last day of 1933, The New York *Times* stated that "No comments on the year's productions would be complete without a word or two concerning the splendid short features made by the redoubtable Walt Disney. One might safely venture that his prismatic 'Silly Symphony' 'Three Little Pigs' has been shown at more theaters simultaneously than any other film, short or feature length." The paper went on to praise other recent Silly Symphonies, among them *Lullaby Land*, *Father Neptune* and *Noah's Ark*, the last of which had been the subject of an invidious comparison to *The Three Little Pigs* by one movie man. He thought he was being gypped because *Pigs* contained only four animals, while the Ark, of course, contained hundreds.

No one else shared these sentiments. The three pigs and the

wolf who pursued them with such dreadful and comic dedication were not only the most finely delineated characterizations Disney's people had yet created—Disney himself wrote his brother, "At last we have achieved true personality in a whole picture"—but their story was subject to a very useful interpretation in this darkest of all depression years. "To many people," Lewis Jacobs wrote in 1939, "this film suggested that only by building an 'impregnable house' can the 'big bad wolf' of hunger and fear be kept out. In a time of spreading bank failures, bankruptcies, and unemployment, the message of The Three Little Pigs was emphatic, especially after Roosevelt's famous appeal to Americans to stick together and not give up hope. The picture's theme song . . . became a national anthem overnight. Originating as a popular child's fairy tale, the film became by force of circumstance and the time spirit a heartening call to the people of a troubled country."

The gloomy statistics of 1932—18,000,000 people out of work; U.S. Steel stock listed at 185 *after* the crash in 1929 now down to 62¼, and that sort of thing—are vivid memories to those who lived through their initial publication, historical clichés to those whose knowledge of the time has been gained through the proliferating volumes of popular social history. What does seem significant, however, is that the spirit of *The Three Little Pigs*, viewed from the perspective of more than thirty years, is more that of Hoover than of Roosevelt. It is true that there is an optimistic tone to the film, a jaunty, sprightly style in drawing, music and action that partakes more of the Roosevelt manner than of the starchy Hoover mode. But philosophically the message is Hooverian, stressing self-reliance, the old virtues of solid, conservative building and of keeping one's house in order. After all, it is the eldest pig, who even looked a little bit like Hoover, who is the film's hero. More important, he follows the main line of conservative thought in the nation at that time, which was that the great national disaster was the direct result of an improvidence not unlike that of the two

154

younger pigs, skipping about, singing and dancing, when they should have been forting up against the very real menace that lurked nearby. As Henry Ford had just finished saying, "The average man won't really do a day's work unless he is caught and cannot get out of it," adding that so far as he could see—which, socially, wasn't very far,—"There is plenty of work to do, if people would do it."

There was also abroad in the land, during this last year of Hoover's unhappy tenure in office, a feeling that we might just be able to talk our way out of our difficulties. Billboards sprouted along the highways, asking, "Wasn't the depression terrible?" as if by putting the question in the past tense the depression itself could be made to vanish. The President periodically rounded up business leaders to confer on the situation, emerging from the meetings not with programs of action but with his famous assurances that things were "fundamentally sound." He was renominated by his dispirited party in a speech that spoke of his career as one that "typifies spiritual values and the vanity of mere earthly things." He accepted the call to duty by, as Robert Bendiner summarizes, "a defense of pure conservatism and congratulated himself for having beaten the Depression without any sacrifice of American principles." Which, of course, is precisely what the eldest pig in Disney's little fable did to beat the wolf. He did not experiment with anything new in the line of defenses: he merely constructed the most solid, traditional house he could, thereby reflecting, as Hoover also did, the conventional middle-class, midwestern wisdom of the day.

This, of course, is a social critic's plausible if somewhat self-conscious reading of what is essentially a charming film, as is the quibble that in the course of attempting to breach the solid defenses of the eldest pig's brick house, the wolf donned the robe, beard and glasses of the long-caricatured Jewish peddler. It was an unfortunate choice for a gag. Despite the film's naïveté and its one glaring lapse of taste, one can still applaud

The Three Little Pigs as a significant advance in Disney's art and, because of its general cheeriness, a socially helpful piece of entertainment in a year that was singularly lacking in good cheer almost everywhere one looked.

The Three Little Pigs was not an unmixed blessing for Disney. To be sure, it established the "Silly Symphony" series in the public mind as nothing previously had, but as with Mickey Mouse, success brought with it the danger of entrapment in the attempt to repeat success. The last piece of writing ever to go out over Walt Disney's signature—the message to stockholders in the 1966 annual report of his company—referred to the matter: "Back in the '30s *The Three Little Pigs* was an enormous hit, and the cry went up—'Give us more pigs!' I could not see how we could possibly top pigs with pigs. But we tried, and I doubt whether any one of you reading this can name the other cartoons in which the pigs appeared." It was a lesson well learned, and he refused to try to follow *Snow White and the Seven Dwarfs* with more films featuring the dwarfs, and, as he said in this letter, he was not going to try to make sequels to *Mary Poppins* either. In an industry that has devoted enormous amounts of energy to scrambling on and off bandwagons it was an admirable and sensible policy.

About the symbolic meanings people kept finding in *The Three Little Pigs*, Disney was sincerely mystified, and even a trifle amazed. Barely on familiar terms with his own—not to mention anyone else's—subconscious mind, he rejected all interpretations of the work which extended beyond what is actually showed. This was characteristic of his response to most criticism; often he repeated variations on the statement "we make the pictures and then let the professors tell us what they mean." If an idea did not either stem from his conscious mind or receive acknowledgment from it, it simply did not exist for him. Of *The Three Little Pigs* he said, "It was just another story to us and we were in there gagging it just like any other picture. After we heard all the shouting, we sat back and tried to analyze what made it good. Then we consciously tried to put some social meaning into *The Golden Touch*. It ended with King Midas surrounded by his gold, hollering for a hamburger. It was a tremendous flop."

It could be argued, however, that Disney's Academy Award winner of the next year, *The Tortoise and the Hare*, and his equally popular *The Grasshopper and the Ants* contained messages for their times, as well as charm (and, in the case of the latter, another hit song, "The World Owes Me a Living"). The first suggested that victory goes to the consistent plodder rather than to the flashy but lazy competitor; the second, that there is virtue in saving against the rainy day. Both were widely acceptable homiletic shields against the kind of disaster that was befalling so many Americans in the years the pictures were in release. Certainly, there was nothing very New-Dealish about the sentiments they expressed, which were more rural and small town than urban and sophisticated. They expressed, indeed, a wish for simple solutions rather than a dynamic plan for action.

But at this point in his career it must not be supposed that Disney was thinking much about politics or economics—beyond his own, of course. Indeed, although he supported Barry Goldwater in 1964 and contributed to the campaign funds of several conservative Republican candidates for office, among them George Murphy and Ronald Reagan, Disney never did think much about political affairs in any programmatic or even pragmatic way. The political conservatism for which he was often attacked by liberal commentators and praised by conservatives was no more than an acting out of an instinctive feeling about life and society, very much on the order of the other fairly simple, even primitive, ideas that formed his work. If he had any politics at all, they were politics of nostalgia, and his instinct throughout his life was to wall himself off from the affairs of nations and governments, the better to tend his own garden in his own fussy style, which was an odd blend of the boyish and the paternalistic. In later years, when it became known that he was backing right-wing candidates, he was often asked if he had political ambitions of his own. Once he registered a shrug and a small-boy scoff: "Naw, I'd spend all my time getting mad at people." On another occasion a reporter from the Dallas *Morning News* put the same question to him, and his response was characteristic: "I don't even want to be President of the United States. . . . I'd rather be the benevolent dictator of Disney enterprises. . . ." By this time, of course, the wisdom of his instinctive individualism had been confirmed by the obvious progress he had made economically—progress that was certainly subject to interpretation as a working out of the classic tenets of the free-enterprise philosophy. Disney's position was much like that of the small manufacturer who has seen his little widget business grow to proportions that have surprised even him—except that Disney worked in a highly public medium. All of which suggests that his politics, far from being surprising, were quite in keeping with his background and experience.

In the middle of the 1930s, however, his political simplicity caused him to make the most remarkable statements. In what appears to have been a speech that was adapted as a magazine article in 1933, Disney's comments on the world political scene make amazing reading. In it he promised that Mickey Mouse would never do anything to hurt or frighten a child—already a few earnest souls were decrying the violence of his adventures —and then went on to point out quite sensibly that The Mouse was not a creation aimed specifically at children. "Mickey Mouse pictures are gauged to only one audience: the Mickey audience," he said. "The Mickey audience is made up of parts of people; of that deathless, precious, ageless, absolutely primitive remnant of something in every world-wracked human being which makes us play with children's toys-and laugh without self-consciousness at silly things, and sing in bathtubs, and dream and believe that our babies are uniquely beautiful. You know . . . the Mickey in us."

158

As an admittedly self-serving analysis it was not a bad one, and if he had stopped there the piece would not have much claim on our attention. But the young man, "bewildered but wholly unspoiled by his sudden rise to fame," as a contemporary chronicler put it, could not resist mentioning the important people who were known to adore The Mouse. "Mr. Mussolini takes his family to see every Mickey picture. Mr. King George and Mrs. Queen Mary give him a right royal welcome; while Mr. President F. Roosevelt and family have lots of Mickey in them, too. Doug Fairbanks took Mickey with him to savage South Sea Islands and won the natives over to his project. Mickey is one matter upon which the Chinese and Japanese agree."

Alas, however, there were still people who had somehow resisted The Mouse's charm, which grieved Disney. "Mr. A. Hitler, the Nazi old thing, says Mickey's silly. Imagine that! Well, Mickey is going to save Mr. A. Hitler from drowning or something some day. Just wait and see if he doesn't. Then won't Mr. A. Hitler be ashamed!"

So much for geopolitics as viewed from Disney's land. (What Hitler's propagandists had actually said was that The Mouse was "the most miserable ideal ever revealed . . . mice are dirty.") The coy style, the determined reduction of the world view to a level even lower than the very simple one Disney privately tended toward, the downright other-worldly quality of the piece—all were fairly typical of the sort of thing Disney's ghost writers and public relations people put out under his name all his life. Judged even by Hollywood standards, the Disney studio's off-screen pronouncements reached a level of ickiness unparalleled anywhere. No matter how self-serving a great man's speech or a great corporation's press release, one can usually find at least the shadow of the man or the institution behind the words. That was generally not the case with Disney. No studio put out more words of public-relations copy, yet none was less informative than this highly secretive organization. Indeed, the function of all those words went beyond that of a smoke screen—the usual *desideratum* for PR—and became a full-scale diversionary action. The words were designed to portray the organization as an open, happy, sunny institution, presided over first by a bashful boy artist, then (as he aged) an avuncular genius of the masses. Neither image could have been further from the truth about this complex man or his remarkable corporation. But despite the style in which his discussion of "Mr. A. Hitler" was couched, the piece is truthful in at least one respect: it revealed a man almost totally disengaged from the realities of the larger world even as that world was reaching out toward him, fairly begging him to let it bestow its favors on him.

19 *I see no reason why there should not be a theatrical season providing my proposed plan for using pressed figs and dates as money goes into effect fairly soon.*
—Robert Benchley, 1933

A THEATRICAL SEASON was begun in the fall of 1933, and there was no need to resort to Mr. Benchley's plan for a substitute coinage or to any of the more seriously suggested proposals that were offered, mostly during the brief bank holiday of March, to tide the country over until more conventional currencies were available. There was, however, a good deal of barter going on in the U.S.: a newspaper offered to exchange subscriptions for bushels of wheat, a hotel accepted "anything we can use in the coffee shop" as room rent, and two tubes of toothpaste were good for a trolley ride in Salt Lake City. Credit, too, was extended in often ludicrous fashion: at one Philadelphia department store you could charge streetcar tokens to your account, and in New York, although toothpaste wouldn't buy you a ride on the subway, it was possible to buy a three-months' supply of Pebeco with a check for a dollar postdated by three months.

The movies, as previously noted, continued to do well through 1934. With admissions at only twenty-five or thirty cents in the neighborhood houses, they provided, next to the thirty thousand new miniature golf courses, where the fee for nine holes was only fifteen cents, the cheapest possible sort of escape. They also provided other come-ons, among them Bank Night (usually Tuesday), when one was rewarded only if the number that one was assigned on the previous Bank Night was drawn and only if one had bought a new admission and could claim the reward personally. Administered from a central office in Denver, the scheme offered prizes sometimes as high as a thousand dollars and had the effect of encouraging habitual attendance on a traditionally slow night at the Bijous and Orpheums. There were also Dish Nights and Bingo games at some theaters, and then that peculiar mingling of pain and delight—the double feature—was introduced in these days as an additional method of luring the penny-wise, hour-foolish out of their homes (and away from that popular new appliance, the radio). In short, though the movie business could be good, it was necessary for one and all to scramble very hard for their shares of those minuscule admission charges.

None had to work harder for his share than Disney, despite the acclaim he was winning. Luckily, he had found, in various sidelines, the equivalent of Benchley's pressed figs and dates, which if he did not use directly as money, he could easily convert into cash. On several occasions he publicly complained that the short subject was far too often short-changed in the marts of his trade. To be sure, Radio City Music Hall, with which Disney quickly established a mutually admiring relationship based on their parallel pursuits of the family trade, paid as much as $1,500 a week for one of his shorts, but the more usual rental fee in the first-run houses was in the neighborhood of $150 a week. This compared very unfavorably to the $3,000 or so which a feature could command in the same house. And when impartial observers in the trade considered that most of his playing dates were not in the first-run houses but in the neighborhoods and the small towns (where for an old short the rental might be as small as three dollars and where the double-feature movement was beginning to cut out shorts altogether), they could detect a certain justice in Disney's complaints. Nor were these the end of them. He admitted that his rentals were higher than those of his competitors, but his costs were more than proportionately higher than theirs. He even groused that *The Three Little Pigs*, his biggest hit till that time, was not really doing very well. It was renting at black-and-white rates, about one-third those charged for color films then, even though Technicolor prints were much more expensive to make. And because of its sudden hit status, Disney had to pay for more prints to satisfy the demand, prints he felt would not be useful once that demand slackened.

He covered his pain on this subject by talking like an artist. "We will continue to follow our rule to put every cent of profit back into the business, for we believe in the future and what it will earn for us," he told an interviewer in 1934. "I don't much favor commercialization. Most producers think it is better to get while the getting is good. We have not operated that way. . . ." And, in that same year, *Fortune* reported that Disney felt that the only way to make short subjects pay was to make his product so good that audiences would demand them in preference to his cut-price competitors.

He did have a few other assets, though, not the least of which was its merchandising program. He had been in it from the moment Mickey Mouse achieved his initial success. In New York on business in 1930, he was waylaid in his hotel lobby by a nameless fellow who wanted to put The Mouse's likeness on school tablets, and offered Disney $300 for the privilege. Needing money, as usual, Disney signed the contract that was thrust at him and was launched on a sideline that was, at times, more profitable than the picture business.

The same year King Features came forward with an offer for a syndicated cartoon strip, and by 1934, Disney had fifteen people employed in his New York office to oversee licensing of products that were either reproductions of his characters or bore their likeness in some form or other. At this point, some eighty U.S. concerns, including such blue chips as General Foods, RCA Victor, National Dairy and International Silver, were moving some seven million dollars' worth of stuff carrying what amounted to the Disney imprimatur. For this they paid royalties in the range of 2½ to 5 percent—occasionally as much as ten percent—and Disney was grossing $300,000 on the operation and clearing half that amount, which made up almost one-third of his net profit. By the 1960s the percentage contributed to the company's profits by its merchandising and publications program has dropped to something less than 10 percent of its gross income, and it has stayed near that level in the years since. It remains, however, a tidy little profit center.

In the early days, Mickey Mouse naturally was the leading figure in these sidelines and performed at least two certifiable economic miracles in the depression. The Lionel Corporation, manufacturers of toy trains, was rescued from receivership by the sale of 230,000 handcars that featured the figures of Mickey and Minnie pumping away at the handles. The Ingersoll Watch Company was saved from deep financial trouble when it put out Mickey Mouse watches, of which something like ten million have been sold to date. (The originals, the ones on which Mickey's pointing fingers told the time, are now collector's items for trivia specialists, bringing as much as fifty dollars in the market. Despite their proliferation the watches were never meant to live past the recipient's puberty, and so they were thrown away, as they were bought, by the millions.) From the start, merchandising was carefully handled by the Disney organization, which exercised more rigid control than was usual in the field over the ethics and the advertising standards of licensees and guarded against price cutting and corner cutting in manufacture. This careful guardianship of the Disney name occasionally reached ludicrous proportions, as when the rights to the "Who's Afraid of the Big Bad Wolf?" tune were denied the producers of Edward Albee's *Who's Afraid of Virginia Woolf?*, presumably on the ground that the song would be injured if it were exposed to the insalubrious moral climate of George and Martha's house. Instead the words were sung in the play to the tune of "Here We Go 'Round the Mulberry Bush," which is in the public domain. But as a general rule, and as anyone who has raised a child during the last thirty-five years can testify, Disney-licensed products have tended to be somewhat more durable, attractive and well-designed than most of the junk with which they compete in the drug and dime stores. But, of course, they remain junk by any intelligent standard of toy manufacture.

In the beginning, The Mouse and his friends did not confine their activities in aid of commerce only to the wares of childhood. Someone put out a Mickey Mouse radiator cap, and for a brief moment in history it was possible to purchase a Mickey Mouse diamond bracelet for twelve hundred dollars. And before Mary Poppins thought of the idea, Mickey was, in effect, the spoonful of sugar helping the medicine to go down; that is, you could glimpse his cheery countenance on the label as you downed a certain brand of milk of magnesia. Later on, no Disney character was allowed to appear on products with an unpleasant connotation for children, and that ruled out most medicines. Beyond setting general policy on merchandising, Disney paid little attention to this endless flow of goods and confessed, after it had reached the flood stage during the prosperous Fifties (when The Mouse alone had appeared on five thousand different items, which had contributed a quarter of a billion dollars to the gross national product), that he simply couldn't keep up with it all. When his own children, Diane and Sharon, were small, he occasionally presented them with a selection of the items at Christmas time, and he often had it delivered in carload lots to the John Tracy Clinic for deaf children in Los Angeles—a favorite charity, founded by Spencer Tracy, a fellow polo enthusiast, and named after the actor's deaf son, who was for a time employed by Disney in a minor capacity. But essentially the toys, so long as they were safe and well made, were of little concern to Disney; they helped him to enlarge his profit margin painlessly and to publicize the work he most cared about—his movies.

By the middle thirties merchandising was extremely useful in broadening the wedge into the foreign markets that Disney's films had begun to open. The cartoons were, of course, universal in their appeal and very easy to understand. By 1934 Disney had opened small offices in London and Paris to aid in the distribution of merchandise as well as film, but as late as 1937 his films were being dubbed into only three foreign languages, French, Spanish and German. Elsewhere, Disney cartoons had to appear with subtitles, at first no great problem since there was so little dialogue, but the growth of verbal humor in the pictures proved an increasing handicap in the quest for easy universal understanding. It was easier to build an audience with the printed word, and so Disney comic strips, comic books and story books appeared in no less then twenty-seven of the world's tongues. It was as a printed comic and as merchandising figures that The Mouse and his cohorts won many of their first audiences in out-of-the-way corners of the world (thus reversing the order of recognition that had pertained at home), and in the process increased Disney's revenue in a way that no other movie maker could so easily and consistently exploit.

By 1937, indeed, The Mouse had become something of a political figure. Hitler, whose wrath had been kindled because in one of Mickey's films his animal friends appeared wearing the uniforms of German cavalrymen, thus dishonoring the nation's military tradition, had been forced, by popular demand, to allow Michael Maus, as he was known in Germany, back into the country. This triumph, however, was balanced by The Mouse's expulsion from Yugoslavia, where he was suspected of representing a too attractive revolutionary figure (the correspondent who reported this extraordinary chapter in the history of bureaucracy's march was also thrown out by the nervous Slavs). The Mouse was never banned in Russia because he was never much of a threat to the new Socialist order there, trade relations between the U.S. and the U.S.S.R. being almost nonexistent in the Thirties, but at one point the Russians denounced him as a typical example of the meekness of the proletariat under capitalist rule, then shifted the line on him and decided his films were "social satire" depicting "the capitalist world under the masks of pigs and mice," then shifted again to call The Mouse "a war monger." Finally they created a competitor known as Yozh, or porcupine, who had a suitably prickly—and correct—Marxist-Leninist attitude toward world conditions.

If nothing else, the political passions occasionally stirred by The Mouse during this decade indicate the folly of overinterpreting essentially innocent popular culture material in the light of any ideology—political, psychological, religious or even literary. Such work has a way of rebounding against the critic in an awkward, even comic, fashion—a curious process that has the unhealthy byproduct of rendering the purveyor of popular culture immune to serious attempts at understanding the effect of his work. In any case, by the middle of the decade, Disney was reaping benefits he had in no way counted on, thanks to the international favor his creations had won. England's King George V refused to go to the movies unless a Mickey Mouse film was shown, and Queen Mary was known to have appeared late for tea rather than miss the end of a charity showing of *Mickey's Nightmare*. At his screening of movies in the upstairs hallway of the White House, Franklin D. Roosevelt usually

tried to show a Disney cartoon; other statesmen who were on
record as favoring Disney in general and his Mouse in particular included Canada's Mackenzie King, Jan Christian Smuts of
South Africa, the aforementioned Mussolini and the Nizam of
Hyderabad. *The Encyclopaedia Britannica* devoted a separate
article to The Mouse, Madame Tussaud included a replica of
him among the figures of the mighty in her wax museum, and
Disney himself had been admitted to the Art Workers' Guild of
London—the first movie maker ever to be so honored. All over
the world there were Mickey Mouse clubs (not to be confused
with the later television version of the promotional gimmick),
whose members carried a Mickey Mouse emblem, took a Mickey
Mouse oath, sang a Mickey Mouse song and used a Mickey
Mouse handshake. There were fifteen hundred of these clubs
in the U.S. alone. In Africa it was discovered that some native tribes would not accept gifts of soap unless the bars were
stamped with The Mouse's outline, while many other primitives
carried Mickey Mouse charms to ward off evil spirits. A trav-
eler in China reported seeing his likeness peering from a window in Manchuli, the transfer point between the Chinese Eastern Railway and the Transsiberian Line. And it was reported
that in Japan he was the most popular figure next to the Em-
peror. As a child, the present Duchess of Alba, a direct descend-
ant of Goya's mistress, had her beloved Mickey Mouse doll included—along with her cat, dog and horse—in her first formal
portrait. Thus, Mickey now hangs in her Madrid palace, along
with works by Goya, Rembrandt, Titian and other masters in
the family collection. In all, Mickey Mouse was available in one
form or another in thirty-eight of the world's nations by 1937,
and the newspapers took considerable pleasure in printing lists
of his foreign aliases. In France he was Michel Souris and, pop-
ularly, Mickey Sans Culotte, because of the shortness of his
pants and because that was the vernacular term for a revolutionary. In Japan he was Miki Kuchi; in Spain, Miguel Raton-
cito; in Italy, Topolino; in Sweden, where one theater ran a

program made up entirely of Disney cartoons for seventeen weeks, he was Musse Pigg; in Greece, Mikel Mus; in Brazil, Camondongo Mickey; in Argentina, El Raton Mickey; in Central America, El Raton Miguelito. "I guess," said Walt Disney, "the cartoon is something everyone knows and likes."

That simple sentence speaks volumes. There was no character in the movies more American than Mickey Mouse, no environment more American than the small-town locale he inhabited with his gang. And yet the appeal of the Disney cartoons was universal. Their international success must be attributed to the surmise that the message of their medium—the animated cartoon—was so easily understood by everyone. Dialogue was minimal; action, drawn in high definition and never needing any verbal explanation, was as easily understood by an Italian peasant as it was by a New York intellectual—more easily perhaps, given the propensity of the latter to look for complications where none exist. To some degree the international popularity of American action films of all sorts—a popularity which has persisted throughout the postwar dolors that have afflicted those films at home—is based in large measure on simple abhorrence of ambiguity, on preference for straightforward action rather than needless, possibly misleading talk. The bold colors of the Disney cartoons, their use of animals, which have no nationality, as the major characters, their broadness and brevity, the commonality of the problems they encountered and the solutions they invented, and above all, their cheerfulness—all contributed to the success of the films in the international market. What is true of high art is also true of mass art to the extent that universality of appeal is based on success with particularities. In their uncomplicated way, the Disney craftsmen caught something of the truth of the American scene and situation at the time and, lo, found that they had touched a chord that set up responsive vibrations all over the world.

By 1935 The Mouse had become, in the words of a League of Nations scroll that Disney traveled to Paris to accept (along with a gold medal), "an international symbol of good will." Disney was accompanied by Roy on the European trip, which produced another of his "aw-shucks" anecdotes. The Disney brothers were told that the award would be presented at a formal garden party at which the accepted dress would be morning coats. The Disneys protested but to no seeming avail and so stopped off in London to have the required formal wear tailored for them. They showed up at the party in their new finery only to discover that their hosts had embraced American ways to the extent of abandoning their cutaways and striped pants in favor of business suits.

But the trip produced more than an anecdote and some free publicity. Abroad, Disney noted that his cartoons often received billing above the features with which they played, and in Paris he and his brother attended a showing of a half-dozen of his cartoons playing alone, without support of a feature of any kind. This confirmed his growing belief that the surest way out of the mouse race was to get into feature production himself.

The story behind the show on which the two Disneys dropped in actually begins almost a year earlier in Stockholm, where a young construction engineer named Willard G. Triest was trying his hand at film promotion after several years of working on extensions of the New York subway system. Disney had been unhappy about his Scandinavian grosses and pressured United Artists for some special action there. Local custom decreed but two shows a day and these, of course, were dominated by whatever feature the theater was showing. Disney shorts thus received only a small number of screenings and only a tiny share of the gross receipts. Triest decided to put together a 55-minute program of Disney cartoons, in both color and black and white, and to play them on a continuous-run basis from one in the afternoon until 11 at night. The innovation was so radical that only a second-class theater could be engaged to try it, and Triest tried some American-style promotion to lure the people. Music shops were talked into playing

"Who's Afraid of the Big Bad Wolf?" on loudspeakers directed at passers-by, little Mickey Mouse and Pig cutouts—a million and a half of them—were distributed to school children. Opening night was a Kliegslighted, red-carpeted gala, with the diplomatic corps in attendance, white tie obligatory and a champagne reception afterward. The result was a 14-week run, a trebling of the theater's house record, and even, one night, attendance by a goodly share of the Swedish royal family. Triest even helped locate two children who had been missing from the Japanese embassy for some eight hours—he discovered them, at nine in the evening, sitting through his program for the seventh time. He was called upon to repeat his success in Paris, and it was his *L'heure Joyeuse de Mickey avec Les Trois Petits Cochons* that captured Disney's eye and imagination late in its run.

He had been toying with the idea for a feature for some time. There had been rumors in Hollywood of an attempt by Disney to make a version of *Alice in Wonderland* combining live action and animation—and starring Mary Pickford. From 1932 onward Disney had increased his staff to a level higher than he strictly needed to maintain his regular schedule, and he was also putting quite a bit of his earnings into an effort to educate his people in the fine arts—again something that was not absolutely required by the sort of film he was producing. Obviously, something was stirring in his brain, and by 1934 he was quietly discussing a proposed feature-length production of *Snow White and the Seven Dwarfs* with visiting reporters. He thought it might cost as much as $250,000 and take eighteen months to make. "We will use a full symphony orchestra and fine singers," he promised and added: "We've got to be sure of it before we start, because if it isn't good we will destroy it. If it is good, we shall make at least a million."

In every respect, Disney's estimates were far too modest.

PART SEVEN

Disney's Folly

20 *Of all the things I've done, the most vital is co-ordinating the talents of those who work for us and pointing them at a certain goal.*

—Walt Disney, 1954

FROM THE TIME—roughly—of *Snow White*'s conception to the time that it was finished, a period of approximately five years, the staff at the Disney studio grew from about 150 workers to some 750. And most of the growth was from the bottom. Unlike most growing industrial enterprises, the largest number of new employees were not in executive or administrative work but were, instead, animators, assistant animators, breakdown men and in-betweeners (the last being the traditional starting point for a young man learning the art, and whose work, logically enough, consisted of doing the drawings that come "in between" the drawings of the main action, executed by the men above him on the ladder). There is no doubt that the animators were the glamorous figures of the infant industry, the men who drew the best salaries ($150 to $200 a week) and among whom were a few who came to work wearing polo clothes, ready to ride with the boss at the end of the day. But there were plenty of other new faces around the Hyperion

171

Avenue studio, on which Disney spent $250,000 before he moved to his new studio in 1940. There were layout and background men, art directors and story men, directors and musicians in profusion. And always there were apprentices— about 20 of them at any given moment—studying in a wide variety of art classes right in the shop, doing routine work on the films and getting paid as little as $18 a week for their efforts.

It was a young shop—Disney himself was only thirty-six when *Snow White* was finished—and full of exuberance. The employees were confident they were working in the best studio of its kind in the world, and full of belief they were in on the ground floor of an art that was going to be one of the important forms of expression in this century. Older men by the dozens who cared about animation deserted New York, the former capital of the art, to lay siege to Disney's door. They resorted to every sort of trick to gain admittance and usually didn't get it until they indicated a willingness to accept a cut in salary and status and perhaps even to join the apprentices in their art classes. Younger men, just out of art school, responded by the hundred to the ads the studio placed in newspapers around the world, seeking recruits. Don Graham, an instructor at the Chouinard Art School in Los Angeles (and latterly its dean), was the man in charge of the apprentice program and also the man who brought Disney into as much contact as he could stand with the finer realms of graphic expression. Chouinard once received, according to an old Disney hand, thirteen hundred pieces of mail—containing sample art—in response to a series of recruiting ads placed in the foreign press: twenty of the senders were invited to join the program and two finally attained the status of animator. The attrition rate was similarly high among domestic recruits, whom Graham found in the course of cross-country recruiting drives.

The studio to which these men reported looked like "a jerry-built bee-hive," as one of them later put it. To accommodate his burgeoning staff Disney was constantly forced to remodel, cramming more and more people into tiny offices, acquiring space in adjoining buildings and then burrowing through the walls in order to connect the outlying rooms with the main building. Even so, the place had amenities that other animation studios did not offer. There were no time clocks because, Disney said, he had hated them when he was a young man. All the equipment the men used was of the highest quality; there were plenty of fifteen-hundred-dollar movieolas (one Disney graduate was shocked when he went to work for Max Fleischer on his Gulliver feature and found there was only one such machine—absolutely vital to editing film—for the entire production), and every artist had plenty of light, a commodity in short supply at some competing studios. Nor was there any minimum footage requirement for the animators. They were, instead, encouraged to throw out a whole day's work if they did not like it. The desire for quality was further stressed by bonuses ranging from four dollars to twelve dollars per foot for especially good bits of animation.

Finally, there was at first very little resentment of the employer, despite the long hours and low pay he enforced. In later years Disney's informality may have seemed a trifle studied, but in those days it appeared to his multitude of bright young men as completely genuine. The Disney brothers, to be sure, had paneled officers fronting on Hyperion Avenue, but they were modest in scale and were reachable through a tiny reception area guarded by just one receptionist-switchboard operator. In any case, Walt Disney spent only a minimum amount of time behind the drawing table he used as a desk. He insisted on being first-named by everyone, and he constantly dropped in on all and sundry to see how they were coming along. His story conferences were models of democratic give-and-take, and everyone who ever sat in on one seems to agree that it was as an editor and critic of stories that he had his finest creative hours. He had a fine sense of pacing, a gift for stretching and embroidering a basic gag or situation that some have compared to that of the great silent comedians, and above all, in infectious enthusiasm for ideas, even bad ones, that kept the ideas bouncing until, somehow, the plot or situation or character was sharpened to a satisfactory but not necessarily preordained point.

For an interviewer of the time, he summed up what he was looking for in these sessions. "We have but one thought, and that is for good entertainment. We like to have a point to our stories, not an obvious moral but a worthwhile theme. Our most important aim is to develop definite personalities in our cartoon characters. We don't want them to be just shadows, for merely as moving figures they would provoke no emotional response from the public. Nor do we want them to parallel or assume the aspects of human beings or human actions. We invest them with life by endowing them with human weaknesses which we exaggerate in a humorous way. Rather than a caricature of individuals, our work is a caricature of life."

Disney was perfectly capable of overseeing the story elements of his operation himself. He had an unfortunate predilection for bathroom jokes, which were usually edited out, and for jokes involving either an assault upon or the adoration of the posterior. (The Rube Goldbergish paddling machine by which the wolf is punished in *The Three Little Pigs* is a classic example of Disney's *derrière*-assault propensity, and the little boy unable to button the drop seat of his pajamas in one of Disney's early Christmas specials is a representative instance of the *derrière*-adoration school of animation. The lad's trouble in maintaining his modesty is the latter film's most heavily emphasized running gag, and the climax of the picture is the present that Santa Claus leaves for him—a tiny chamber pot. Even when he was not being as explicit as this, Disney's interest in the posterior was a constant in his films. Rarely were we spared views of sweet little animal backsides twitching provocatively as their owners bent to some task; often were the buttocks of some child or sprite, like Tinker Bell, emphasized in the character's basic

174

design.) But within his own terms, Disney performed his editorial tasks with undiminished enthusiasm until the end of his life. He was not a terribly articulate man and often resorted to pantomime, mimickry and the sketching of vague shapes with his hands, which were often described by colleagues as "restless" or "constantly in motion." Subtle changes in the rhythm of a tapping pencil were studied by aides as an indication of shifts in his mood. In later years certain of his associates seemed to do little more than read and interpret statements of opinion and desire that were often Delphic in their ambiguity. ("I want black on black," he told the people animating the fight between the stags in *Bambi*—which is, of course, impossible. But the artists were able to give a black-on-black impression by keeping colors dark and illuminating the scene with lightning flashes.)

At all times Disney remained remarkably unwilling to release scripts or storyboards to the production people. He liked to huddle over them as long as possible, hoping they might be improved in some way that was not entirely clear, even to him. In the days when Technicolor facilities were limited and one had to sign up months in advance for their use, these shooting dates served as arbitrary deadlines, forcing him to give projects up to the fates even though they did not fully satisfy the ideal version that existed only in his mind and that he could never express. Later, the demands of his carefully worked-out releasing schedule had somewhat the same effect on him, though here he could sometimes juggle things around to gain more time. Somehow, however, he made what can only be termed the literary elements of his films work—and he did it largely through his own efforts. One animator later recalled a session at which Disney acted out the entire story of *Snow White*, playing all the parts in a performance that required several hours to complete and was to serve as the basic guide to the studio. It was referred to throughout the film's production whenever anyone had a creative question.

Strangely, for a man who was generally thought of by the

public as an artist, it was with the graphic elements that he depended on others to do the hardest labor, both practical and theoretical. He, of course, sat in on everything, most particularly on the "sweat box" sessions (so-called because the projection room at the Hyperion Avenue studio was tiny and lacked air conditioning), where all the animators gather to criticize one another's rushes, often no more than pencil sketches of what was to come. There he was very much like the amateur gallery-goer who knows little about art but knows what he likes. What Disney wanted was more and more imitative realism in the movements of his characters, more and more detail (and lushness) in the backgrounds, greater and greater fidelity to nature in special effects ranging from lightning to the fall of raindrops. It is worthwhile remembering that Disney's first experience in show business was doing "impressions" of Charlie Chaplin at amateur nights. One animator has said that Disney's taste in art was for work at approximately the level of a competently illustrated nineteenth-century children's storybook—perhaps too narrow a judgment. Disney achieved something of this quality in *Snow White* and *Pinocchio*, and it had a distinct charm on the screen. The trouble was that he kept trying to improve upon it without ever breaking cleanly away from it. Some peculiar mishmashes resulted from this development. For instance, *Bambi*'s forest had some of the green-and-gold lushness of the antique style, but the deer themselves were rather too carefully naturalistic in appearance while many of their smaller woodland friends turned out to be conventionalized, commercialized images of cuteness—fluffy and cuddly and saucy. Indeed, it is fair to note that with the smaller creatures Disney and his animators never had much success. In the early days of animation it was believed that circular forms were the only ones that could be successfully animated. The Disney studio did much to disprove this theory but somehow clung to it when drawing the smaller animals—chipmunks, squirrels, rabbits and so on. If anything, they grew rounder and softer and therefore cuter as the years wore on. At first glance they were natural representations, but over the course of a long film it became clear that the true intention of the artists was easy adorability. Their use in the typical Disney film was always to reduce dramatic tension at any point where it excessively threatened audience sensibility. In *Snow White*, for instance, the gathering of the little creatures around the exhausted figure of the girl, after her frightened dash through the woods, assuages not only her alarm but that of the audience as well. Later on, the animals join the dwarfs in their attempt to rescue Snow White from her wicked stepmother, and their gamboling presence on the mission serves to reassure, even to provide a few small laughs, despite the desperate urgency of the situation.

To some degree the style of the earlier animators, who combined rubbery stick limbs with the round heads and bodies of their animal creations, served to check this tendency toward the cuddlesome; those creatures were much more clearly—if crudely—cartoon conventions, bearing only superficial resemblance to real animals. You knew where you stood with them; they did not encourage you to want to gather them to your bosom or to think of them in human terms. In fact, it would have been impossible to do so: they were too spiky, too hard in outline, too weird. The animals of the Disney features films, as they grew more real, paradoxically grew more subtly false—Thumper, the rabbit, and Flower, the skunk, for instance, in *Bambi*.

This tendency to adorableness was the most consistent problem of Disney's later work, and one suspects that the style in which the animals were drawn dictated the dialogue they spoke and the situations in which they found themselves. Sweetness called forth sweetness. There were, however, other problems, too. For a while, in the late Thirties and early Forties, he and his artists attempted to push on to styles new to them. There was, for instance, the massively "modernistic" manner of parts of *Fantasia* and the wartime *Victory Through Air Power*, with which they never achieved more than mechanical competence.

177

Dumbo, in the same period, was essentially an attempt to use the bright, uncomplicated style of the Mickey Mouse cartoons in an almost feature-length production and was quite successful in its unpretentious way, though apparently not exciting enough creatively for Disney and his people to stay with exclusively in their future films. Sequences were done in this manner in *Peter Pan* and *Alice in Wonderland*, stories to which it was not nearly so well suited as it had been in *Dumbo*, but the basic drive was toward an extensive elaboration of the old storybook style. In films like *Cinderella* and *The Sleeping Beauty*, detail was piled on detail, technical effect on technical effect, until the story was virtually buried under their weight. It was an art of limited—some would say nonexistent—sensibility, a style that labored to re-create the trifles of realistic movement, that fussed over decorative elements, that refused to consider the possibilities inherent in the dictum that less is more. The wonderful simplicity that Disney's graphic art naturally possessed in the beginning and that he may have distrusted as betraying its humble and primitive origins, disappeared. In the late films complexity of draftsmanship was used to demonstrate virtuosity and often became an end in itself, a way of demonstrating what was a kind of growth in technical resourcefulness but not, unfortunately, in artfulness.

But however one disagrees with his goals, Disney's ability to analyze what he wanted—however unclearly he sometimes expressed his analysis—and his ability to find the people who could give them to him must be admired. He was probably quite right in believing that an audience's attention could not be held over the span of a long film done in the crude—if forceful —style of the early Mickey films and that he would have to add something to the art itself if he was to grow beyond the short subject.

The first thing he understood—and it was a basic insight— was that he would have to train his men himself, as none of his competitors was willing or able to do. "I decided," he said, "to step out of their class by setting up my own training school. We had enough revenue coming in so we could plan ahead, and I laid out a schedule of what I want to accomplish over the years." "It was costly," he added on another occasion, "but I had to have the men ready for things we would eventually do." Some have placed the cost of his art classes at $100,000 a year.

At first he sent his artists to Chouinard itself for night classes, occasionally, in the early days, driving them to the school himself in his car and then returning to pick them up afterward. Then, with the advent of prosperity and the discovery of Graham, the classes were held within the studio. They learned, in some cases relearned, the basics of art—the essentials of capturing the illusion of three-dimensionality in a two-dimensional medium, those tricks of exaggeration and perspective that are necessary to capture the illusion of reality whenever one seeks to re-create it in an artistic medium.

Disney had, in addition, a special problem, one that was never faced by any other serious graphic artist in quite the way he had to face it. That was the problem of movement. The techniques of suggesting it in the static art forms had, of course, been worked on for centuries; the problem of simply capturing it on movie film had been refined in a matter of decades. But motion in animation was a new challenge. And it was not a simple one at that. Photographic realism, oddly enough, looked unreal in animated films. It was a subtle matter to obtain a realistic effect that lapsed into caricature only intentionally. "Look, pull your hand across your face and you'll see what I mean," Disney told one interviewer. "You don't see a single hand; it's sort of stretched and blurred. We had to learn the way a graceful girl walks, how her dress moves, what happens when a mouse stops or starts running."

To begin with, Disney's animators studied motion by attempting to have models break down a simple movement into a series of poses representing each of its components. But this resulted in a style of animation that lacked a smooth flow. Graham's answer to that was what he called "action analysis," and the basic technique of teaching it—to apprentices and senior staff members alike—was to have a model execute a full motion and then have the animators attempt to sketch it from memory, giving the impression of the movement rather than an overly detailed rendering of it. The same technique was applied to the problem of drawing the movement of the mouth as it speaks. The trick here was to avoid overanalysis of its workings, which led to a constant twittering of lips as the artists attempted to draw the shapes they assumed in pronouncing each word. Instead, they were encouraged to draw an impression of a whole phrase. Finally, there was work to be done on the whole repertory of animal movement, which is the basic vocabulary of animation. For a while Disney kept a small zoo in the studio so the artists could draw from nature. Then it was noted that a zoo is not exactly a natural habitat and that the captive animals responded differently to stimuli then did their wild brethren. So he employed nature photographers to bring back footage of the animals in their natural surroundings. This was, incidentally, the genesis of his highly regarded series of nature films, which he began releasing in 1949.

Disney was especially eloquent on reasons why animals dominated the animation field and why animators, at their very best, were never very successful with people. It was because, he said, the reactions of animals to stimuli were always expressed physically. "Often the entire body comes into play. Take a joyful dog. His tail wags, his torso wiggles, his ears flop. He may greet you by jumping on your lap or making a circuit of the room, not missing a chair or a divan. He keeps barking, and that's a form of physical expression, too; it stretches his big mouth.

"But how does a human being react to stimulus? He's lost the sense of play he once had and he inhibits physical expression. He is the victim of a civilization whose ideal is the unbotherable, poker-faced man and the attractive, unruffled woman. Even the gestures get to be calculated. They call it poise. The spontaneity of animals—you find it in small children, but it's gradually trained out of them.

"Then there's the matter of plastic masses, as our animators put it—mass of face, of torso, and so on. Animation needs these masses. They're things that can be exaggerated a little and whirled about in such a way as to contribute the illusion of movement, you see, like a bloodhound's droopy ears and floppy gums or the puffy little cheeks and fat little torsos of chipmunks and squirrels. Look at Donald Duck. He's got a big mouth, big belligerent eyes, a twistable neck and a substantial backside that's highly flexible. The duck comes near being the animator's ideal subject. He's got plasticity plus.

"For contrast, think of the human being as the animator sees him. It takes the devotion of a whole boyhood to learn to wiggle an ear as much as three-sixteenths of an inch, which isn't much. The typical man of today has a slim face, torso and legs. No scope for animation, too stiff, too limited. Middle-agers tend to develop body masses—jowls, bay windows, double chins. But you can't very well caricature a fat man. Nature has beaten the animator to the punch."

This uncharacteristically long speech, delivered in the 1950s, represents a theoretical summary of some two decades of hard, practical work at the Disney studio to learn the techniques of an art and then to refine them into a style that existed at first only in the mind of Walt Disney. The unfortunate thing was that when his people finally achieved what he wanted, it was not, by any objective standard, as excellent as he thought it was, though he continued to cherish it. What was missed by him—though not by some of his associates—were a good many promising stylistic possibilities that developed out of the natural limitations of their previously unexplored art. These, unfortunately, were consumed by the drive for that realistic surface, that mechanical slickness that Disney desired and that evidently pleased his audiences. Even so, the foundation was laid in those days for an art the possibilities of which have still to be fully explored; both a technology and techniques applicable to almost any problem one can imagine arising in animation were formulated.

In the 1930s Disney was willing to investigate almost any possibility that promised to bring him closer to his goal. His mind was still open and educable. He hired Rico LeBrun, the well-known muralist and an expert on animal anatomy, to instruct in his school. He brought in guest lecturers of all sorts to speak on all manner of subjects. There was, for example, an academic with a heavy German accent, hired to deliver a talk on the theory of humor. He began his lecture with the declaration, "Ve vill now explain vot iss a gak"—and quite unintentionally brought down the house of assembled gagmen, rendering them incapable of attending the finer points of his analysis.

Alexander Woollcott fared somewhat better before this tough audience, and so did Frank Lloyd Wright, though the latter somewhat nonplused Disney. The architect had in his possession a Russian animated cartoon that Disney was anxious to see, and since this was late in the decade, it is possible that Wright was interested in getting the commission to design the new studio Disney wanted to build. In any case, a meeting was arranged, and Wright was full of enthusiasm for the work he observed going forward as he toured the studio, though Disney was reportedly puzzled by the architect's suggestion that he ought to distribute his animators' black and white roughs that were projected for his edification and not bother with polishing them to the customary high gloss—an excellent idea, by the way, since the roughs are full of a vitality and an individuality that the overrefined finished products lack once they have passed through the factory.

Then Wright showed the Russian film, announcing, by the way, that its score was by Shostakovich, which caused Disney to inquire, "Who the hell is he?" When it was over, the studio's artists were abuzz with excitement. As one of them later recalled it, the shapes in the film were deliberately flattened, forcing them out of normal perspective and imparting an expressionistic quality to the work. Wright thereupon stood up and cried, in his most imperious manner, "Walt Disney, you too can be a prophet!" To which the honest rustic replied, in genuine perplexity, "Jesus Christ, you want me to make pictures like that?"

Stories of Disney's naïveté in matters of high and traditional art are legion. His daughter reports his leafing through a book of paintings, stopping to study a page and remarking, "I like this guy. Who is he?" Informed that the guy was Goya, Disney registered recognition and added comfortably: "Good man, Goya." One of his animators kept in his office a Cezanne reproduction, which Disney spotted one day. He asked the name of the artist and commented that "the fellow can't draw—that vase is all crooked." Some time later, however, the same animator was having trouble getting a scene just the way Disney wanted it. Finally, in desperation, Disney told him to "get some of that 'Seezannie' quality" into the work, which, it developed, was exactly what was required to create the desired mood. The mispronunciation, the alertness to the useful possibilities in artistic traditions alien to him and the ability to store intellectual and aesthetic oddments he might someday find useful were all characteristic of Disney's role as coordinator and ultimate arbiter of studio activity. He was trying—and he was learning. The trouble was that he borrowed from the great traditions of art only what was immediately useful to him, the superficials of manner and style. Nothing that he saw in it broadened or deepened his sensibility.

This limitation in him did not seem to affect the spirit of the young men who learned animation in his studio in the short golden period that was probably over by 1940, when Disney opened his new plant in Burbank, and was certainly finished by the strike of 1941. In the memories of those who worked there in the great days the experience is regarded as something far more than a merely educational one; it created a sense of community among them that is felt only by those who have shared the excitement of exploration and experiment, those who have known what it is like to be young in a young field. It sets these men apart, "as if we were all members of the same class at West Point," one of them recently said.

There was, as a result, a passionate commitment to the new art on the part of many of the employees that far exceeded the kind of loyalty most companies can command. Particularly when *Snow White* began to overtax the studio's facilities, Disney was able to obtain overtime in huge amounts with no more than a vague promise of bonuses, in unnamed amounts, if the film succeeded. The impression is that he could have got the extra time even without dangling this dubious carrot before his workers. The desire to do the work well was—at least to hear them tell it—goad enough. Visitors to the studio were always amused by the sight of animators endlessly trying out facial expressions and movements before their mirrors and then trying to get down on paper what they had just done. One tourist recalled recently: "You'd see a guy sitting quietly at his animation board [different from an ordinary drawing board in that it could be illuminated from below and in that the glass circle on which the paper was placed could be revolved a full 360° so the artist could gain easier purchase on difficult lines] and when your guide asked him to do the thing he had just invented for Donald or The Goof he'd suddenly jump up and start bouncing around the room, his face working like a maniac and emitting these weird sounds. When he was finished he'd sit down quietly and pick up his pencil as if nothing had happened." They were, as the cliché went, "actors with a pencil," and they would risk any loss of dignity to study their lines, as it were. One of them was once arrested by the police for lying down on a suburban sidewalk in the midst of a rainstorm; he claimed he was studying the lightning and he escaped punishment.

For many this period ended in the bitterness of layoffs and strikes; for others, even—perhaps especially—those who stayed on with Disney, there is a sense of alienation that has grown as the corporation has grown and animation has passed from the center of its life to the periphery, where its expense has been tolerated (at least while Walt Disney lived) out of sentiment and a desire to keep the organization alive in the field where it began and with which it is still closely associated in the public mind. For a very few there is an anger—about the way it all ended, the way animation as an art has slipped once again to the edge of everyone's consciousness, the way they feel Disney treated them—that the passage of time has only slightly dulled. They speak in the passionate tones of unrequited love. But one senses, talking to all of them, that however the experience ended, nothing can really touch or spoil the intrinsic quality of those days. Mack Sennett, whose work, incidentally, Disney unwittingly helped drive from the screen, once said of his apprenticeship with D. W. Griffith: "He was my day school, my adult education program, my university." Many of his animators had the same feeling for Disney. Just before he died, one of these men wrote to Disney, for whom he had not worked and whom he had not seen in some thirty years. He said, in effect, that he had lived an extraordinarily happy life as an animator and that he felt he owed both his happiness and his success in the field to the training he had received at the Disney Studio and that he simply wanted Disney to know what he had done for him.

Which is not to say that all was seriousness or that emotional and intellectual intensity was the prevalent personal style at the Hyperion Avenue studio. It was hard work, especially for the younger men, who had their regular duties to attend in the office plus a full educational schedule (more than one of them remembers that "you had to fight to hang on in the classes" even as you were "fighting off the resentment of the older men who had never had any formal training and thought it was pretty effete"). But the place had, in compensation, "something like the mood of a college fraternity house." Disney himself had a reputation as a practical joker—though no one seems to remember any he played—and the pail poised to fall from the top of a half-open door when it was swung open appears to have been a basic tool of interpersonal relations around Hyperion Avenue, while the art of throwing push pins at targets attached to the cork boards with which the place abounded attained one of its highest flowerings there: several of the artists actually learned to fling four push pins at once and make them stick. Given the small size of the pins and the awkwardness of their balance, one's admiration of their dexterity is boundless.

As for more elaborate japes, there were too many of them to relate here. But a couple may give the flavor of the institution. There was, for example, the sad case of the artist who had an obsession with clean water and insisted on having a water cooler of his own, which no one else was allowed to drink from. One day he came to work to discover a school of goldfish using it as a swimming pool. Then there was the naïve and nervous gagman, not long out of high school and so tense at having to present his first storyboard at a conference with Disney that he fell victim to what is now known as "distress of the lower tract." His colleagues solemnly told him that the only sure cure for his condition was to drink a can of sauerkraut juice immediately before entering the conference. It had a predictable effect on him, and he had to break off in midsentence to dash for the nearest bathroom—which had been locked by the conspirators. He has his revenge, however. He acquired a large washtub, wedged it into the back seat of the car belonging to his principal tormentor, ran a hose in through the window, filled the tub to the brim with water and sat back to enjoy the man's efforts to extricate the tub without damaging the car (an enormous siphoning operation was finally undertaken).

Obviously, controlling an organization abounding in such youthful high spirits was no easy task, and through the years memos designed to establish clear lines of authority and efficient production methods fluttered down from the front office in an unending snowstorm. In his early study of Disney, Robert

D. Feild quotes two such documents, which give some sense of the seriousness of Disney's effort to get things organized:

> In order that the Supervising Animators may be relieved of as much management responsibility as possible, a secretary-manager of this function is maintained who works in close collaboration with the Production Operations Manager, who (under the direction of the Supervising Animators on the productions with which they are concerned) has the responsibility for maintaining a supply of work for all animators, which involves the making of the necessary contacts to see that men are properly and promptly cast, and the maintenance of statistics relative to productivity, the issuance of deadlines, the operation of adjusted compensation systems, and the formation of such routines, procedures, etc., as are necessary for the uniform movement of production.

All clear? If not, consider this definition of the "Advisory Function to Production" of the Director of Technical Research:

> He is authorized to hold direct contact with any Production Department Head in whose department he sees the opportunity for instigating technical progress. In order that a single control of each department may be maintained, he works through the department head involved, advising the department head of ways and means of achieving desired technical results. The department head is responsible for making an analysis of the suggestions offered and for submitting same to the Production Supervisor. In the event that a routine necessary for the accomplishment of a technical advance affects more than one department, the establishment of that routine is to be discussed at the earliest Production Board meeting.

The trouble with all this was that it was a studio that constantly discussed problems around the water cooler or in the courtyard or over lunch, which meant that everyone was always stepping out of the narrow channels Disney was trying to dig for them. He was himself one of the great offenders in this matter, being unable to resist peering over people's shoulders or just dropping in to see how things were going in this office or that. Thus one artist, unhappy at his assignment as a storyboard sketcher, looked up one day to see Disney in his door and, replying to the inevitable question about how things were going, replied that they were just terrible and that he hated his work. Asked what he thought could do, he replied, simply, "Pluto." He was given a one-month trial with the team that had the dog in hand (or on a leash), succeeded, and thereafter was one of the studio's three Pluto experts.

Gradually, although he was trying to stay on top of an organization that could not help outrunning its organization charts, Disney, with the indubitable but immeasurable help of Roy Disney, began to bring everything under control. The rapid influx of new employees, though they presented a housing problem, actually helped in this process. With so many people to oversee there was an obvious rationale for bureaucratizing the chain of command without hurting the feelings of the old hands, who were used to a more informal method of doing business. The art instruction, far from being the boondoggle many thought it was, contributed directly and soon to the efficiency of the new order. Besides providing cheap labor for the low-level jobs, its students achieved a technical mastery that eliminated a great deal of waste effort. One of its graduates said recently, "Before I started there I animated well and badly both. But I couldn't reproduce the former at will and I couldn't fix up the latter. What the classes did for me was to give me consistency." His sentiments are often echoed by his fellow students. Very simply, Graham's efforts produced, more quickly than anyone predicted, a studio style of steadily high technical quality, and those who could not meet the new standards were either weeded out—though Disney always hated firing people—or, if they were lucky, a small niche in one of the new specialty occupations was found for them.

Specialization was the new watchword on Hyperion Avenue. Without, apparently, giving a moment's conscious thought to the matter, Disney in the late Thirties was recapitulating the history of the entire industrial revolution behind his Spanish stucco walls, breaking down film production into smaller and smaller components, just as all other forms had been broken down since Eli Whitney began experimenting with the production line. Some of this was inevitable; obviously a sound effects man could not perform the tasks of a musician or the actors who did voices. Neither was it entirely reasonable to suppose that an animator could necessarily swing around and do backgrounds or special effects or camera work. It would have been equally wasteful to put high-priced creative artists to work on such routine chores as inking and painting the cels, which are the finished products that the animation camera photographs, and which, in any case, were best completed by feminine hands. It is also clear that the natural gifts of the artists within all departments would vary, making one man more successful with Donald Duck than with Mickey Mouse (known to the artist who usually drew him as "The Varmint"), another better with chipmunks than with turtles.

On the other hand, something distinctly valuable is lost in overspecialization—namely, the artist's personality. Ruskin, writing as the flood of industrialism reached its first great crest, said that when evidence of the single, shaping hand disappeared from an object intended as art, its aesthetic value also vanished. It is a tenet of criticism now so deeply ingrained that most people are scarcely aware of its comparatively recent origins or that Disney's production method had ample precedent in the ateliers of the Renaissance masters and in those remarkable products of community artistic endeavor, the cathedrals of Medieval Europe. If he had been interested in such abstract matters, Disney

189

could have said that The Mouse Factory (as people took to calling it) was compromised from the beginning, as all film studios are, because the art begins in machinery (the camera) and because it depends on instant public acceptance for survival. Looked at in this light, his efforts become only the next logical extension of the trends within his art *cum* business and, indeed, of the trend toward mass production that has been the central fact of existence in Western culture since the end of the eighteenth century.

But of course Disney was both too preoccupied by practical matters and too uninterested in theory to join any such high-flown discussion. David Low, the great English political cartoonist, in effect spoke for him when he said, in a much quoted statement: "I do not know whether he draws a line himself. I hear that at his studio he employs hundreds of artists to do the work. But I assume that his is the direction, the constant aiming after improvement in the new expression, the tackling of its problems in an ascending scale and seemingly with aspirations over and above mere commercial success. It is the direction of a real artist. It makes Disney, not as a draftsman but as an artist who uses his brains, the most significant figure in graphic art since Leonardo."

All of which has a certain validity. But it is not the whole truth, for as the decade wore on and Disney's artists and artisans began to see the shape of things to come, resentments grew. There were whimsical variations in the pay of people who were performing essentially similar tasks, and these appeared to be the result of favoritism on the part of the modern Leonardo. Then there was the matter of credit; excepting only Ub Iwerks' brief appearance on the credit card, no name but Disney's ever appeared on his films, a rule that perhaps was good showmanship but not one calculated to win the hearts of the employees. With *Snow White* he finally yielded on this matter. But on his first feature he carefully gave so many credits—and his name, in contrast, appeared in such very large type—that the effect was the same. Lost in the crowd, the individual craftsman merely suffered a new form of anonymity. Finally, and perhaps most dangerous of all for the future, the system had the effect of crushing individual initiative. The best artists chafed under the restraints of their specialities and, undoubtedly, began to withhold something of themselves from the group creative process (some took to moonlighting for other producers or working on children's books of their own). Others grew more and more vocal in their resentments of Disney. The seeds of what now seems an inevitable revolt were planted and growing.

Disney appears to have been unaware of the subtle change in the atmosphere. He continued to see that his men had the best available equipment and appointments and occasionally dreamed of a new studio that would be more than just a place to work. He seemed to think of it as a community of artists, a variation on the old American dream of a Utopia, where work and leisure—perhaps even family life—would be totally integrated to the benefit of all. He seemed not to notice that some of his men were no longer offering him ideas and executions of ideas representing their best judgment on the correct solutions to artistic problems. They were instead beginning that familiar, dispiriting process endemic to all mass media—attempting to read the boss's mind, anticipate what he wanted and give it to him without his knowing it. The little stratagems for sneaking things past him were also beginning to be devised. For example, if you wanted to distract Disney from some element on the storyboard that seemed weak you did the sequences around it in bright colors, hoping his eye would miss the trouble spot. There was a variant on this technique: to create a problem, indicated by a blank sheet in the board, which at Disney's insistence (he could be childishly stubborn on the point) always had its lower right hand corner turned back and pinned up. He would then focus on filling in this blank and—it was hoped—skip lightly over the areas about which the artists were insecure.

Such foolery was dangerous, for Disney had a fantastic

memory for the details of a story, and woe indeed to anyone who tried to skip over some story point or bit of characterization Disney remembered having agreed to. One screenwriter, sitting at rushes of a day's shooting, recalls Disney's noting that a small piece of business prescribed in his script was missing from the scene as shot. The writer had not noticed the absence himself, but Disney insisted on the point, the script was checked and he was proved right. He ordered the scene reshot. Indeed, he would order almost anything reshot, at no matter what cost, in order to get a film exactly the way he wanted it to be. He may have paid low salaries, but when it came to the product to be sold under his name and, psychologically, made his own through his incessant interventions, no corners could be cut.

Of course, for a man as intense as Disney in his desire to control his environment, the childlike desire to make a little world all his own, animation was the perfect medium psychologically. You can redraw a character, or even a line in his face, until it is perfect; you need never settle as the director of the ordinary film must, for the best an actor—imperfect human that he is—can give you. If the best an animator gives you does not meet your standards, you can get a new animator and set him to the problematic task. And another. And another. They are infinitely interchangeable, and operating as Disney was, with everyone cloaked in anonymity and working within the confines of a house style, no one except those directly concerned knew where one pencil began and another left off. As a writer who worked for Disney in the great days of animation recently put it: "Animation is where screen direction gets down to matters of detail unheard of in live action. In animation you deal with the glint in the eye, the twitch of an eyebrow, the tic of a muscle. You're dealing with microscopic fractions—if you want to." Disney wanted to, perhaps even needed to. For animation, to borrow from the unfortunate jargon of psychology, is a compulsive's delight.

21 *During the nineteenth century artists proceeded in all too im-*
pure a fashion. They reduced the strictly aesthetic elements to
a minimum and let the work consist almost entirely in a fiction
of human realities. In this sense all normal art of the last cen-
tury must be called realistic. . . .

Works of this kind are only partially works of art, or artistic
objects. Their enjoyment does not depend upon our power to
focus on transparencies and images, a power of the artistic sen-
sibility; all they require is human sensibility and willingness to
sympathize with our neighbor's joys and worries. No wonder
that nineteenth century art has been so popular; it is made for
the masses inasmuch as it is not art but an extract from life.
Let us remember that in epochs with two different types of art,
one for minorities and one for majority, the latter has always
been realistic.

—José Ortega y Gasset, *The Dehumanization of Art*

The film is, moreover, an art evolved from the spiritual founda-
tions of technics. . . . The machine is its origin, its medium
and its most suitable subject. . . . Films . . . remain tied to
an apparatus, to a machine in a narrower sense than the products
of the other arts. . . . The film is above all a "photograph"
and is already as such a technical art, with mechanical origins
and aiming at mechanical repetition, in other words, thanks to
the cheapness of its reproduction, a popular and "democratic"
art.

—Arnold Hauser, *The Social History of Art*

THE ARISTOCRATIC PHILOSOPHER and the Marxist his-
torian, so opposed in their opinions of the validity of realism as a
mode of artistic expression, at least agree that popular art tends
to be realistic and that the artist who wishes to be popular must
be realistic. From this, much unhappiness has followed, especially among artists and aesthetes. It must never be thought,
however, that Walter E. Disney shared this unhappiness. "All
we are trying to do is give the public good entertainment," he

193

said late in the 1930s. "That is all they want." And that was all he wanted, for he *was* his public, and when he knew his own mind—which he usually did—he knew theirs. It generally pleased them to think of his works as magical creations rather than technological ones, and that did not bother him in the slightest. Indeed, he took a great deal of pleasure in allowing publicists and journalists to reveal the technical secrets of his magic making. He was proud of it, and he knew that all of us are rather like children, so intrigued by the magic of clocks that we must take them apart in an attempt to divine the secret of their trick, yet still able to retain our awe at the total effect even when the pieces are strewn all over the floor around us.

Superficially, this may seem something of a paradox, since the content of Disney's work was usually the highly unrealistic fairy tale or children's story often folkish in origin—that is, its authorship was probably communal in the first place and whatever the circumstance of its creation, it was, by the time Disney got to it, community property. Writing in what some impressionable commentators have been pleased to call the Age of McLuhan, this is a less troublesome point than it might have been in the dark ages prior to 1965, when the Canadian professor came into vogue and taught us that the content of a new medium (as the movies still were in the 1930s) is nearly always the product of an older culture. We may add to this the basic insight that the fantastic is always more acceptable to plain people—and sometimes to sophisticates—when it is rendered in the most realistic possible style. So, when offering time-tested mythic material, Disney was careful to present it in every day, down-to-earth artistic terms that offered no difficulties of understanding to the large audience—that in fact gentled them with the familiar instead of shocking them with the aesthetically daring. It was the way he personally preferred to arrive at the state in which disbelief is willingly suspended.

And so the enormous effort at art education, the enormous expenditure on improved sound and color film processes, the care lavished on the details of production, must be seen always as a drive toward realism, no matter what subject matter Disney chose to feed into the elaborate and expensive machine he was constructing. As he went to work on *Snow White* he began developing another technological breakthrough, a new camera that he believed would mightily enhance the believability of *Snow White* and, indeed, of all his future work. It was called the multiplane camera, and though it was not an achievement of the magnitude of sound or color film, it was a most useful device for Disney. So it will be for the student of his work, for by analyzing the effect of the camera on the Disney Studio's product as well as the symbolic meaning of the effort that went into the development of this, the only important technical device to be created solely at his studio, we gain an important insight into Disney's sensibility.

Until the perfection of the multiplane camera, the conventional animation camera, even in its most advanced state, had an important defect. We can begin to understand this defect by drawing on a contemporary account of the customary animation camera in operation:

"When all of the celluloid drawings for the entire footage have been finished they are sent to the camera room. Each camera is mounted above a table lighted by mercury bulbs. A frame the size of the cels is ready. First the background is laid down. Then a cel with Mickey, another with Minnie, a third with the villain and a fourth that is blank are slipped over the pegs, which hold them in perfect register (and which were, and are, the same everywhere in the studio, from the animator's board through the ink and paint department to this point). To the eye and the camera the picture appears to be on one sheet.

"Compressed air clamps a glass pane over the drawings to remove wrinkles, the operator's hand touches the control button of the camera, a click is heard as the lens shutter blinks, a tiny bell rings, the air lifts the glass and the photographer removes the cels and replaces them with the next set. . . ."

The trouble with this method of photography—if, indeed, it was a trouble—was that the camera could not truck into the frame without spoiling such small illusion of depth as it presented. In particular, there was a problem with objects at infinity. Foreground objects could simply be removed cel by cel in order to give the illusion that the camera was moving past them. But what about objects that were supposed to be behind the object or character toward which the camera was supposed to be moving closer and closer? Obviously they would grow in size, as this movement continued, at exactly the same rate as the foreground object.

The answer to the problem posed by the disconcerting visual effect of the early technique was obvious, theoretically at least. Separate the cels, putting each object on a separate plane and arrange these planes in a scale corresponding to the natural order of things. Thus, a cel representing a foreground tree might be only an inch or two in front of the camera's lens, while the cel on which, say, a house was drawn would be six inches from the lens. The horizon line, in turn, might be a foot or more behind the house. With a setup of this kind the camera could obviously prowl at will through a scene just as it could through a full-scale, three-dimensional setting or a natural location, or, indeed, just as the human eye observes the world.

But the multiplane camera, as it was called, was more easily described than built. Ub Iwerks had made a primitive model of the machine during his time of independence from the Disney organization (using, it has been said, railroad tracks with a jalopy mounted on them respectively to guide and to power the camera). When he came back to Disney he led the team that perfected first the vertical multiplane camera, which peered down through an iron framework fourteen feet tall, through layers of cels set in grooved shelves "like a baker's pie-wagon," according to early description. Later Iwerks participated in the development of the horizontal multiplane, which allowed the camera to pan simultaneously across the frame as well as into it,

It cannot be said, of course, that the multiplane camera was a sensation. Indeed, most people were probably unaware of its use in Disney's later films. Nor is it possible to apply Arnheim's arguments *in toto* either to the movies in general or to the work of Disney in particular. He wrote in a historical moment when the art of film photography was in a regressive state, with the camera imprisoned in an unwieldy booth where its whirrings could not be picked up by the microphone and when the director's authority was temporarily superseded by that of the sound technician. This imparted to the first talkies a static quality, visually, that was extremely disconcerting to some aestheticians of the film, and for a time, the theoreticians were inordinately fearful of the new technology. This basic fear informs Arnheim's work to a degree greater, perhaps, than even he was aware.

Then, too, the addition of sound to film brought the film closer than it had been to the traditional literary arts, a disappointing development to critics who had been schooled in the visual arts and were predisposed to interpret film largely in terms borrowed from them while ignoring the fact that even silent film contained heavy elements of plot, characterization and drama, which, however unsuitable to painting, do have a right to live in a mixed medium like film. From this, however, it should not be imagined that the sound film was generally welcomed by the literary intellectuals, either. Some of them did noble service in its cause, but many were as hostile to the talkies as their ancestors had been to the printing press, which converted literacy from a mark of class distinction to a universal right. Since, as Eric Hoffer says, it is "natural for the scribe to limit proof of individual worth to fields inaccessible to the mass," intellectuals who had come to regard the novel and the drama as private preserves tended to look with dismayed distrust at a medium that made something like the pleasures of these arts available to a wider audience.

More directly to the point, Arnheim's theory—and it must be

199

emphasized that his work was quite typical of the period—did not take into account the rise of a new grammar of film, a process that has greatly accelerated since 1945 and has now quite transcended his original objections. The addition of sound and color were not, in practice over the years, nearly so restrictive as he predicted they would be. Even as they came into wider and wider use, film makers, largely through the development of bold new editing techniques, discovered ways of telling a story that were uniquely cinematic. And these had the effect of marking off the boundary between film art and life's reality far more effectively—and interestingly—than did his rather narrow proscriptions. Anyone seeing the highly personal statements of a Resnais, an Antonioni, a Bergman, a Fellini, a Truffaut, even an Orson Welles, can have no doubt that what he is seeing is the statement of an artist in film, not the simple reproduction of real life. Nor can he doubt that these men have constructed a new and more flexible aesthetic of the film than Arnheim ever dreamed of.

Still, with all these *caveats* entered, Arnheim's work has a peculiar applicability to Disney, who once said "When we do fantasy, we must not lose sight of reality." So, like his audience's, his principal definition of art as an imitation of life and the drive toward greater and greater realism, carried out at such vast effort and expense throughout the Thirties, begins to seem needlessly, heedlessly narrow. To be sure, the desire to reproduce nature more accurately led, at first, to a higher quality of work at every stage of the film-making process, and the Disney Studio must receive credit for seizing upon technical advances of all kinds, developing many of its own and then synthesizing all the discoveries in the field into a method of production that was commercially viable and wildly attractive to the public. Indeed, Disney's position became so dominant so quickly that it is fair to say that without his efforts it would not now be possible to call animation either an art or a profession; it would still be merely "the cartoon business." Moreover, as we have seen, color added an element to the cartoon that no artist, even the most abstract abstractionist, can do without, while the synchronization of visual imagery with musical sound definitively separated the film cartoon from its heritage, the newspaper cartoon, and gave it an expressive potential far above that of its ancestor.

But once launched on the realistic course, Disney was unable commercially and unwilling artistically to deviate from it, or to press beyond its limits as he had earlier, when he was trying to move beyond the limits of the short, silent cartoon. After *Snow White* there were no breakthroughs comparable to those that preceded it; there were only fussy improvements on the basic structure Disney and his people had already built. The multiplane camera thus becomes a symbolic act of completion for Disney. With it, he broke the last major barrier between his art and realism of the photographic kind. He could at last give his audience the illusion of three-dimensionality, and he was exceedingly pleased.

In animation—at least at the Disney Studio—the rest was clean-up work. A man who worked on *Bambi*, which went into production shortly after *Snow White*'s release, even though it was not finished and publicly shown until 1943, said recently: "He might as well have gone out and taken pictures of real deer, that was the quality he was driving for in the animation." During the war years animator Ward Kimball, who had been called by one of his colleagues "Disney's artistic conscience," began experimenting with limited animation, which is deliberately two-dimensional in style and makes no attempt to copy movement from life (and is therefore quite inexpensive compared to full animation). He used it successfully in the "Baby Weems" sequence of *The Reluctant Dragon* and in parts of *Victory Through Air Power*. But the style did not appeal to Disney.

If the freshness, the sense of excitement that had once attended Disney's efforts in animation diminished, so did the quality of the humor contained in his short films. With many of his best men gone and those remaining concentrating on features, the little cartoons responsible for his first fame suffered seriously. The Warner Brothers cartoon department, which had among its directors the gifted Friz Freling and a genius named Chuck Jones, moved into what has been termed "La Grande Epoque." Its star, Bugs Bunny, was as urbane as The Mouse was rural, and infinitely more versatile than any of the Disney gang, each of whom had limits. The Duck, for example, was barred from verbal humor because of his deliberately garbled voice; The Goof had, built in, a stupidity problem; Pluto, of course, had neither voice nor brains; Mickey, finally, was now too nice to be a comedian. Bugs, on the other hand, could do everything. The inimitable voice, supplied by Mel Blanc, could push home a punch line in the same deft manner that the radio comedies of the time had taught us to appreciate; the body was built for speed, and the chases that were the high points of his films were masterfully constructed. Finally, and most important, The Bunny's personality perfectly suited his times. He was a con man in the classic American mold, adept in the techniques and ethics of survival, equally at home in the jungle of the city and in Elmer Fudd's carrot patch. In the war years, when he flourished most gloriously, Bugs Bunny embodied the cocky humor of a nation that had survived its economic crisis with fewer psychological scars than anyone had thought possible and was facing a terrible war with grace, gallantry, humor and solidarity that was equally surprising.

Around Bugs the Warner craftsmen created a memorable stable of similarly breezy spirits—most notably the maddest fantasist—victim in all cartoon land, Daffy Duck, and later, the greater cartoon comedy team, Wile E. Coyote and The Road Runner. The aforementioned Fudd, with his angry lisp and his ever-present shotgun, was the perfect foil for Bugs and Daffy, and for the generation that passed its prepuberty in the Forties, they were the super stars of the cartoon screen. The Disney stable—slower, less wildly inventive, possibly more subtle—were distinctly of the second rank. As for the rest of the competition—the mindlessly sadistic Tom and Jerry created by the Hanna-Barbera team (in those pre-TV days working out of M-G-M), Walter Lantz's hopeless Woody the Woodpecker—they were out of sight.

Thus, in the short-cartoon field, the popularity contest was lost by Disney to his competition by 1950. Shortly thereafter, the failure to develop stylistically cost him his artistic leadership as well. In the early Fifties it passed from him to UPA, a small firm founded by former Disney employees during the war. Using limited animation against backgrounds both impressionistic and expressionistic, the firm produced cartoons splashed with bold colors and enlivened with caricatures of motion as delightful as those Disney had offered in his early works. Though Disney paid grudging compliments to his new competitors and his brother, feeling that well-produced competing films made by commercially solid concerns were good for everyone, was free with advice and assistance on financial matters, many felt that Disney was quite hurt by his loss of artistic leadership and critical acclaim.

He fought back in a sulky, unprogrammatic and desultory fashion. He allowed Kimball's unit to produce a film in the new style, *Toot, Whistle, Plunk and Boom*, and it won an Academy Award as the best short cartoon of 1952, but he allegedly told Kimball no film like it would ever again be produced at his studio. He was not quite so unrelenting as that, for a number of limited animation shorts have since been produced at the Disney Studio as educational films and as features of various attractions at Disneyland. Limited animation is also frequently used to tie elements of the Disney television show together. But Disney never let Kimball set up a purely experimental unit, as many animators, both within and without the studio, hoped he would. Instead, he grew more and more preoccupied with Disneyland, where, ironically, Kimball found a part-time outlet for another of his talents—as director of the "Firehouse Five," a Dixieland band originally formed as lunchtime recreation at the studio but soon professionalized and turned into an "attraction" of some power at the amusement park.

By the end of the decade he was out of the short-cartoon field entirely. It had become too chancy and—as those who survived him for a while discovered—its profits were too small to bother about. By that time no major studio had an animation unit working on films for theatrical release. Friz Freling has gone into partnership with David De Patie and they spun a reasonably successful theatrical series off the title sequence they did for *The Pink Panther*. Released through United Artists, the Panther was an excellent creation. He did not speak and all his humor was, therefore, visual. Backgrounds were simple, bright and imaginatively used; indeed, a splash of color—a pure, formless abstraction—was frequently used almost as a character, as a foil or a partner in the Panther's activities. He was, in short, a character who lived only in and on film, never in a simulacrum of reality as the Disney gang did. De Patie-Freling became the only firm—as a small one—then doing interesting work in the theatrical-cartoon market on a consistent basis. A former Disney employee, the late John Hubley, in partnership with his wife, Faith, did an occasional exquisite short film that got a commercial release, but did the bulk of his business as a producer of TV commercials. Occasionally one of Norman McLaren's fine abstract shorts got imported from Canada, and, even less frequently, American audiences got a chance to see in their theaters some of the excellent animation being done in France and in the Iron Curtain countries. But, since the best American animators refused to be locked into a series with a running character, and since the distributors only wanted packages with such characters, and since profit margins remained as thin as ever they were in the post-war period, no one offered the animators much commercial encouragement. The gifted Ernest Pintoff, having made two splendid shorts, *The Violinist* and *The Interview*, for example, left the theatrical short-subject field and tried without great financial success, to make the transition to features.

Lacking the government subsidies that kept the art healthy, or at least alive, in other countries, most American animators could be found hiding out in television in the 1960s. As Neil Compton has pointed out, the best of their shows—the non-horrific ones aimed at the younger children—were regarded by the networks as Saturday and Sunday morning fillers and often escape the attention of their vice-presidents in charge of blandness. As a result a certain amount of satire went on down there in the bargain basement. It was not great stuff, but it was often more lively and pointed than what went on in prime-time situation comedies. Bullwinkle, Dudley Do-Right of the Mounties, and Roger Ramjet (whose very short films were sold in syndication and dropped into cartoon shows at the whim of local stations) were healthy spoofs of traditional mass-media heroic attitudes and one was grateful for them as small favors, slight correctives to the steady drip-drip-drip of banality in most children's TV programming. One also wished that budgets had been a little more generous so that the creators of these shows could offer a new generation something akin to the elaborate visual humor that earlier generations took for granted at the Saturday matinees.

As for Disney, his television program contained only a modicum of animated work—much of it quite weak—and in the Fifties the number of animated features he produced for the theaters dropped to one every four or five years, and they were of indifferent quality. Indeed, so locked into the patterns of the past were these features that the animal characters of the latest film looked almost exactly like the animals of the first full-length efforts to come out of the studio. There was, very simply, a Disney bear, a Disney deer, a Disney chipmunk and so on, predictable and unvaried from film to film. By this time their relationship to their natural models was vague indeed; their relationship to past Disney products, all-important.

There was also a structural rigidity about the Disney animated features that grew increasingly obvious as the years passed. The editing principles applied to *Snow White* were those of the conventionally well-made commercial film of the time. There was nothing particularly daring about the way it was put together: its merit was based on other skills. In general, a scene would open with an establishing or master shot, then proceed to an intermediate shot, then to close-ups of the various participants, with conventional cut-aways to various details of scenery or decor as needed. Confusing flashbacks or dream sequences were avoided, and special effects were introduced in such a way that every child was aware that something out of the ordinary was about to happen. It was a good enough way to shoot a film, but, especially in recent years, a far more flexible editing principle has come into play, particularly in the foreign films. It has been discouraging to see the Disney Studio cling to the old conventions of telling a story on film, particularly when the animated film and the stories it usually adapts seem particularly suited to the deftly allusive new style, with its bold leaps through time and space, its sudden juxtapositions of seemingly unrelated material, its quickness of mind and spirit, its sheer pleasure in the film as film. The fact that children are constantly amused by this style as used on television commercials, and seem completely able to understand it, would seem to undercut most arguments in favor of the clarity of traditional editorial techniques.

Again, Disney knew what he liked and refused to change with the fashion. About the only development one sees in his films is the increasingly heavy use of what has come to be known in the trade as "Disneydust," those sparkly highlights that burst from any object touched by any magic wand in any

Disney animated film. Of late years the dust seems to have
settled on almost every flat surface in sight, and it is, of course,
a very close cousin to the stardust that flakes off any Disney
rendering of a heavenly phenomenon. Walt was known to have
liked the effect.

22 *Clearly, mythology is no toy for children.*
—Joseph Campbell, *The Masks of God:*
Primitive Mythology

IN RECENT TIMES most people have preferred to think of
mythology in general and the folktale in particular—the latter
is admittedly not quite such a serious matter—as children's
playthings. In a much quoted simile, J. R. R. Tolkien has
pointed out that the fairy tale has been retired to the nursery as
old furniture is retired to that place, not because the children
like it so much, but because their elders no longer care for it.
They have thus achieved, in our time, a kind of cultural neutrality, particularly in the minds of the unbookish, mass audience.
They are considered safe, moral, entirely suitable for innocent
eyes. It is a very naïve view, as Disney was to discover once he
began trying "to lick" the story (as they say in Hollywood) and
as at least some members of his audience were to discover when
their children had to be carried from the theater screaming at
even the fairly mild, often gently charming version of *Snow
White* that Disney finally made.

It is necessary to conceive of fairy tales in a more complex
way if one is to understand the way they work on us. As C. S.
Lewis observed, "Many children don't like them and many
adults do." Which means, of course, that their appeal is more
universal in one way than many people suppose (it is not confined to a single age group) and less universal in another way

(there are some people who are constitutionally unable to respond to them no matter what their age, education or station in life). It is easy to see what Disney liked about the form. It imposes on the teller certain restrictions cited by Lewis—"brevity, its severe restraint on description, its flexible traditionalism, its inflexible hostility to all analysis, digression, reflections and 'gas.'" These were criteria Disney insisted upon in all the works that emanated from his studio, no matter what their subject matter. Liking the fact that folk stories are the most nonliterary of all literary forms, he also appreciated the informality of their composition, for as Joseph Campbell says, the folktale is "told and retold, losing here a detail, gaining there a new hero, disintegrating gradually in outline, but re-created occasionally by some narrator" in an entirely democratic fashion—"an art on which the whole community of mankind has worked."

Disney, in the ineffable style of his early days as a theoretician of aesthetics, seemed to agree with this definition when he offered his own definition of culture to a wandering scholar. The very word, he said, "seems to have an un-American look to me—sort of snobbish and affected—as if it thought it were better than the next fellow. Actually, as I understand it, culture isn't that kind of snooty word at all . . . a fellow becomes cultured, I believe, by selecting that which is fine and beautiful in life, and throwing aside that which is mediocre or phoney. Sort of a series of free, very personal choices . . .

"Well, how are we to recognize the good and beautiful? I believe that man recognizes it instinctively. . . ." How could a man holding such views avoid the fairy tale? Even more deeply ingrained in him, however, was nostalgia for the vanished past, and this, too, surely played a part in his choice of material. Study of the origins of myth and of folklore was begun intensively almost precisely at a time when the world that supported the creation of legends and fairy tales ended—that is when the rise of rationalism, then of science, then of mass industrialism and urban life called into question the primitive systems of belief that had sufficed to explain the natural world and its workings to earlier generations. Then, says Ralph Harper, "it was appropriate that, when all old values and beliefs were being discredited by revolution and by the new confident bourgeois civilization, some men should go back, surreptitiously, to the past, for help in surviving in a time when everything spiritual had disappeared but self-confidence." The brothers Grimm worked at their self-appointed task of systematically collecting European folktales even in the midst of the Napoleonic wars, and throughout the nineteenth century, with its wars and revolutions, mass migrations and intellectual upheavals, others continued in the same vein. The disciplines of philology, anthropology and archaeology made vast strides in less than a hundred years, in the process cutting a trail to man's communal past that we continue to widen.

Paradoxically, this effort has all along been aided by the very forces that had exploded the old world in the first place. Improved methods of transportation opened up previously obscure corners of the world, and improved medicine made it safer for explorers and scientists to visit them, while the need for raw materials of every kind drove the Europeans into the most all-encompassing effort at colonialism the world has ever witnessed. Meantime, scientific advances of all kinds gave the scholars and scientists who followed in the wake of this effort—and whose work was often used to justify it—a set of tools with which to examine the phenomena of the past with a new sophistication. Finally, the self-confidence of the times, of which Harper speaks, filled all who participated in this last great age of exploration with a missionary zeal, an eagerness to convert distant brethren not just to Christianity but to an entire way of life. The other side of this coin was an unwavering belief in the superiority of Western ways, which led to an almost casual expropriation of tons of primitive art and artifacts and its convenient placement in institutions like the British Museum, which to modern eyes is a veritable monument to the spirit of cultural rape that characterized so much of colonialism.

Out of this vastly important intellectual movement there slowly evolved a popular nostalgia for the life of an imagined past—a nostalgia that had its basis in a superficial reading of the results of scholarly and literary endeavor and in an innocently enthusiastic approval of the spirit in which the work was carried out. This nostalgia informed much of the new popular culture—also a product of industrialism—and it continues to inform present-day popular culture as well as the critical effort to understand it. (This applies both to defenders of it, like McLuhan, and to opponents of it, like Marya Mannes and Dwight Macdonald; the chief difference between them is the past cultures they select for invidious comparison to our own.) In effect, this nostalgia for communities past is an antidote to the pace and disruptive quality of modern life as well as the pressure it places on the traditional, individualistic values of the nineteenth century—factors that have spawned alienation, the disease of our time, which is often expressed, as Harper puts it, "in personal homesickness and longing for lands never seen." What we are dealing with here is a short chain of paradoxes, summarized by Harper in this way: "If fulfillment must somehow precede longing, it is nevertheless fitting that an understanding of homelessness must precede an understanding of longing and fulfillment." In other words, one of the great functions of culture, both high and low, in both the nineteenth century and the twentieth century, has been to make the links in this chain easily visible. It has, in effect, given us a detailed and not entirely erroneous vision of a past, a previous fulfillment, the loss of which we can sorrow for, the recapture of which we can work toward.

Very little of this is consciously expressed by any of us, and certainly it was never articulated by Walt Disney. Yet, viewing his work and his life, it is impossible to doubt that it was operating in him, and on two levels at that. He was not, as we have seen, a very well-read man or a very subtle observer of the society around him. Yet almost from the beginning of his career he presented us with images of longing. There was the barnyard and small-town environment of Mickey Mouse and his companions, and then there were all the adventurous uprootings of The Mouse that caused him so much trouble and that he overcame principally by asserting the so-called old-fashioned virtues. There was, all along, the emphasis on the innocence and playfulness of life in the forests and fields where every prospect pleased and only man was vile. There was the determinedly uncomplicated statement of aesthetic aims and beliefs of Disney himself, harking back inevitably to simpler times. Finally, there was the seemingly deliberate isolation of the man and his studio from the major currents of his art and his industry and his times, for it must not be forgotten that in the very period that he was creating his first major statement of the nostalgic theme in *Snow White*, the rest of the film industry was turning toward a kind of documentary realism about comtemporary life that was unprecedented in its short history. Arthur Knight puts it this way: "As the thirties wore on . . . growing tensions produced a notable series of films that rode the mounting wave of liberalism without recourse to either the 'fantasy of good will' or 'screwball' subterfuge. Labor unrest, slum housing, unemployment and dislocation aggravated by the dust storms of the mid-thirties—all of these were put on the screen with a directness that stressed the social and economic sources of such hardships. There was sympathy for the common man and new hope for a better tomorrow. In place of the contrived and improbably 'happy endings' of the depression musicals and 'back to the soil' films, there was now a forthright expression of belief in the inherent strength of democracy. . . ." The fierceness of the embrace in which both the public and the intellectuals wrapped Disney in this period resulted, not from any conscious effort by him to state social themes, but because his fantasies were capa-

ble of interpretation as dream works symbolizing and allegoriz-
ing the feelings that other film makers, other artists of all kinds,
were then expressing in more direct terms—and, of course, because his visions appealed to the longings for the vanished past
that were universally present in the national psyche.

The second level of Disney's appeal was stylistic rather than
ideational, and it was also present in his work from the beginning of his fame. We have already spoken of his concern for
realism and of a conception of beauty very close to the style favored by illustrators of nineteenth-century children's books.
These were part of a larger kind of cultural conservatism to be
found typically in small-town, middle-class Americans. It is
necessary to note only in passing the predilection of this class
for building banks and public buildings in the Greek and Ro-
manesque styles, their strange admiration for home architecture
in styles even less congenial to the American landscape—the
gothic and medieval structures affected by the well-to-do, and
the Tudor and Colonial homes their less affluent neighbors
began building early in this century. In this tradition also fits
the suburban "ranch house" of today, momentarily re-creating,
for their more imaginative owners, the vision of a more spacious
style of life, now vanished. Nor is there need to dwell on the
other cultural ideals of this middle class—the genteel tradition
of its literature, the Romanticism of the music it preferred to
hear at its concerts and musicales, the preference for sentimen-
talized portraits and nature painting in its art. All of these were
"culture" to the striving middle class of America. All partook of
an element of nostalgia and all remained in lively vogue, at least
away from the urban centers, until very recently.

All of them represented "culture" to Disney too, even if he
did find the word snooty and un-American—which, in fact, it
sometimes was as some people used the term. All these examples of culture found expression in his work—in the sentimental
cuteness of his characters, in the studio's corporate artistic
style, in his unremitting desire to juxtapose his art with "classi-

cal" music—remember the "Danse Macabre" in *The Skeleton Dance* as early as 1929—and, most important, the choice of *Snow White* as the subject for his first feature. Its use of the sleeping beauty theme automatically makes it a work that caters to nostalgia, for all of us would like to go to sleep, as Snow White does, and then awaken to find the world unchanged, indeed improved, since it is her lost lover's kiss that awakens her. Moreover, as a nursery story, first heard in childhood, it is bound to stir the sweetest memories when it is revisited in adulthood, especially with one's own offspring in tow.

But there is something more to this tale and to all folk literature than the matters we have so far discussed—a much deeper current that Disney himself could never catch and that he would never allow his employees to toy with either. It was the inability—or was it unwillingness?—to see folk literature as "the primer picture-language of the soul," to use Campbell's phrase, which, of course, guaranteed the success of Disney's film. But it was also the factor that kept it—and him—from greatness. The limitations of his background provided an excuse for this ultimate failure. And so did the conditions under which he created his first long film.

23 *We've bought the whole damned sweepstakes.*
—Roy O. Disney, 1937

IF HE HAD NOT been in the midst of *Snow White*, 1936 might have been the best year of Disney's life, financially speaking. In bargaining to renew their distribution contract with United Artists that year, the Disney brothers insisted that they must control the future television rights to their products—a remarkable piece of technological foresight, since most Hollywood independents were signing those rights away even after the new medium was well established. Unable to secure them from UA, they turned to another studio, RKO Radio, and made the best deal they ever had. The distributor advanced the full cost of each short production to them and, in return recouped its investment and turned its profit out of a kitty limited to 30 percent of the gross. Without the killing overhead *Snow White* added to their operations, the Disneys would have been—temporarily at least—as secure as it is possible to be in the motion-picture business. On the other hand, they would have achieved stability at the price of future growth, and they knew—better than many of their critical competitors—that they dared not stop growing. At first they had financed *Snow White* out of the accumulated earnings of the studio, but Disney's first cost estimate of $250,000 was soon surpassed, as was the $500,000 figure next projected. By the time the shooting was done, the negative cost of the film was to be in the neighborhood of $1.7 million and the total gross needed before it would become a Disney asset was placed at $2.5 million.

Racing to get the picture into the theaters in time for the 1937 Christmas season—traditionally the best movie-releasing time—Disney finally had to go to his principal backer, The Bank of America, and request an additional $250,000. In an incident he loved to retell, Disney was forced to show an unfinished print of the film to one of the bank's vice presidents, Joseph Rosenberg, in order to secure the fresh backing. The print available was not color-corrected, and many of the most important sections were not finished. So that Rosenberg could get some idea of the film's continuity, pencil roughs of the unfinished sequences were inserted throughout. Disney recalled the Saturday he showed *Snow White* to Rosenberg as a nightmare. For once, it was cold in the sweat box—or at least he *felt* cold—and he kept up a desperate line of chatter to explain and perhaps distract the banker from the film's uncompleted moments. The session must have been agony for a man as compulsive as

Disney was in his love for finished products of perfect smoothness and technical brilliance. Rosenberg appeared unmoved, responding to Disney's line with grunts and monosyllables. When the ordeal was finally finished Disney took Rosenberg on a tour of the plant, on which the banker volunteered not a single comment about the movie he had just seen. Finally, as he was getting into his car, he turned to Disney and said, "Good-bye. That thing is going to make a hatful of money."

Rosenberg later confessed to Disney that he was new to the film business and afraid to trust his instinctive response to *Snow White*. He was also discouraged by several very dubious opinions among rival producers he polled about the project. Among them, the only one he later recalled as optimistic about the commercial possibilities of a full-length animated cartoon was Walter Wanger. Also on Disney's side was the manager of Radio City Music Hall, who booked the film sight unseen, and a United Artists promotion man named Hal Horne, who had stayed friendly with Disney even after he had taken his business elsewhere. He told Disney that the speculative gossip about *Snow White*—some of it openly derisive—was in fact good publicity, bound to heighten curiosity over it and to pay off ultimately at the box office. He also advised Disney to follow his own instinctive desire and sell the film as a fairy tale, not as a prince-and-princess romance, which many promotion people, with the love of the cliché sales device endemic to their craft, were urging him to do. It was, after all, a fairy tale, and that form, however new to movies, had had a certain popular appeal through the centuries.

This handful, however, were the only people outside the studio whom Disney could later recall as standing by him in the loneliest of his many lonely periods. Even his own wife was dubious about the project. When he told her he was going to do a story involving dwarfs, her immediate reaction was one of repulsion. "There's something so nasty about them," he later recalled her saying. But that was the least of his worries. He admitted, after the fact, that "when we did *Snow White*, we weren't really ready." To begin with, the story as the Grimms set it down was quite a violent one, difficult to tell in visual terms acceptable to the commercial audience. There was the bloody business of the substitution by the huntsman of the stag's heart for Snow White's to prove to the wicked queen, her stepmother, that he had carried out her instructions to kill the girl. Then there were no less than three attempts on Snow White's life by the stepmother herself—disguised as a peddler crone—after the girl found refuge with the dwarfs. Each of these was bound to make for unpleasant viewing—choking her with a corset, giving her a poisoned comb and, finally, the successful gift of the poisoned apple. Then, too, there was the Grimm ending, calling for the stepmother to attend Snow White's wedding to the Prince and then undergo a fatal torture: "But iron slippers had already been put upon the fire, and they were brought in with tongs, and set before her. Then she was forced to put on the red-hot shoes, and dance until she dropped down dead."

The solution to this multitude of grisly problems was to emphasize the roles of the dwarfs, who were not even named in the Grimms' tale, and to play down the Queen's part. There is infinitely more footage devoted to the funny little men than there is to the stepmother, whose attempts on Snow White's life are reduced, in the movie, from three to one. Nor did Disney linger long over the scene with the huntsman. The grieving of the dwarfs over the death of Snow White is also sharply cut. And, of course, the original ending was totally eliminated (Snow White and her Prince simply ride off singing).

Added to the film were some brilliant animated sequences—in particular, Snow White's flight through the forest after her escape from the huntsman, during which the trees seem to reach out to hold her back. Delightful, too, were her discovery of the animals who guide her to the dwarfs' home and their ingenious cleaning of the place: in which a squirrel's tail becomes a bottle brush, a deer's becomes a duster, the birds trim pie crust with their beaks or use them to reel up a cobweb. Finally, there were the famous characterizations of the dwarfs—Doc, Happy, Grumpy, Sneezy, Bashful, Sleepy and Dopey—which became almost a comedy of humors.

The original balance of the tale, however, was destroyed by these inventions, as well as by the songs for which Frank Churchill, who did "Who's Afraid of the Big Bad Wolf," contributed the music (lyrics were by Larry Morey). Three of them were hits—"Whistle While You Work," "Heigh-Ho," and "Some Day My Prince Will Come"—and most of them integrated fairly well into the Disney version of the tale, although like the tamperings with the original story, they made the film fundamentally different in mood from the tale the Grimms told.

Nor were the story and its mood the only problem the studio faced. It was feared, for example, that audiences could not tolerate, for the length of a feature, the hard brightness of color that was customary in the short cartoons, and so the entire tonal range had to be adjusted. After much experiment a muted palette, with browns and greens predominating, was arrived at—and it remains one of the most pleasant aspects of the picture. Equally difficult problems were presented by animation. The house-cleaning sequence, very long in relation to its importance to the plot, was probably the finest sustained choreography of movement achieved up to that time by Disney, and it remains to this day a classic of its time and its field. Watching it, one senses not the industrial pressures one feels in some Disney studio work but a kind of inspiration that is as rare in this field as it is in any other. Infinite, expensive care was lavished on it as well as on some other, shorter pieces of animation that approximate its quality—in particular, the scenes of the dwarfs washing up for dinner, the dance in which they celebrate Snow White's arrival and acceptance in their house, and their chase through the forest in a vain attempt to rescue her from the wicked queen—and it was by no means wasted. This material was drawn and redrawn, and Disney confessed that "I had to use different artists on various scenes involving the same dwarfs, so it was hard to prevent subtle variations in each dwarf's personality." Some of the other graphic problems were never solved. For reasons suggested earlier, it was impossible to do Snow White and her Prince Charming in acceptable fashion. They could not be caricatured because they had to meet conventional standards of beauty and handsomeness, and except for Snow White's race through the woods and her dance with the dwarfs, the plot did not provide them with actions and movements of the sort that animation is notably successful in rendering. As a result, all the prince's action and most of Snow White's were Rotoscoped—a process that has remained one of the deeper secrets of Disney's land, never admitted to in public. Very simply, it is a process of photographing live action against a blank background and then integrating these shots into animated sequence by tracing them frame by frame onto the film and inking and painting the photographed figures so they will look as if they were animated. No matter how subtly done, these figures never look quite right in the context of an animated film. Their movements are jerky and hesitant, lacking the smoothness, force and purposefulness of figures that are wholly the creation of an animator's pencil. In later years reliance on the Rotoscope was sharply reduced, but whenever the animators have had to deal with conventional human beauty, they have resorted to the device. Disney's publicists have always claimed that the photographing of live models—word of which got around Hollywood, particularly among the aspiring actors who accepted the work—was only for "study," never for actual use in a film. Apparently it was felt that knowledge of this process would spoil the purity of the studio's image.

Indeed, in the context of the total film, few of its momentary imperfections mattered. Otis Ferguson of *The New Republic*, who was perhaps the most sensitive film critic of the time, noted, for instance, that when the queen transformed herself into a crone, she bore a rather uncomfortable resemblance to Lionel Barrymore (shortly thereafter Disney went through an embarrassing phase of caricaturing well-known movie stars in his short subjects). Ferguson also stated his disappointment in seeing the comedy occasionally falter. "Such things as running into doors and trees on the dignified exit, the jumbled consonant (bood goy, I mean goob doy, I mean . . .), headers into various liquids, etc., are short of good Disney." But Ferguson found, in contrast to these lapses, many examples of finely observed comedy, based on the detailed study of both animal and human behavior: "Take the young deer in the little scene where the forest life first gathers around Snow White: shy but sniffing forward, then as she starts to pat it, the head going down, ears back, the body shrinking and tense, ready to bound clear; then reassurance, body and head coming forward to push against the hand—half a dozen movements shrewdly carried over from the common cat. Or take the way (later) the same deer moves awkwardly and unsteadily on its long pins in the crush of animals milling about, as it should, but presently is graceful in flight, out in front like a flash."

In the last analysis the distinction of the film—and for all its imperfections, it is a major cinematic achievement—rests on hundreds of details of this sort, small touches that one scarcely notices on a first viewing but that must finally be seen as the movie's true subject matter. In the end, they disarm all criticism in much the same casual way that Disney brushed aside the dark mists that enveloped the basic legend. It does not matter that there is an occasional lapse into overly broad humor or sentiment. There is a genuine sunniness of outlook here, a sense that one sometimes gathers from works in the higher arts, of the artist breaking through to a new level of vision and technical proficiency and running joyously, freely before this wind of change, the agony of creation for a moment at least in a state of remission. Ferguson found the film to be "among the genuine artistic achievements of the country" and, in general, that opinion was echoed by other critics. Audiences responded—for the most part—with uncomplicated delight.

To be sure, there was one subartistic current of criticism that has plagued all of Disney's animated films. That was the claim that the film was too violent, too frightening, for children. Journalist Bill Davidson, for example, claims that "the witch in Snow White probably has caused more children's nightmares than Frankenstein's Monster and 'Godzilla' combined." Dr. Benjamin Spock, discussing the alleged terrors of the film, went so far as to tell an apocryphal story against it: "Nelson Rockefeller told my wife a long time ago that they had to reupholster the seats in Radio City Music Hall because they were wet so often by frightened children." All over the country there were earnest debates about the appropriateness of *Snow White* for children, and everyone seemed to have a story about someone's child who had hysterics in the theater or bad dreams for weeks after seeing the film. Disney received hundreds of letters from protesting parents. Typically, his reply was that "I showed *Snow White* to my own two daughters when they were small, and when they came to me later and said they wanted to play witch I figured it was all right to let the other kids see the witch." (Actually Diane Disney remembered *Snow White* a little differently: "When the wicked old witch flashed on the screen I was so terrified that I hid my face in my hands.") Indeed, of the many criticisms leveled at Disney throughout his long career this one about the scares he gave children seems the least valid, though the most widespread. (In the same way, the most common criticism of movies in general—which has to do with their alleged sexiness—also seems the least intelligent, for the moral transgressions of movies are much too complicated and interesting to be discussed in such simple-minded terms.)

In any case, the offending moments of *Snow White* occurred when the queen-stepmother transformed herself into a crone (not really a witch, as most people seem to remember her), and when the huntsman's knife seemed to flash down on the girl and it was unclear, for an instant, whether or not he had killed her. Most children recall these scenes with a kind of delicious shudder—the sort of thing that, before psychology and do-gooding liberalism combined in attempt to smooth all the interesting edges off childhood, used to be the source of our best remembrances. A good many youngsters—those who knew their own limitations—were wise enough to do exactly what Disney's daughter did: avert their eyes and request a companion to tell them when the scary part was over (children are remarkably more sensitive to their own fears than most people credit them with being). Only a few found themselves so startled by fear that traumatization followed, for as Donald Barr has observed, "Disney terror is mere scare. Unless it happens to touch on a particular child's particular phobias, it simply does not disturb children, for it has no reference to any of the unease and tension that arise from a child's private trials."

Disney's critics seemed to forget several things about *Snow White* and about the other animated features to which similar objections were raised (notably *Pinocchio*, with its tiny hero being swallowed by a quite enormous whale, and *Dumbo*, with its frightening storm and ensuing separation of the mother elephant from her baby). The first and most obvious of these things is that the majority of children should not be denied the very real pleasure of exposure to the quickly and pleasantly resolved excitements of these films because a minority cannot deal with them. Then, too, there is the simple fact that we need to learn to deal with things that frighten us, even as children. The ability to separate that which is, after all, "only a story" or "only a picture" from that which is reality is not a bad one to cultivate early. Nor is it wrong to introduce children to symbolic representations of evil, in restricted doses and in the right context of course, in the hope that it will provide them with the imaginative tools to deal with it intelligently when they encounter it in its more chilling manifestations in life. As for the bad dreams *Snow White* was supposed to have caused, it is a simple fact that it is humanly impossible not to dream, that the materials entering into them are many and varied, and that no child and no adult can escape this particular working of his unconscious. If Disney had not been putting things into the child's stream of consciousness the day he saw *Snow White*, someone else would have been, perhaps to better effect, perhaps to worse, but certainly to *some* effect. One cannot protect a child from experience, and it seems preposterous to protect him from one as generally innocuous, as often rewarding, as *Snow White*.

Indeed, looking back on *Snow White* from the perspective of thirty years, one is inclined to believe that its defects are unimportant in terms of the film itself; it easily triumphed over them. Their real effect was on the future when, uncorrected and allowed to deepen, they vitiated much of the potentially promising work that emanated from the Disney studio. Large numbers of people who knew very little about the movies were encouraged to make sweeping statements about Disney's genius. Mark Van Doren for instance, wrote that "his technique, about which I know little, must of course be wonderful, but the main thing is that he lives somewhere near the human center and knows innumerable truths that cannot be taught. That is why his ideas look like inspirations and why he can be good hearted without being sentimental, can be ridiculous without being fatuous. With him, as with any first rate artist, we feel that we are in good hands; we can trust him with our hearts and wits." The professionals of film criticism sensibly confined themselves to the work at hand, which Frank Nugent of the New York *Times* summarized as "delightful, gay and captivating." If it was not quite fit to rank "with the greatest motion pictures of all time," as Howard Barnes of the New York *Herald Tribune* thought it did, it certainly did "more than match . . . expectations," as Nugent put it. But it also raised expectations for the future, and amidst the chorus of unmeasured praise only one voice was raised to point out the already obvious—but still correctable—defects in the Disney technique.

That voice belonged to Gilbert Seldes, who was one of the best critical friends Disney had. Seldes deserves recognition not only for acumen but for prescience, for he observed and isolated the difficulties Disney had with folk material *before* the release of *Snow White* and based his strictures on two short cartoon renderings of traditional tales, *The Golden Touch* (in which King Midas begged for a hamburger) and *The Country Cousin*, an adaptation of the country mouse-city mouse tale. His immediate concern was a statement by another dabbler in the popular arts—Mortimer Adler. In his book, *Art and Prudence*, the Chicago philosopher declared that Disney's work "reaches greatness, a degree of perfection in its field which surpasses our best critical capacity to analyze. . . ."

Seldes begged to differ. You could at least "murmur a word of warning," he declared, and he did so through a quite precise analysis of the folkish films in comparison with three recent Disney originals involving The Mouse, the duck and the incomparable Pluto. The Mickey Mouse film was *The Band Concert*, which Seldes called "Disney's greatest single work," a judgment that stands the test of time. "It has," wrote Seldes, "comedy of detail—such as the sleeve of Mickey's oversized uniform continually slipping down to conceal his baton; it has comedy of structure based on the duck's persistent attempts to break up the concert by playing a competing tune on the flute—a tune to which the band, against its will, has to turn; it has comedy of character in the stern artistic devotion of Mickey contrasted with the unmotivated villainy of Donald; it has comedy of action when the tornado twists the entire concert into the air and then reverses itself and brings the players back to the grandstand. In no other picture have I observed so many flashing details—during the tornado itself there is the general line of comedy that in the whirlwind or caught on treetops, all the players continue to follow their music, but there are moments in this scene when the screen seems to be animated by dozens of separate episodes. They are miraculous if you catch them and even if you do not, the total effect is miraculous still." He goes on to pay deserved tribute to *Mother Pluto* and *Alpine Climbers*. In the former the good-natured, slightly moronic dog conceives "the fantastic idea that he might by accident hatch a brood of chicks and far from being aghast comes to be more protective than the chicks' legitimate parents." In the latter the ineffable duck and that magnificently shaggy, unnamed St. Bernard who frequently appeared with him encounter a series of angry mountain fauna in the course of an expedition that is a great comedy of errors and terrors.

To these films Seldes contrasts the folk adaptations—"a little pretentious and a little dull," with their heavy backgrounds and "absence of hilarious fun." He correctly sensed what was troubling Disney and his artisans. The bright, simple style of the Mickey Mouse cartoons, despite the great strides that had been made in them, was not suited to traditional folk material; you could not suggest with it the depths the folk material often contained. Neither was the answer to be found in standard storybook illustration, which is where Disney now seemed to be turning. He needed, Seldes implied, more eclectic taste in his study of models. A wide-ranging, informed animator might profitably study Tenniel's great drawings for *Alice in Wonderland* or even those of Peter Arno or James Thurber. Then, too, there were Goya and Hogarth and Adolf Dehn and even George Grosz—if not precisely to copy, then to indicate the range of possibilities available. Disney had found, said Seldes, a gold mine in legend and myth, but he must not confine his operations to rapacious strip mining. He must be prepared to dig deeper and farther. And for that he needed graphic tools of greater range and greater subtlety than he then possessed.

It was sound advice. Perhaps *Snow White* presented too many difficulties, financial and technical, to apply it immediately. And immediately thereafter, Disney found himself on a sea of economic troubles that were not conducive to thoughtful experimentation. But Disney was a man capable of infinite effort, under all sorts of pressures, when he wanted to do something new. The inescapable conclusion is that he was perfectly content with his artistic style and saw no reason to expand its capabilities or its flexibility or even its terms of historical reference.

What one might have dared to hope for—what his critics implicitly did hope for—was not a slavish imitation of the great masters of drawing but rather an expanded capability of fitting a variety of styles to a variety of stories in many moods. Sometimes these styles might have been borrowed, sometimes they might have been invented on the spot. The point is that such eclecticism might have served as a brake on "Disneyfication," that shameless process by which everything the studio later touched, no matter how unique the vision of the original from which the studio worked, was reduced to the limited terms Disney and his people could understand. Magic, mystery, individuality—most of all, individuality—were consistently destroyed when a literary work was passed through this machine that had been taught there was only one correct way to draw.

What was consistently wanting in all the Disney versions of folktales and classic children's stories was something of the spirit with which the brilliant young English actor and director, Jonathan Miller, recently approached *Alice in Wonderland*. Sensibly declaring that there is no good reason to be loyal to the text with which one begins since "the book remains after all," he points out that "the scriptures . . . have survived the creative depradations of the Renaissance painters, and the Greek myths are reborn each century through the imagination of a Seneca, a Racine or a Joyce." The best children's books are like these sources in that "they have a simple, imaginative hospitality which somehow invites the mind to make them over again." The point is, however, that these timeless images must "excite some sort of answer" on the part of their re-creator that is similar to the original work in imaginative intensity and depth of feeling. This is precisely what *Snow White* failed to draw from Disney and his craftsmen, though in the general excitement over what they were attempting, this was overlooked. Disney, the man who could never bear to look upon animals in zoos or prisoners in jail or other "unpleasant things," was truly incapable of seeing his material in anything but reductive terms.

Joseph Campbell has offered a brilliant description of folk stories which can and should be extended to include other material Disney chose to animate later, works like *Pinocchio*, *Bambi*, the Uncle Remus tales (used in *The Song of the South*), *The Sword in the Stone*, *The Jungle Book* and *Winnie-the-Pooh*. Says Campbell: "The tale survives . . . not simply as a quaint relic of days childlike in belief. Its world of magic is symptomatic of fevers deeply burning in the psyche: permanent presences, desires, fears, ideals, potentialities, that have glowed in the nerves, hummed in the blood, baffled the senses, since the beginning. . . . Playful and unpretentious as the archetypes of fairy tale may appear to be, they are the heroes and villains who have built the world for us . . . all are working in order that the ungainsayable specifications of effective fantasy, the permanent patterns of the tale of wonder, shall be clothed in flesh and known as life."

This knowledge need not be intellectualized. Indeed, it better not be, since in the overthought adaptation "the spiritual sap of the work dries up, and the whole thing falls apart like so much dead wood," as Jonathan Miller says. But it must be present, it simply must be present, in some form or another. Perhaps if Disney's psyche had been a little less the product of *petit bourgeois* striving, perhaps if he had had a little less education of the wrong kind—had been more truly a primitive—he might have found the inner spirit to comprehend the power of the material he was going to depend upon and then have found the graphic style, or styles, suitable to it. Perhaps if he had had a little less technological imagination—and a great deal less business acumen—to distract him, he might have found a way to be faithful not to the letter of his material, which is a feckless demand for any movie maker engaged in the process of translation from one medium to another, but faithful instead to its true spirit, its *animating* spirit. Unfortunately, he lacked the tools, intellectual and artistic, he needed for this task. He could make something his own, all right, but that process nearly always robbed the work at hand of its uniqueness, of its soul, if you will. In its place he put jokes and songs and fright effects, but he always seemed to diminish what he touched. He came always as a conqueror, never as a servant. It is a trait, as many have observed, that many Americans share when they venture into foreign lands hoping to do good but equipped only with know-how instead of sympathy and respect for alien traditions.

PART EIGHT

Troubled Times

---

24 *When banks came into pictures, trouble came with them. When we operated on picture money, there was joy in the industry; when we operated on Wall Street money, there was grief in the industry.*

—Cecil B. DeMille

WALT DISNEY AGREED. Not long before he died he fell to discussing bankers with a reporter and declared, "They are fellows who don't understand your business—my problem all along. I don't mean to be heavy on bankers, but they just don't understand." He was fond of declaring his sympathy for his brother, who had to spend so much time with the money men and once told him, "You've got to get away from those fellows. They'll get you down. Stay as far away from them as you can."

Had they chosen to, the Disneys could have been in a position to avoid "those fellows" for years, perhaps for the rest of their lives after the success of *Snow White*. For the people set aside whatever fears for their children's mental health the film stirred and seemed to have none of the other reservations since expressed about it. Six months after its release, *Snow White* had returned a gross of some $2 million to the Disney studio and was on its way to grossing the $8.5 million it produced on its first run. (As of 1985, the picture had returned $41. $4 million to the studio's coffers.) It would have been possible to finance a modest, steady expansion of the studio out of its profits alone. But Walt Disney saw a chance for a next leap forward. "Success is hard to take," said Roy Disney. "We thought we would do two animation features a year." Before *Snow White* went out into the world, Disney was already beginning work on two features—*Pinocchio* and *Bambi*—and, shortly after they were placed in full production another project began to grow—and grow—in his mind, a project that would wed animation to serious music on a scale never before attempted, in an effort to popularize such music for a very wide public. The result was, of course, *Fantasia*.

All this naturally required huge outlays of money, and as if the films were not enough, the Disneys decided to go ahead with the construction of Walt's $3.8 million dream studio. As a result, by 1940 not only had Disney run through most of the *Snow White* profits, but his organization found itself in debt to the banks by roughly $4.5 million. Worse, the prospects of paying off such an amount grew dimmer by the hour as the spread of World War II closed off the foreign markets where Disney counted on gaining about 45 percent of his return. And this was not the end of his troubles: he had labor unrest to contend with; *Bambi*, in which he wanted animation of almost photographic naturalism, was seriously delayed by technical problems, and *Fantasia* turned out to be at least a temporary financial calamity.

What appears to have happened is that in the first flush of big success, Disney set aside his habitual, populist distrust of bankers and plunged ahead with a recklessness unprecedented even for him. In 1938, for the first time, the banks were genuinely receptive to him, even encouraging. And, after all, their aid had been instrumental in the completion of *Snow White*. Why not use them again to press forward in this most propitious of all moments? Times were, if not good, certainly better than they had been in a long while. And the worth of Disney's labors had been blessed not only by an honorary degree from the University of Southern California but by similar honors from those citadels of the eastern intellectual establishment, Harvard and Yale. At the latter, no less a personage than William Lyon Phelps declared, in writing the citation, that "one touch of nature makes the whole world kin, and Walter Disney has charmed millions of people in every part of the earth. . . ." Why, he was even a Chevalier of the French Legion of Honor. Best of all, it was beginning to seem that he was gaining acceptance from Hollywood's power elite. When *Snow White* premièred at Hollywood's Carthay Circle Theater in December, 1937, he at last had a full-length feature that could be given a klieg-lighted send-off of the sort the older moguls habitually gave their pictures. "A long, long time before," his daughter wrote, "he had promised himself that someday a cartoon of his would have such an opening. . . . So . . . with Hollywood's brass turning out [it] was a triumph for Dad." The same may be said about the special Academy Award that was presented to the studio in 1939 for *Snow White*. It came in the form of one big Oscar and seven little ones—for each of the seven dwarfs—and it was presented by none other than Shirley Temple. Disney's head was turned: to a reporter who referred to *Snow White* as a cartoon he allegedly snapped, "It's no more a cartoon than a painting by Whistler is a cartoon." It was a very blunt statement, somewhat at odds with his modest public character of the time. Still, Disney was entitled to his euphoria, and to relish his new power, even though the mood was to prove costly.

Of all the projects in hand, only *Pinocchio* presented no insuperable problems. This film was shot entirely on the multiplane camera, and indeed, its opening sequence, with the camera panning in at night across the rooftops of the village where the toymaker Geppetto lived and then down on a dusty, wayfaring cricket named Jiminy, who was looking for a place to sleep, was regarded as something of a marvel. No less than twelve planes were employed. The shot cost about $25,000, and the accountants talked Disney into using less elaborate setups in the rest of the film. The problems Carlo Collodi's original story presented were not so easily resolved. The Italian writer had written his book directly for magazine serialization, and since he had been paid, as was the nineteenth-century custom, on word rates, he had allowed himself to ramble considerably. As a result his tale of a puppet, given life by a Blue Fairy but denied real boyhood until he proved himself "brave, truthful and unselfish," needed considerable pointing, though even in its sensibly trimmed version, there was plenty of action to fill the scenes. Before the film was finished the puppet fell in with such comically evil companions as J. Worthington Foulfellow, a con-man fox; his henchman, Gideon, who was an avaricious cat, and a juvenile delinquent named Lampwick. He gave himself up to the debaucheries of Pleasure Island and was very nearly turned into a donkey before he escaped. Finally, he was transported on the wings of a great dove to the middle of the ocean, where he allowed himself to be swallowed by the great whale, Monstro, in the hope of rescuing his foster-father, Geppetto, who had suffered the same fate in the course of a voyage to save Pinocchio from the evil temptations placed before him.

One must suspect that Disney found in this story elements of autobiography, since he had himself been a child denied the normal prerogatives of boyhood. It is certainly possible that at least some portion of his drive for success was a compensation for his failure to find the father who had, in the psychological sense, been lost to him since childhood. This may also explain why he so relished the paternal role he was now beginning to play with such earnestness—and such ineptitude—with his employees. In any case, such an interpretation suggests why *Pinocchio* is the darkest in hue of all Disney's pictures and the one which, despite its humor, is the most consistently terrifying. The menacing whips that crack over the heads of the boys who are turned into donkeys after their taste of the sybaritic life may have had their origin in his recurrent nightmare of punishment for failure to deliver his newspapers. And, of course, one suspects the dream of winning the neglectful father's approval by a heroic act—such as rescuing him from a living death in the whale's maw—must have occurred to Disney at some point in his unhappy youth.

Whatever problems the range and sweep of the story presented, it had a rhythm and a drive far stronger than *Snow White* and more like that of the short cartoons. There was more adventure in it, more spectacle and, perhaps, a better balance among all its elements. The most sympathetic and animatable characters were also the main characters in *Pinocchio*, as contrasted to *Snow White*, in which the heroine's role had to be cut back in favor of the dwarfs' because of the difficulties she presented to the artists. In addition, the art, in all its aspects, was smoother and more elaborate, though not yet overslick— perhaps the high point of Disney's chosen mode and, this time, well adapted to all the film's moods instead of just a few of them, as had been the case in *Snow White*.

The picture was also notable for its introduction of a device that was to be employed frequently in future Disney animated features in order to make them more easily palatable to the family audience. In the original Collodi story, there was a cricket who offered to serve as the puppet's conscience but who was indifferently squashed by Pinocchio after very little discussion. It was not exactly an endearing gesture, nor did Pinocchio's character prove entirely winning as the story proceeded: he was, from Disney's point of view, too much the out-and-out delinquent. He was consequently softened into a good-natured lad, easily led astray but trying in his inept way to discover the principles of correct behavior. More important, the cricket was not squashed but developed. Appointed the puppet's conscience by The Blue Fairy, he became Pinocchio's worldly wise mentor, ally and rescuer—serving him, in fact, in rather the manner that Roy Disney served his younger brother. He also served as a kind of chorus commenting on the action and as an admirable foil to the hero. Most important, he was an adorably bright little creature, cute as a bug as it were, and probably more popular with audiences than Pinocchio, who was rather square and simple in manner (the cricket also had the film's most memorable song, "Give a Little Whistle").

The success of this wee creature showed Disney and his people a convenient way to brighten and lighten any story they feared might grow too serious or unpleasant for audiences. Jiminy Cricket's direct spiritual descendants were thereafter rarely absent from Disney's animated films. In *Bambi* there were Thumper the Rabbit and Flower the Skunk, who introduced the young deer to his woodland environment and instructed him in matters of safety and convenience; in *Dumbo* there was Timothy the Mouse, who was both conscience and theatrical manager; in *Cinderella* there were the mice who were the heroine's only friends; in *Peter Pan* Tinker Bell, who had always been a tiny light on the stage, was characterized as a midget (but physically well endowed) nymphet; while a talkative owl was luckily present in the original of T. H. White's *The Sword and the Stone*, the least well known of Disney's animated films. It is perhaps significant that Disney's greatest animated failure, *Sleeping Beauty*, contained no tiny creature for audiences to love or to tell them how to respond to what they were seeing. In that film they were left floundering among the ambiguities like so many intellectuals. In the first instance, however, Jiminy Cricket was an effective little character and an effective little storytelling device as well.

The reviews of *Pinocchio* were almost as ecstatic as those accorded *Snow White*. Indeed, Frank Nugent thought *Pinocchio* "superior to *Snow White* in every respect but one: its score. . . . [It is the] best thing Mr. Disney has ever done and therefore the best cartoon ever made." His colleague on the *Herald Tribune*, Howard Barnes, thought it "a compound of imagination and craftsmanship, of beauty and eloquence, which is to be found only in great works of art." But one senses in all the notices a slightly reserved note, almost as if the critics were prisoners not only of their previous enthusiasm but of the general unwillingness to criticize the works of such a universally esteemed citizen. Barnes noted, for instance, that the new film "lacks the element of surprise and something of the emotional depth" of its predecessor. Franz Hollering in *The Nation* said that "one misses the lyrical parts of *Snow White* . . . and also its stronger central idea." It seemed to him, therefore, "smaller than its parts," which was the exact opposite of the common response to *Snow White*, where technical difficulties were ignored because the total effect was so enchanting.

Such minor reservations were not the cause, however, of the film's failure to return more than its $2.6 million cost on its first release. The trouble was that by the time it was released, Germany had marched into Poland, beginning World War II. *Pinocchio* therefore became the first Disney film to feel the effect of the curtailment of the overseas, though ultimately it would gross a handsome $30.4 million. For the moment, though, it represented the beginning of a squeeze that was to grow tighter and tighter in the next few years.

The inability of *Pinocchio* to perform at the box office did not prevent Disney from moving into his new studio, but it certainly darkened what was a major event in his corporation's life. Here, at last, was the rationally planned factory he had wanted for so long, here at last was a structure symbolizing a stability and an importance never achieved before by an animator. To be sure, he had been forced to make some compromises. Delighted as they had been by *Snow White*'s acceptance, Disney's bankers were still not absolutely certain he was here to stay. They would advance him money for a new studio only on condition that its principal structure (still called the animation building, but nowadays housing mostly executives) could easily be adopted to some other use. This particular section of Burbank needed a hospital, and so the bankers insisted that the building be constructed for easy conversion into such a place. As a result, it is one of the oddest edifices to be found on any movie lot. The central corridor on each of its three floors is about twice the normal width, the better to trundle beds and wheelchairs about. Scattered along it are niches that nowadays hold Coke and candy machines but that could easily serve as nursing stations. Entrances to eight short wings, four on either side of the hallway, are placed at regular intervals, and one of them, on the top floor, was given over completely to Walt Disney's suite of offices. It, like all the other wings, could be turned into a ward with the greatest of ease. In fact, this peculiar design entails no great inconvenience for anyone, although the ease with which movement along the corridor could be controlled—so important to hospitals—was to become a sore point among the employees in very short order. It should also perhaps be noted that the bankers were right about the need for a hospital in the area, for St. Joseph's, where Disney died, was built directly across the street from the new studio a few years later.

There were two other major compromises with Disney's initial vision. The first of these was immediate: the idea of an amusement park was abandoned. Resident archaeologists have found rough sketches for such a park dating from the early 1930s in the files. It was to have been two acres in size, containing train and pony rides, and there was talk around the studio, according to veterans, of singing fountains and perhaps statues of Mickey Mouse, Donald Duck and the rest of Disney's stars. This conceit, at least, was carried out to a modest degree by naming the studio's principal streets Mickey Mouse Boulevard, Minnie Mouse Boulevard, Donald Duck Drive, Snow White Boulevard and Dopey Drive. The main building stands at the intersection of Mickey and Dopey, where the wrought-iron signboard has a tendency to tilt in an untidy fashion. The second compromise with the dream came later on, when the building designated on the original ground plan as a school became, ignominiously enough, the headquarters for the publicity department.

Still and all, it was—and is—a neatly functioned place, "a mass of clear-cut buildings, with a horizontal emphasis of design, not self-consciously asserting what we are told at school is the 'modern functional style' but merely workmanlike," to quote an early description. "Under the California sun they show up clean, in tones predominantly pink, cream-colored and gray, with the sun glinting on the dull metal used in conjunction with brick." Such lack of true architectural distinction as the place may have was compensated for by pleasantries of landscaping. Plots of well-tended, very green grass separate the buildings, cheerful flower beds abound, and there are plenty of areas useful for various informal games. Disney was wise enough to purchase enough land—forty-four acres—for uncrowded expansion, and over the years three sound stages have been added to the original single stage as the bulk of production has switched from animation to live action. Reflecting the same trend, a scene dock has been added, along with an expanded carpentry shop; a warehouse has become a casting office, and the short-subject building has become the makeup and costume room serving the influx of actors. Even with this change in emphasis, however, the place still fits the criteria that were, according to Robert D. Feild's constantly burbling study of the man and his works "inseparable in Walt's mind"—"formal planning, which would allow the picture to be manufactured as efficiently as possible, and an arrangement whereby those employed could retain the greatest possible amount of creative independence." Feild's line was that "it may be a factory, but in this twentieth century, by so becoming, it has dignified the artist's calling." As he saw it, the studio was a step toward breaking down "the tradition that art is only messing about with paint; that the artist is normally to be found in an 'attic' or a 'barn'; and that studio or art school must center around a model, in the nude perhaps, regardless of whether its activities are 'pure' or 'applied' or 'commercial' or

237

'industrial.' " He wrote this in 1942, and the involuntary wince with which one reads these words today is a measure of how the hoped for marriage of art and technics has failed under the perverting pressure of worldly concerns.

Disney's pride in the new plant was immeasurable. But, ironically, the assaults against that pride were incessant. His father, for instance, was unimpressed. "When the new studio was finished," a contemporary chronicle reports, "Walt took his father around and proudly pointed out all the gadgets. The little boy who had carried papers was grown up now and this was his dream come true. 'It's all air conditioned,' he boasted. 'You can get any kind of weather, any time you want.' The old man thought it over. He seemed unimpressed. Taking in the whole architectural triumph with a wave of his hand, he inquired: 'What else is it good for?' " Disney is elsewhere reported to have replied, with some weariness, "A hospital." Of this same visit, Disney later said, "Pa was of the generation that didn't believe in borrowing money, and he offered to help me out with $200 when I was eight million dollars in the hole trying to build my studio." The last figure is an exaggeration, but the tone of the reminiscence rings true; Disney appears to have seen as little of his parents in these years as was decently possible.

25 *Oh*, Fantasia! *Well, we made it and I don't regret it. But if we had it to do all over again, I don't think we'd do it.*
—Walt Disney, 1961

Fantasia BEGAN TO preoccupy Disney before either *Pinocchio* or the new studio were finished. It has been said that the film grew out of a meeting between Leopold Stokowski and

Disney at a Hollywood party, where the former repeated an oft-made wish to work with Disney on something and requested a tour of the Disney studio. At the time, Disney was in the midst of one of his periodic, sentimental attempts to restore Mickey Mouse to something like his early popularity. The instrument of this rehabilitation was to be a short subject based on Paul Dukas' scherzo for orchestra, "The Sorcerer's Apprentice." Stokowski was entranced, and agreed to conduct the score. He persistently wondered, moreover, why Disney should stop there. Why didn't he make a full-length film, using several other musical works to suggest "the mood, the coloring, the design, the speed, the character of motion of what is seen on the screen," as the conductor later expressed it. In short, a fantasia, in the precise sense of the musical term, which means a free development of a given theme. (In the beginning the word was merely a working title for the film, but no one could improve on it, so it stuck.)

Among the first ideas the oddly matched collaborators had was to dispense with written credits. Their wedding of art and music was to be uncluttered by any dependence on the literary arts. So Deems Taylor, sometime composer and musicologist then at the height of his fame as an explainer of music for the masses on the Metropolitan Opera broadcasts, was hired to give a spoken introduction to the film. Soon he was sitting with Stokowski and Disney in a three-week conference attended by the heads of various Disney departments, at which hundreds of recordings of hundreds of pieces of music were played in a search for the film's program. By 1939 Stokowski was recording the selections they had made, working in Hollywood and in Philadelphia, where he was nearing the end of his long tenure as conductor of The Philadelphia Orchestra.

Not unnaturally, it was decided to open the film with the maestro's own transcription of Bach's "Toccata and Fugue in D Minor." Stokowski had begun his career as a church organist.

he had built and conducted his orchestra so that critics often spoke of its organ-like sonorities, and his transcription of Bach's great work for the organ not only had been a labor of first love but was well received by audiences right from the start, despite some purist quibbling by critics. Indeed, it is not too much to say that the elevation of Bach to a proper place of esteem among American music lovers in this century began with the popularity of Stokowski's lush and viscerally exciting work, so different in its effect from pure Bach, whose appeal lies in austere intellectuality.

In any case, the "Toccata and Fugue" was followed in *Fantasia* by excerpts from "The Nutcracker Suite," "The Sorcerer's Apprentice," "The Rite of Spring," "The Pastoral Symphony," "The Dance of the Hours," and a sequence that combined "A Night on Bald Mountain" with the "Ave Maria." Musically speaking, it was a very mixed bag, and it was even more so as a piece of animation.

As Stokowski said, "*Fantasia* was created and drawn by artists most of whom have no knowledge of, or training in, music." He thought that as "enthusiastic listeners" they were able to penetrate the inner character of the music, there to discover "depths of expression that sometimes have been missed by musicologists." Even he had to concede, however, that the visions contained in *Fantasia* were just one way "out of many possible ways" of visualizing the music. All too often, these were the crudest ways. In the opening sequence, for example, Mickey Mouse appears, shakes hands with Stokowski (in silhouette) and welcomes him to Hollywood. The orchestra, also in silhouette, begins to play the "Toccata and Fugue," and images suggestive of musical instruments being played by hundreds of hands begin to appear on the screen. These shapes grow more and more abstract, then clouds begin to form into strange shapes, comets flash, a rippling mass fills the screen and finally shapes itself into a pipe organ—just in time for the climax of the piece—when it disappears, as Deems Taylor later put it, in "a blaze of light, against which stands the tense, vibrant silhouette of the conductor. A last great chord. Bach has spoken."

Someone—or something—surely has. But it is a travesty to imply that it is Bach, since the music heard is a transcription of his work and the animation is a transcription of the transcription, into another medium entirely. Disney enjoyed working on the sequence, perhaps, because its basic concept was his: "I said, 'All I can see is violin tips and bow tips—like when you're half asleep at a concert." He thought they were abstractions, but they were not, of course. They were merely a form of literalism different from any he had attempted before.

But if the opening sequence was unsuccessful, it was at least not offensive in *Fantasia*. There is some debate about which one really represented the nadir of its taste. Some hold for the animated vision of the creation of the world with its garish volcanic eruptions, its cheaply scarifying dinosaurs, its attempt to set general-science level education about geology and evolution to Stravinsky's "Rite of Spring." Others are most distressed by the revel on Mount Olympus, which formed the "story" for a truncated version of the Beethoven *Sixth Symphony*, a cheerful nightmare compounded equally of the oppressively cute and the depressingly heavy-handed. To make sure everyone got the idea that this was art, the girl centaurs were originally drawn barebreasted, but the Hays office insisted on discreet garlands being hung around their necks, a decision that satisfied puritans but did nothing to hide the grotesquery of their conception. The torsos and heads that topped the horse bodies of these creatures belonged to adolescent girls styled to resemble the teen-ager down the street—surely the weirdest blend of classicism and Americanism ever observed in a nation too long devoted to the feckless enterprise of reconciling these irreconcilable impulses. The sequence ends with the most explicit statement of anality ever made by the studio, which found in the human backside not only the height of humor but the height of sexuality as well. Two of the little cupids who scamper incessantly through the sequence finally—and blessedly—draw a curtain over the scene. When they come together their shiny little behinds form, for an instant, a heart.

Probably the worst thing in the film is its conclusion, in which the terrors of "A Night on Bald Mountain"—bats and gargoyles and devils and the other creatures of the gothic demonology engage in a black mass—are dispelled by the coming of dawn and a procession of the churchly singing the "Ave Maria"; it is essentially the structure of "The Skeleton Dance" enormously elaborated. Taylor thought that "incongruous as this juxtaposition may sound at first blush, it is astonishingly successful; for the two works are so antipodal in mood that they complement each other perfectly . . . an engrossing tone picture of the struggle between good and evil, and the ultimate triumph of the good," which proves that nothing is sacred, not even the sacred, when an eager popularizer gets busy. In itself, the idea of this juxtaposition is not offensive, but as the climax of the film it seems insincere—a conventionalized invocation of religiosity, an arbitrary resort to a surefire sentiment, rather like the placement of a brassy patriotic number at the end of a musical review. The execution of the sequence is arty, the musical arrangement throbs with false emotion achieved through an excess of stringed instruments and a lush choral setting of Schubert's song, which is, of course, intended for a solo voice.

Having observed all this, it is only fair to point out that there is much in *Fantasia* representing a distinct advance in the studio's work and some small things that succeed on almost anyone's cinematic terms. There are a couple of pleasant things in "The Nutcracker" animation, especially the dance of the Chinese mushrooms; "The Sorcerer's Apprentice" sequence, featuring Mickey, with which the whole project began, is a very good one, full of wit and invention, and "The Dance of the Hours," with its ostrich and hippopotamus ballerinas remains a lovely piece of low comic animation, a joke on a piece of music that had become something of a joke itself as well as a broad satirical comment on the absurdities of high culture. Indeed, in the context of the film this short section can be seen as a mockery of the very material that surrounds it. Finally, even in the most pretentious of *Fantasia*'s sequences there is an eclecticism, a reaching out beyond the studio's standard style that is most welcome. The massive renderings of the earth in upheaval in "The Rite of Spring" and the battle of the dinosaurs that follows do have a certain rude power one might not have thought the animated film capable of attempting, however flawed the results. And up until the tasteless modulation into the "Ave Maria," Disney's venture into the tradition of the grotesque in "A Night on Bald Mountain" is a rewarding one. Wolfgang Kayser points out that there is a relationship—and not one of opposites, either—between Disney's chosen métier, the fairy tale, and the grotesque. Indeed, the former appears at first glance to be very like the latter, a world where we are exposed to the "alienation of familiar forms." On closer examination we see that those elements of the fairy tale that are already familiar to us are usually not transformed; they are comfortingly familiar as they are in our own experience. Only the truly imaginary creations of the tale are strange to us—imaginary toads in a real garden, as it were. The genuinely grotesque takes us only one significant step farther, transforming everything, the familiar and the unfamiliar alike, into terrifying symbols that have as their goal "a secret liberation." "The darkness has been sighted, the ominous powers discovered, the incomprehensible forces challenged," leading to a definition of the grotesque as "an attempt to invoke and subdue the demonic aspects of the world," as Kayser puts it. Until the willful intrusion of the Pilgrim chorus, this is precisely what Disney's artists attempted in the last moments of *Fantasia*, and it is because they succeeded so well—though not perfectly—that the "Ave Maria" intrudes so disturbingly on their work. It is as if Disney could not bear the implications of what they did—or was afraid that his audience could not. To intrude religious sentimentality on such a potent vision of blackness is to spoil it, to negate all the good work that went into it. Had Disney not pulled back, it is possible that, at least with the sophisticated audiences, he might have swept aside, in one last burst of power, all the objections that the earlier sequences of the film raised. Instead, he merely reinforced them.

It is possible, of course, to say that if the studio had not been ready for *Snow White* it certainly was not ready for *Fantasia*. If after his first exposure to the centaur sequence Disney could—as he did—comment, "Gee! This'll make Beethoven," one is entitled to wonder if his organization would ever be ready for a work of this kind. A fawning respect for cultural tradition is not what was required. What was needed here—as in all adaptations of high culture to mass culture—was respect for the integrity of the forms he was seeking to make over. Without that respect, it is impossible to turn out a work with any integrity of its own—and that is why *Fantasia* is such a disturbing jumble.

The experience of Igor Stravinsky is apposite in this respect. He reports getting a take-it-or-leave-it offer from Disney's New York office of five thousand dollars for the use of "The Rite of Spring" in the picture. If he refused the money, he was informed, the music would be used anyway, since it was copyrighted in Russia, which did not protect it here because the U.S. had never signed the Berne copyright convention. Stravinsky decided he was faced with a *fait accompli* and gave permission for the use of the music. "I saw the film with George Balanchine in a Hollywood studio at Christmas time, 1939," he wrote later. "I remember someone offering me a score and, when I said I had my own, the someone saying, 'But it is all changed.' " It was indeed. The instrumentation had been improved by such stunts as having the horns play their glissandi an octave higher in the 'Danse de la terre.' The order of the pieces had been shuffled, too, and the most difficult of them eliminated—though this did not save the musical performance, which was execrable. I will say nothing about the visual compliment, as I do not wish to criticize an unresisting imbecility. . . ."

At the time, Stravinsky made no protest; he even submitted to having his picture taken with Disney. The latter apparently mistook resignation for approbation and he recalled Stravinsky's emerging from the screening "visibly moved"—as perhaps he was, one way or the other. He claimed, in any case, that Stravinsky made two visits to the studio and had, on the first one, approved all the changes and cuts that were made, an allegation the composer denied on the ground that he was confined to a tuberculosis sanitorium in Europe prior to and during the recording of his work. The point is that what happened to Stravinsky happened to all the composers represented in *Fantasia*. His misfortune was that he was the only one still alive and able to take offense. He therefore encountered the producer at his entrepreneurial worst. Had Disney actually possessed the soul of an artist—as his more ardent and ignorant supporters liked to claim he did—he could not have treated Stravinsky as he did and he would have approached the entire *Fantasia* project in a different spirit.

Superficially, *Fantasia* seems to put Disney's critic in a contradictory position. If the basic objection to his work in general is that its style and viewpoint too quickly and too narrowly solidified into a minor mold, how can one criticize his only large-scale effort to break out of his self-imposed limitations? The answer, of course, lay in the attitude Disney took to *Fantasia*. Had he been able to see it as a genuine artist sees his failures, as instructive experiences from which one learns something about the limits and possibilities of his art, then he might have gone on from it to create something that fully satisfied the promise that was scattered throughout the picture but never satisfactorily integrated. But, as *Time* later wrote, "though Walt learned a lesson from *Fantasia*, he learned the wrong one. Mistaking for culture what Stokowski and Taylor offered him, he decided that culture was not for him."

Worse, he was denied even his customary technological pleasures. He had planned to shoot *Fantasia* in a wide-screen process, complete with stereophonic sound and to play it on a reserved-seat basis for a long period of time before going into a more customary releasing pattern. Under pressure from his bankers, he was forced to abandon his new projection system entirely, to forego stereophonic sound in all but a few key cities and to shorten the film considerably so it could get quickly into the neighborhood houses, where the bulk of Disney's profits were traditionally made. "The bankers panicked," Disney said later, "*Fantasia* was never made to go out in regular release. I was asked to help cut it. I turned my back. Someone else cut it." Ultimately he was vindicated. Revived several times since the end of World War II, and shown at its full length, the picture has more than returned its $2.3 million investment, earning some $4.8 million in the U.S. and Canada alone.

But it still fared very badly in its initial run. The critics were fairly enthusiastic. Bosley Crowther of the New York *Times*, for example, found that it sometimes wearied the senses, that the color was occasionally too pretty and the dominance of visual imagery over the music could be annoying. Nevertheless he declared that "motion picture history was made last night" by a film that "dumps conventional formulas overboard and reveals the scope of films for imaginative excursion. . . . *Fantasia* . . . is simply terrific." Over at the *Herald Tribune*, Howard Barnes was less ecstatic. Calling the film "a brave and beautiful work," he felt constrained to add an objection that was to become a commonplace in discussion of *Fantasia*. "Being one who does not believe that one artistic medium needs translation into terms of another, it seems . . . Disney is attempting the impossible. There are times when his breaking down of music into animated art strikes me as definitely pretentious . . . the images on the screen are not apt to match with your reactions to the score." Still, he viewed it as a "fascinating new experiment . . . a courageous and distinguished production." The trouble was that the public was uninterested in experiment from Disney. They simply stayed away from *Fantasia*, more frightened by its reputation, perhaps, than they would have been had they tasted its comparatively mild pleasures and perils firsthand.

From Disney's point of view, they could not have picked a worse time to shy away from one of his products. When he undertook *Fantasia* he had not had any reason to suppose that it would be as economically important as it was turning out to be. Indeed, in 1938 he had every reason to believe that he could afford a money-losing experiment. But with *Pinocchio* unable to perform as expected abroad and with the potentially profitable but difficult *Bambi* put aside in order to devote full effort to *Fantasia*, he was suddenly in perilous straits. Far more than should have depended on *Fantasia*.

And the situation worsened even as the film approached completion. Early in 1940 the banks shut down the Disney credit line entirely, and in order to raise operating capital he was forced in April, 1940, to offer stock to the public for the first time, thus diluting ownership—a step he feared would mean dilution of his control over the enterprise. Although the latter never came to pass, it was a psychological blow that was perhaps harder for him to take than it would have been for other men. Indeed, shortly after the stock went on the market Disney was passing through Detroit and was told that Henry Ford liked his work (it was almost inevitable that he would). A meeting between the inspiration of *Fordismus* and one of his great, though unconscious, disciples was arranged. When Disney told the old man that he had just put his stock on sale, Ford commented sourly, "If you sell any part of an enterprise, you should sell it all." He, too, had recently been forced into the clutches of the money market, which he naturally identified with his fantasy of the worldwide Jewish conspiracy and which he had long fought to avoid. He more or less exactly summarized Disney's worst fears about the matter in his single-sentence comment.

Disney tried, at least, to keep some of the stock close to home by announcing that about 20 percent of the shares that had been set aside for himself and his brother would be distributed to employees. The stocks were 6 percent cumulative convertible preferred shares with a par value of twenty-five dollars. This and future distributions were to be in lieu of the holiday bonuses previously awarded employees, and the basis of the distribution was to be what it had been in the case of the bonuses—the length of the individual's service with the company and the value of those services as determined by the management. It is possible, as some former Disney employees have charged, that the gifts of stock were intended to assuage a worsening labor situation in the studio. It is also possible that no such thing was intended. The public record is silent on the point.

What is clear, in retrospect, is that the arbitrary distribution of stock deepened one of the grievances that most rankled the employees. If Disney seems to have been high-handed and insensitive with people like Stravinsky, he was doubly so with those who worked for him. There was no consistent policy in the studio regarding wages, and the ability to obtain raises was based, so far as the employees could see, purely on one's current standing with the boss. (Some say that they were encouraged to think of Roy Disney as the heavy in this situation, with Walt Disney, in effect, hiding behind his brother's skirts when requests for wages or favors were turned down.) The stock distribution was, to the rebellious employees, one more example of this system—or nonsystem—in operation. They saw only the stick in the offer, not the very real carrot. In the quarter century since, the shares have split several times, and the new shares have, as previously noted, soared to a level four times that of the original offering. In the years immediately after 1940, however, the trend was mostly down, and in the aftermath of the bitter strike that afflicted the studio in 1941, the stock slumped to a price as low as three dollars, driven there at least partially because employees dumped them in a gesture of displeasure with Disney. Like many such gestures, it backfired. Disney's faith in the future of his company was unwavering, and he picked up stock bargains by the hundreds during the dark years. Still, the gesture was understandable, for if the strike was not a violent one in its overt manifestations it was a wrenching experience psychologically for all concerned.

26

Come all of you good workers,
Good news to you I'll tell,
Of how the good old union
Has come in here to dwell.
Which side are you on?
Which side are you on?
—Labor song, popular in the 1930s

IF HIS FATHER's response to the new studio had been disappointing, the reaction of his employees when they moved in in 1940 was an unpleasant shock for Disney. However luxurious their new accommodations, they did not assuage a sense of disappointment that psychological conditions were not similarly upgraded. Indeed, they were worsened by the move, for now the production units were isolated from one another, and at the entrance to each group of offices sat a young lady whose duty was to ask the destination and mission of anyone desiring to leave his work area to visit another. Assistant animators and in-betweeners were isolated on the first floor of the animation building, which became a hotbed of discontent, verging on re-

249

bellion. Thus the easy give-and-take camaraderie of the Hyperion Avenue studio was threatened, and there appeared to be no compensation in the offing for its loss. The sense of foreboding that had gripped the studio ever since the completion of *Snow White* was mightily increased. Many of the employees had given Disney large quantities of free overtime when he was driving to complete that film, and instead of getting the bonuses they had been vaguely promised if it succeeded, they were now faced with a string of layoffs. Rumors that time clocks would be installed—despite Disney's previously well-publicized personal dislike of the instruments—did nothing to allay fears. The salary structure remained crazy-quilt, and the only general wage increase Disney granted in these years was self-serving: he brought a number of workers up over the forty-dollar-a-week level, at which point, under the Wagner Labor Relations Act, they ceased being entitled to time-and-a-half for overtime. Worst of all, Disney himself responded gracelessly to the pressures of his increasingly difficult economic situation. The conversational coinage of the story conference and the sweat box had always been rough, but now it seemed to grow unbearably brutal. One animator, working on *Fantasia*, decided to take piano lessons—at his own expense—in an attempt to gain a better understanding of musical structure and thus improve his work on this difficult project. When Disney found out about it, he snarled, "What are you, some kind of fag?" In the increasingly tense atmosphere of the studio, such remarks rubbed feelings very raw.

To the employees the answer seemed to be some sort of union. If Disney was so intent upon rationalizing his productive capacity, and if that process was going to destroy the informal style that had previously sufficed in the area of industrial relations, then it was necessary for them to do a little rationalizing of their own. Disney, in a move to avoid the possible intrusion of labor racketeer Willie Bioff—whose distressing presence, it should be added, in fairness to Disney, was actively encouraged by other producers—had already formed a company union. Like so many of its peculiar breed, the union was devoted mainly to smoothing things over in a manner favorable to management. Now, however, some of the more restive employees began talking to representatives to the new Screen Cartoonists Guild, which was affiliated with the AFL painters and paperhangers union. Under the goad of this competition, the company union took a somewhat more militant stance toward management, and battle lines were drawn for what Disney later preferred to think of as a jurisdictional strike.

Throughout the thirties, of course, Hollywood had been moving toward the unionization of all sorts of crafts not covered by the traditional theatrical unions, as well as toward the strengthening of many weaker labor unions. Indeed, the transformation of one of these, the Screen Actors Guild, from a tiny and ineffectual debating society into a tough and powerful union was not without its moments of high and hilarious drama. Early in the depression the actors had taken voluntary paycuts, believing the producers when they said the cuts were necessary to avoid layoffs. Shortly thereafter, layoffs were instituted anyway, and the actors, led by such worthies as the Marx Brothers, Frank Morgan and Eddie Cantor, fired off a two-thousand-word telegram to President Roosevelt, detailing their grievances and bringing considerable public pressure to bear on the producers. The actors managed to get Guild shops at all the studios by the simple expedient of having a delegation, headed by Robert Montgomery, who was the Guild's president, and Franchot Tone, call on Louis B. Mayer and present him with an ultimatum: grant the Guild shop immediately or face a strike the next day. Mayer had plenty of arguments to muster against his polo-coat proletariat: he was in the middle of a bridge game, he had two hundred guests for lunch, a number of his fellow producers were at the racetrack and therefore unreachable for polling on their intent in the matter. Worst of all, it was Sunday and therefore there was no secretarial help to draw up an agreement. The unionists were made of stern stuff, however—and as many have testified, it took stern stuff to stand up to Mayer—so they eventually came away with a hand-written document of surrender from the biggest of the big bosses. The scene was not exactly reminiscent of Walter Reuther's battle with Ford's goons at the overpass at River Rouge, but each man fights a different battle and in a style suited to his condition.

Enough has been written about the peculiarities of the class struggle in Hollywood to indicate that no one but its participants or a Yahoo congressman investigating it well after the fact could take it seriously. There is, for example, the well-known story of the status-conscious thousand-dollar-a-week screen actor afraid to enter a party given to raise funds for loyalist Spain because it had been made known that only those in the fifteen-hundred-dollar-a-week-and-above bracket were welcome. There was the leftist screenwriter who slipped a few lines of La Pasionara's into a coach's pep talk in a football movie. There were the words of the more hard-bitten comrades who let it be understood that the writers and directors and stars of Hollywood were valuable for nothing but their guilt-ridden cash—"fat cows to be milked," as one of them put it. There was Daniel Bell's contemptuous summary of the mass-media hacks of the 1930s as slightly feeble intellectual drifters "for whom causes brought excitement, purpose, and, equally important, answers." There was Murray Kempton's cruelly truthful observation that "the slogans, the sweeping formulae, the superficial clangor of Communist culture had a certain fashion in Hollywood precisely because they were two-dimensional appeals to a two-dimensional community." There was, finally, as an ironic footnote, the "Labor Hall of Fame in Hollywood" which *The Nation* published without its tongue getting anywhere near its cheek. On it, in addition to Montgomery, who was later to be Eisenhower's television Svengali, were such luminaries as Joan Crawford, later of the Pepsi-Cola board of directors, Adolphe Menjou, whose latter-day politics would match the elegance of his haberdashery, and George Murphy, the dancer who turned out to have two right feet when he was elected to the U.S. Senate.

However loony the forms of its expression, there is little doubt that the attitude toward politics as it was expressed in the upper strata of the movie colony was as genuine as it was ingenuous and that it exerted its influence on others in the industry who were less well situated economically. The farther down the economic ladder one ventured, the more real the grievances became for film workers. The fact is that many were underpaid and insecure in their jobs, just as their cousins in less glamorous industries were. It is also true that Hollywood, like that other great one-industry, company-dominated town, Detroit, was particularly vicious in its anti-union tactics. In such places, where industry leaders have ready access to one another, a solid management front is easy to create, and the blacklist becomes an appealingly easy weapon to use. Its threat seemed very real to the anonymous craftsmen within the industry whose talents were interchangeable and for whose special individual abilities there was no public demand of the sort that protected the stars and directors who took a stand on the great issues. One man who was active in the formation of the Screen Cartoonists Guild recalls parking his car blocks from the places where meetings were scheduled and then cutting through back streets and over fences and across backyards to make sure that he was not followed and would run into no one who might ask him any embarrassing question about his destination. Maybe it was melodramatic and unnecessary, but such was the mood of the place and the time that it seemed a perfectly sensible precaution to him then—and it still seems so to him now as he looks back upon it.

He, along with others who were members of the Guild, freely admits that, in general, conditions at Disney's studio were better than they were in the animation departments of the other studios, where salaries at the lower levels were sometimes as little as eighteen dollars or twenty dollars a week for people who were by no means beginners in the art and where, of course, working conditions were generally not as good and the work itself was not nearly as interesting or as prestigious. But Disney was to animation what Metro-Goldwyn-Mayer was to movies in general. It was, indeed, despite its comparatively modest size, the General Motors of its field. If it could be organized, the rest of the industry would almost automatically follow its lead. Thus, to some degree, Disney was the victim of his own success.

There were indeed issues at stake that were overripe for resolution, and so organization of a Screen Cartoonist Guild unit at Walt Disney Productions proceeded, to the excessive displeasure of Walter E. Disney. He viewed the organization drive by "outsiders" as a personal insult—an attitude quite blatantly provincial. Throughout the 1930s, as unions of all kinds gathered strength, they penetrated areas where trade unionists had rarely been seen, let alone allowed to share power over wages, hours, working conditions, even hiring and firing, all previously considered management's exclusive prerogative. The larger concerns fought them, yielded grudgingly and slowly, and finally depersonalized their relationship with their employees until today, as it is often pointed out, it is difficult to tell the difference between the executives who represent the great corporations from the union executives who sit across from them at the bargaining table. The issues between them can easily be expressed in the statistics contained in the cost of living index, the company's current balance sheet and the productivity tables. From these encounters the human element has largely been excluded. But the transition to this state of affairs has been much more difficult for the smaller concerns, many of which, like the Disney Studio, were managed by their owners and sometimes by their very founders—men who took a certain pride in knowing most of their employees by their first names, and perhaps even their families and sometimes their personal problems as well. For them, a future of depersonalized employee relations was unimaginable, just as the invasion of outsiders to bargain over matters the owners had always decided unilaterally was unthinkable. Despite his public position, even though he could be hurt by bad labor relations in a way that a backwoods widget manufacturer could not be, even though he could easily have had access to far more sophisticated advice about labor relations than many employers, Disney could not help himself. He reacted to the threat of the Screen Cartoonists Guild like a stern father faced by the rebellion of youth. And in the process he became as a child himself.

Years later, one of the leaders of the strike and a man who had suffered much during and, in particular, after it said, "I don't think Disney was a bad person. I think if he had been left to his own devices he would eventually have recognized the Guild. But he was poorly advised, and he was naïve as far as politics and all related subjects were concerned." The studio's lawyer, Gunther Lessing, is often singled out as the man who influenced Disney to fight the union with such ferocity.

It may also be said, in Disney's defense, that he was under far heavier pressure than many of his employees knew. The layoffs of the period were not lightly undertaken. With *Pinocchio* doing slow business and *Fantasia* an outright box-office flop, with no cash on hand with which to begin large-scale future projects, and with no new credit available, Disney had little choice but to cut back and keep a relatively small staff working on *Bambi* and *The Reluctant Dragon*, the latter a hastily conceived promotional effort, in which two preexisting cartoons were stitched into a live-action script that had actor-writer Robert Benchley taking a wondering tour of the new studio. It was obviously no more than an attempt to get feature-films receipts flowing into the studio as quickly as possible—though of course it did allow Disney the pleasure of showing his latest toy to the world. Disney was, quite simply, hanging on, hoping conditions would improve.

255

His pride, though, did not allow him to admit this to his employees. Instead of talking about his troubles and asking his team (or family, or whatever it was) to help out, he listened to advisers like Lessing who convinced him that the weak young union could not hold out long if he took an intransigent line. At meetings with the men he alternately wheedled ("I only make $200 a week myself") and threatened (if they persisted, he would shut down the whole studio and they would all be out of work together). He even hustled around to the ink and paint department, a large one full of politically and economically unconscious ladies, who were only too willing to take tea with Mr. Disney and listen to his dire predictions of what would happen if the Cartoonists Guild should gain a foothold in his newly created paradise.

What he did not understand was that many of his employees were locked into his psychological condition with him. If he was the father figure, they were, in fact, his spiritual sons. "The strike was a psychological revolt against the father figure," one of them recalls. "We were disappointed in him, in the promise of the big happy studio where everyone would be taken care of that was simply not working out in reality." Instead, all the men saw were layoffs, an assembly-line style of production that promised less rather than more creative freedom, and an industrial design that seemed to have as its goal the ending instead of the encouragement of the old sense of community which had pervaded Hyperion Avenue. Another animator recalls that "Daddy wouldn't talk to us. We had the feeling that if he'd really listen to us, the dream of the paradise for artists would have come true." By the same token, he says that if Disney had taken his men into his confidence about the true state of the company's affairs, they would have been willing to compromise many of their differences with him in the hope of better times to come.

The causes for the strike as they went into the public record are ambiguous. Disney claimed that he was willing to put the whole matter to a vote: in a studio-wide election supervised by the National Labor Relations Board, his employees could choose as their bargaining representative either the Cartoonist Guild or the company-encouraged union, and he would abide by the results. It was his contention that this offer was rejected by Herb Sorrell, who was the organizer for the Guild's parent, the painters and paperhangers union. Sorrell, according to Disney, told him that he had once lost such an election by one vote and that he would not submit to the process again. Disney claimed that Sorrell threatened to "make a dustbowl" of the studio by organizing a secondary boycott against its products. It is possible that he did so, since such techniques were not uncommon and, indeed, were not illegal until the passage of the Taft-Hartley Act. It is also quite possible that the Cartoonists Guild would have lost the bargaining election. The Guild later claimed that about 55 percent of the studio's employees went out on strike, but the figure might have been inflated. In any case, before the vote the relative strength of the unions was very difficult to determine since a large number of employees had signed up with both in order to hedge their bets.

It should, of course, be pointed out that however effective the studio union was made to appear, it was still not a true labor union that could genuinely protect its members in the event of serious difficulty or obtain for them, through collective bargaining, significant improvements in the terms of their employment. Such company-created unions are perfectly legal and they were a device much favored by managements in the 1930s as a way of delaying recognition of genuine unions, even keeping them out entirely. They made the employer look as if he were offering his employees a choice of representation and allowed him to appear before the public as a democratically spirited citizen, awaiting the will of his electorate before deciding an important matter. Legality is not, however, morality, and the number of such company unions that ever attained the stature of a true countervailing force to management is small, if it exists at all.

Nor should it be believed, given the covert pressures that an employer can bring to bear on his workers, that a vote in favor of such a union, even when it is duly certified by a government agency, is a truly fair vote.

Nevertheless, the situation at the Disney Studio might still have been resolved had another series of layoffs not begun. Among those put temporarily out of work there were a suspiciously large number of men who had joined the Cartoonists Guild. This heated the atmosphere considerably, and it reached the boiling point when Disney fired Arthur Babbitt, a gifted animator whom Disney had marked down as a troublemaker. Babbitt had been an executive of the company union and instrumental in getting it to take a tougher line with management when the Cartoonists Guild had come on the scene. He had also had a rather serious personal confrontation with Disney in an attempt to get the producer to adjust the wage differential between himself and his assistant. At the time Babbitt had been making in the neighborhood of three hundred dollars a week, while his assistant had been getting no more than fifty dollars a week. Finally, disgusted with Disney's intractability, he had switched allegiance to the Cartoonists Guild. Shortly thereafter Disney fired him and was foolish enough to state, among the reasons for Babbitt's dismissal, his union activities. Dismissal for this cause was specifically prohibited under the Wagner Labor Relations Act, and the union forthwith took a strike vote, which was overwhelmingly carried, and agreed to go out on May 29, 1941. Contributing to the urgency of the occasion was a rumor—it was true, he later admitted—that Disney was going to lock them out.

At first, he surprised them by keeping the studio open. "Since it wasn't an authorized strike, my artists walked right through the picket line. All of the other union men who worked for me walked through those lines, too—even the musicians. But I was afraid some of my people would get slugged," he later said, justifying his subsequent lockout in humanitarian terms. The union people remember it somewhat differently. They claim that a government mediator worked out a compromise by which the union was granted a substantial share of its demands but only on the proviso that it absorb the strikebreakers of the company union into their own Guild. They refused and only then did Disney shut down, hoping the pressure generated by the general unemployment would force a settlement. In two weeks, he was forced to reopen under legal duress, and the strike dragged on until August—nine weeks in all.

In the beginning, there were friendly relations between the members of both unions. After all, they had shared much, and in good spirits, in the past few years. There was more binding them together than separating them. The good relations did not survive the lockout however. The Guild's refusal to let the other workers join it peacefully and their immediate loss of work in the aftermath of that rejection surely soured the picnic spirit, as someone in management well knew it would. When the studio was reopened, the threat of violence on the picket lines was omnipresent. One day, according to Disney's reminiscences, some members of the company union poured a ring of gasoline around a Guildsman who was manning a bull horn and one of their number stood with a lighted cigarette poised over the gasoline, daring the speaker to repeat something he had just said. On another occasion Disney himself attempted to drive his open Packard through the line. Before the shutdown it had been his habit to wave gaily to the demonstrators, showing that he was unbothered by the situation. This time, however, Babbitt called out to him, "Walt Disney, you ought to be ashamed of yourself." Disney, it is reported, made as if to attack Babbitt physically, and the gate police had to intervene quickly. Some recall that Disney later called out to Babbitt, then struck the boxer's fist-up stance, though it is unclear if he was serious, joking or somewhere in between when he made this gesture. In his attempt to keep up an optimistic front, Disney also had an aerial photo taken of the studio and published in the Los Angeles newspapers. For it, he had all the studio's vehicles moved from their garages to the streets to create an air of unabated activity.

Naturally, the strike against the beloved magic maker of the movies, as the public saw him, was well publicized, and the union was at pains to see to it that would-be patrons of Disney films were aware of the situation in his studio. Rather obviously, no lasting damage was done to the Disney image, and it also seems clear that the "worldwide boycott of his films," which some Disney supporters claimed was Communist-inspired, was more of a fantasy than fact. The Cartoonists Guild did manage to get picket lines up around some of the larger theaters in the major American cities where *The Reluctant Dragon* was playing. (At one of them a group of sympathizers crawled into a dragon costume bearing the legend "The Reluctant Disney" and snake-danced down the street.) The picture was not designed to be a very big hit in the first place; in those labor-conscious days a few patrons undoubtedly passed it by, but their number was not significant. If the strike had a serious effect on any group outside the studio it was on the liberal intellectuals who found this demonstration of their idol's political views at surprising variance with the folkish merits of his films. The contradiction, difficult to digest, signaled the beginning of the end of good relations between the producer and his most articulate appreciators, many of whom had seen in the group creativity of the Disney studio the logical extension of their belief in collective political action of all kinds.

In the end, the mediators settled the strike. "The negotiators gave Herb Sorrell . . . everything he wanted," as Disney saw it. And it was true that the Screen Cartoonists Guild became the bargaining agent for the whole studio, though the union was eventually to undergo a debilitating internal struggle to purge itself of a leftist, possibly Communist-dominated, faction. After that it lost the right to bargain for Disney's employees to a union affiliated with the International Alliance of Theatrical Stage Employees, all of which seemed to justify Disney's belief that he had been, as a friend phrased it "one of the first targets of the Communists in Hollywood."

Talking about the strike many years later, Disney was pleased to point out that Sorrell was later "hauled" before the California Un-American Activities Committee (a notoriously unreliable entity in a notoriously unreliable field) and asked "some pointed questions." He added: "At the time I took photographs of those picket lines and studied those photos. I'd never seen half of those faces. They'd never been near my studio. When I showed them to the FBI and to the investigators for the California Un-American Activities Committee, I was told, 'The fellows in those photos have been in every strike Sorrell has called.' " Many employees who were involved in the strike, however, still resent the implication that they were used or taken over by outside agitators. "There weren't more than three or four leftists in the whole studio," one of them said recently. Their grievances were real and their immediate problem was to ameliorate them. They turned to the only source of help available, and as one of them put it, "Disney should have been the adult in the situation. If he had been, all of us could have had what we wanted."

When he was not choosing to regard the strike as part of the great Communist design for subverting the nation (what better place to start?) Disney was inclined to see it as an ill wind that blew him some good, after all. "It was probably the best thing that ever happened to me," he told his daughter, "for it eventually cleaned house at our studio a lot more thoroughly than I could have done. I didn't have to fire anybody to get rid of the chip-on-the-shoulder boys and the world-owes-me-a-living lads. An elimination process took place I couldn't have forced if I'd wanted to. Our organization sifted down to the steady, dependable people. The others have gone."

This, of course, is utter nonsense. A large percentage of his most independent and creative artists left him after the strike. Not all of them did so in overt protest. Some were drafted away

261

from him after the U.S. entrance into the war; some merely drifted away in search of a better atmosphere in which to exercise their talents. Among them were the group who formed the nucleus of UPA, the little studio that wrested leadership in the animation field from Disney at the end of the war; among them, too, were such gifted cartoonists as Walt Kelly, Sam Cobean and Virgil Partch. It is impossible to say if any or all of them might have stayed on with Disney if the climate of the studio had been more salubrious, but it is clear that the strike irreparably widened a breach that had begun to open long before the picket lines went up. As *Time* said in summary: "Whatever the rights of the affair . . . Walt handled it badly and lost the decision gracelessly." Ironically, the one man Disney was forced to retain was the man whose dismissal precipitated the strike—Arthur Babbitt. He went into the armed forces while his case, alleging unfair labor practices against the studio, went through the courts. At the end of the war, Disney was forced to pay him back salary and to give him back his old job. Babbitt was set to work on a film that, he later said, the studio never intended to produce. But he insisted on carpeting for his office and that it be tacked down so it could not be removed in the dark of some night. He stayed on for two years, then left for another studio—the last of the "chip-on-the-shoulder boys" and, in the opinion of his peers, a great animator, too.

PART NINE

The Long Pause

---

27 *Walt Disney, at his best an inspired comic inventor and teller of fairy stories, lost his stride during the war and has since regained it only at moments.*
        —James Agee, *Comedy's Greatest Era*, 1949

DISNEY WAS AWAY from the studio when the strike was finally settled. The office of Nelson Rockefeller, then coordinator of Latin American Affairs in the State Department, approached Disney with a plan for him to make a goodwill tour of South America. His pictures were extraordinarily popular there, and in these early days of the Good Neighbor Policy and these last days of American neutrality, it was thought that he would be an excellent cultural ambassador. Disney at first demurred. He did not want to make a simple grand tour. Typically, he wanted to have some real work in hand to justify the trip. Besides, the strike was in progress. State suggested, in turn, that he might find something down there about which he could make a movie—maybe several movies. The Department would underwrite each film he made up to fifty thousand dollars and would, no matter what happened, underwrite the traveling expenses of Disney and his party (his wife and seventeen people from the studio eventually accompanied him) in the amount of

263

seventy thousand dollars. They also agreed, as Disney remembered it, to put pressure on federal mediators to get the strike settled. All in all, it was a propitious offer—getting Disney away from the strike scene, which had more than once caused him to weep (whether in rage, frustration or genuine sadness is unclear), and giving him a new project to occupy his mind, a sense of new horizons to conquer.

The therapy worked. And while he was away, Disney did work. He told the American ambassadors to the countries he visited not to entertain him, since he was there on a mission that included no time for play. He set up a little, temporary animation shop in Brazil and invited local artists to drop in and see how the work was done. He even entertained the crowds of fans who followed him about by literally standing on his head, his rather engaging substitute for learning the customary few gracious phrases of greeting and thanks that most dignitaries polish up for visits to lands where they don't know the language. After six weeks in Argentina, Brazil, Chile and Peru, El Groupo, as the Disney party took to calling itself, sailed for home on a leisurely voyage through the Pacific that allowed plenty of time for story conferences on the four short films they decided to make, one for each of the countries they visited.

Arriving back home, Disney found the strike settled. There appears to be little doubt that his removal from the scene and his subsequent distraction into new directions cooled his passions considerably. And, removing the object of their love and hate cooled those of the strikers too. There were some personal awkwardnesses to overcome, but by and large the studio was functioning well by the time Disney returned.

Some say, in fact, that it functioned better than it ever had while the boss was absent. They point to the speed and ease and inexpensiveness with which a little film called *Dumbo* was finished in this period. There were no delays while Disney would wrestle over each story point, each gag, each piece of design that flowed from the artists' desks. It may be observed that, whatever the reasons, *Dumbo* was the least pretentious as well as the least costly of Disney's animated features. Only sixty-four minutes long, it told the comic tale of a baby circus elephant rejected by his peers because of his enormous ears, then raised to stardom after he learns to fly by using the outsize appendages as wings. Based on a contemporary children's story (published by the Roll-A-Book publishers), *Dumbo* carried far less cultural weight than the major Disney films that had preceded it, and the artists seemed grateful to be relieved of the burden. Their work recaptured some of the freshness, exuberance and innocence of the short cartoons as well as their pure and simple fun. The gossipy lady elephants who attend the baby's birth and then reject him for being different are good, satirical versions of a standard comic device, the tongue-wagging middle-aged, middle-class feminine moralist. The hugeness of the beasts contrasted gorgeously with the smallness of their souls. The scene in which these giant creatures attempt to construct a pyramid of pachyderms for a new act, all the while bitching to one another about their weight and clumsiness, is a delightfully funny one, a high point in the Disney *oeuvre*.

There was one distasteful moment in the film. The crows who teach Dumbo to fly are too obviously Negro caricatures. It held its terrors, too, among them a storm sequence, a drunken revel by the clowns (some strikers have claimed that the strikebreakers, while working on it in their absence, caricatured strike leaders in the scene) and the enforced separation of Dumbo from his mother. Enraged by the snickers of some little boys observing Dumbo in the menagerie tent, she spanks one of them soundly with her trunk, setting off a panic in the crowd, then turns on the keepers, who try to quiet her. In effect falsely charged with having reverted to the wild state, she is isolated and locked up, away from Dumbo, in a prison-like boxcar. The scene in which she runs amuck is not, in itself, terrifying, but her fate is, particularly to small children who tend to have a strong anxiety about separation from their mothers. A matinee audience, dominated by small children, tends to stir very uneasily over this sequence. It is the most overt statement of a theme that is implicit in almost all the Disney features—the absence of the mother. Very often she is either dead before the film begins or dies while it is in progress (as in *Bambi*) or is represented by a substitute—the cruel stepmother. It is, of course, true that the absence of one or both parents is one of the long-lived conventions of children's literature and that much of the material Disney naturally worked with deliberately dispenses with adults (the freedom implied by their absence is as delicious in a child's fantasy as the terror of their absence in real life is authentic). In this context, it seems fruitless to criticize Disney for adhering to convention. What is worth remarking, in passing, is the similar absence of his own mother in any of his reminiscences. His father, however difficult his relationship with him, was a force in Disney's life. His mother seems rarely to have been present.

Disney resisted blandishments to lengthen *Dumbo* and thus make it easier to sell as a feature. It went out to the world short and modest in its demands, and Bosley Crowther was pleased to note that "this time Mr. Disney and his genii have kept themselves within comfortable, familiar bounds." The result, he thought, was "the most genial, the most endearing, the most completely precious cartoon film ever to emerge from the magical brushes of Walt Disney's wonder-working artists." Otis Ferguson in *The New Republic* was equally enthusiastic. "Every time that you think the Disney studio can't do any more because they have done everything, they turn around and do it again, the new and never dreamed of, the thing lovely and touching and gay. . . ."

Another magazine praised *Dumbo* "for its freedom from the puppeteering of *Snow White*, the savage satire of *Pinocchio*, the artiness of *Fantasia*, and the woolgathering of *The Reluctant Dragon*," and added that "seldom has Disney articulated his characters so aptly." By Christmas Dumbo was, as *Time* put it, "all over the place. His name was up in lights on some 200 cinemansions, he was getting a big play in big city department stores. Toyland was his without a struggle. He was selling giant green peas and bottles of ink, gasoline and women's collars. As a children's book, he was sensational—50,000 copies at $1 each." "Dumbo," the magazine noted, "could only have happened here. Among all the grim and forbidding visages of A.D. 1941, his guileless, homely face is the face of a true man of good will. He may not become a U.S. folk hero, but he is certainly the mammal-of-the-year."

In short, the film was a hit. It was, perhaps, impossible for Disney to score as heavily as he had with *Snow White*, now that the novelty had worn off; and surely the fact that the U.S. entered World War II on December 7, 1941, some six weeks after *Dumbo*'s release, hurt it as well as all the other movies then in release. But in relation to its $700,000 cost—one-half to one-third of the normal cost of a Disney animated feature—it did very well, but not well enough to rescue Disney from his accumulated debts.

Neither did *Bambi*. It finally went into release in the summer of 1942, five years after it was begun. It grossed only $1.23 million, more than a million dollars less than its cost. To date, the film has grossed $28.4 million domestically, but in 1942 its future potential at the box office was no help to Disney. Neither was an extremely perceptive review of the film that appeared in *The New York Times*. Signed only with the initials "T.S." it stated that *Bambi* "left at least one grown-up more than a little disappointed. . . . Mr. Disney has again revealed a discouraging tendency to trespass beyond the bounds of cartoon fantasy into the tight naturalism of magazine illustration. His painted forest is hardly to be distinguished from the real forest . . . in 'Jungle Book' [the film, starring Sabu, was in release at the same time]. His central characters are as naturalistically drawn as possible. The free and whimsical cartoon caricatures have made way for a closer resemblance to life, which the camera can show better. Mr. Disney seems intent on moving from art to artiness . . . in trying to achieve a real-life naturalism [he] is faced with the necessity of meeting those standards, and if he does, why have cartoons at all? One cannot combine naturalism with cartoon fantasy. . . . [It] throws into relief the failure of pen and brush to catch the fluent movement of real photography . . . . In his search for perfection Mr. Disney has come perilously close to tossing away his whole world of cartoon fantasy."

The failure of the film cannot be laid to the indifference of critics. Most reviews were far kinder than the one in the *Times*, and in any case, critical evaluation was—and is—largely irrelevant to the performance of Disney films at the box office. The trouble appears to have been that a woodland fancy was simply too distant from the immediate concerns of his audience. They wanted escape, all right, but they wanted a different variety from what Disney seemed to be offering. They wanted realistic-*seeming* war dramas or, in a lighter vein, the straight comedies and musical comedies that were such staples during the war years. For Disney, *Bambi* represented the end of an era. He made only one animated feature—*Victory Through Air Power*—between *Bambi* and the release of *Cinderella* in 1950, and that, of course, was a special project, far out of his usual line. By the time he got around to *Cinderella* he had transformed his operation from one devoted completely to animation to one in which animation was becoming only a sideline.

The war years, seemingly unkind to Disney, were actually of tremendous significance to him. Surely he lost his original stride, as Agee said, but he was provided with the time to experiment with a new one—live action—and to contemplate entirely new directions, thanks to a flow of government contracts for training and propaganda films of all sorts. These did not return large sums of money to Disney, but they did keep cash flowing through his studio, allowing him to keep it open and to keep his name before the public at a moment when it was entirely possible that, without this subsidy, he might have been forced to shut up shop entirely.

Since he was a man who prized his freedom of enterprise, it cannot be said that Disney suffered gladly his enforced relationships with the various bureaucracies of the government. Indeed, the harassments and the financial embarrassments to which they subjected him undoubtedly deepened his inbred distrust of big government. His first contact with Washington after the outbreak of war was, in fact, downright unpleasant. On December 8, 1941, Disney received a call from his studio manager telling him that the army had commandeered a portion of his studio as headquarters for a seven-hundred-man antiaircraft unit assigned to man the guns protecting the defense plants of the Los Angeles area. Without so much as a by-your-leave they moved in, took over Disney's only sound stage to use as a repair shop (like all such stages it could be sealed against light leaking in or out, which meant the shop could run at full capacity during blackouts) and stayed for seven months. The army is, if nothing else, almost as compulsively neat and tidy about its domiciles as Disney was, but the intrusion of so many strangers on his lot, not to mention the business of identification passes and armed sentries, must have galled him.

The hard-outline precision possible in animation makes it an ideal educational medium, and the government was quick to realize its potential. On the day the soldiers moved out of his studio, Disney received a call from the Navy, offering him a contract to produce a series of films dealing with aircraft spotting, a serious matter for fighting men and an innocent way to occupy small stay-at-home boys whose traditional game of identifying the new model cars had been, perforce, suspended for the duration. Disney managed to make a 10 percent profit on the eighty-thousand-dollar contract, and he was able to deliver the first film within the ninety-day deadline it specified. By the time the series was complete, Disney had contracts for all sorts of educational films—directed at pilots, navigators, nurses, technicians of every kind. He did four hours' worth of films on the care and use of the Norden bombsight alone, a series on the topography of the islands to be hit by the marines in the South Pacific campaign, another on the causes and prevention of airplane crashes. Within a single year he turned out four hundred thousand feet of government films. While he was adapting a tome called *The Rules of the Nautical Road as Applied to Ship Traffic in Harbours and Confined Areas*, he even permitted its technical advisor to sleep in one of the two offices in his suite, where, he later recalled, the officer ran a tight ship—even to the extent of doing his laundry on the premises.

Perhaps Disney's most famous contribution to the war effort was a short subject commissioned by the Treasury Department, which under the new tax law of 1942 and the upsurge of wartime prosperity had suddenly placed fifteen million new taxpayers on its rolls. It was anxious to persuade them into voluntary cooperation rather than alienate them by a heavy emphasis on its powers to force compliance. Disney rushed to Washington for conferences, rushed home to begin planning the film, which starred Donald Duck, then rushed back east with story boards just prior to beginning its animation. These he was obligated to show the Secretary of the Treasury, Henry J. Morgenthau, Jr., acting out the dialogue as he showed the drawings.

Morgenthau was a banker, which did nothing to endear him to Disney, and he was unimpressed. He had hoped Disney would create a new character, a sort of Mr. Average Taxpayer, who would take a somewhat more sober tack than the duck did in dramatizing the virtues of paying taxes in full and on time. Disney argued for making the painful business seem to be as much fun as possible. The Secretary countered by claiming that he did not like Donald Duck. There are at least two versions of Disney's reply, but in effect he noted with some heat that his giving the Treasury the duck was the equivalent of M-G-M's giving the Treasury Clark Gable; he was the studio's top star.

Disney added that because the duck would be going out into the theaters in a film that was to be supplied free, receipts from his other Duck shorts, which had to be rented at full fees, would be hurt. Morgenthau finally yielded, and *The New Spirit* went into production.

At the same time Disney started another Duck film which, though it had no formal connection with the government, was certainly intended as propaganda. Originally titled *In Nutzy Land*, later known as *Der Fuhrer's Face* (after the title song), it won an Academy Award; it contained the studio's major contribution to the country's arsenal of propaganda: the sound of flatulence. "We heil [Bronx cheer], heil [Bronx cheer], right in der Fuhrer's face."

Except for *Der Fuhrer's Face*, Disney's predictions of the effect of *The New Spirit* on the receipts of other Duck cartoons proved more or less correct and, more galling, the Treasury Department did not pay its full bill for the cost of the film. Disney had obtained from it a letter of intent calling for return of his expenses, which came to $47,000, and in addition, Treasury had to pay Technicolor for prints, which raised its total costs to $80,000. Somehow, however, it could not find the money within the funds Congress already had appropriated for its operations and so had to go back to The Hill with a deficiency appropriation bill to cover a number of projects like Disney's. There it encountered a storm of objections to the $80,000 total. Disney was even accused of being a war profiteer. Ultimately—and largely because the Treasury wanted to use his studio's talents for other projects—a payment of $43,000 was squeezed out to him and he glumly pocketed his loss.

It was by no means the only government contract Disney lost money in fulfilling. He remained, as always, a perfectionist within his special definition of the term, and perfection cannot be achieved on anything but an unlimited cost-plus basis. He kept pushing beyond the cost estimates on which contract terms were based. He was not, after all, an anonymous maker of parts for war matériel—he was Walt Disney, and his government films were to be seen by the people who had been the audience for his commercial films and would be his audience again. He had to keep up standards. The outraged congressmen might have been interested in the figures on one of his most popular wartime activities—the creation of comic insignia for military units. He did some four hundred of them at a cost of twenty-five dollars apiece and received not a dime for the service.

About the only government-supported project that worked out profitably was *Saludos Amigos*. The four short films Disney had planned to make after his South American trip were rejected by the State Department, which claimed that, separately, each film could be released only in the country with which it specifically dealt. He was asked to stitch the four into one impressionistic film covering his entire adventure south of the border. He did so by using the sixteen-millimeter film of his party on tour that he had taken for souvenir and promotional purposes. This linked together the animated sequences dealing with the legends, natives and national characteristics of the places he visited. The result was part travelogue, part fantasy, and it was perhaps, as Howard Barnes put it in a notice that was typical of the general response, "singularly beautiful and diverting as well as a striking bit of propaganda for Pan-American unity." James Agee, just beginning his famous tour of duty as *The Nation*'s film critic, disagreed. Save for "a few infallible bits of slap-stick and one or two kitschy ingenuities with color," he found it depressing. Addressing himself to the intent of the propaganda, he stated that "self-interested, belated ingratiation embarrasses me, and Disney's famous cuteness, however richly it may mirror national infantilism, is hard on my stomach." The merit of the argument between this point of view and the more commonly expressed one of Barnes is now impossible to determine for oneself, since prints are unavailable and a childhood memory is notoriously unreliable, but for Disney the film turned out to be one of the few profitable ventures of the period. It returned almost $1.3 million in grosses.

Taken together with his previous experience with *The Reluctant Dragon*, it also suggested a new possibility to him—the combination of live action with animated cartoons. Perhaps he could retain the profit potential of feature production without losing the magical qualities of the increasingly expensive animation process. It did not bother him that this, in effect, took him back to his technical starting point, the Alice in Cartoonland series. That had been long ago, techniques had improved, and there was a whole new generation from whom the combination film might be a technical novelty of the sort that had proved so successful for him in the past. There was another appeal equally potent in Disney's mind—the chance to make a smooth transition for himself and for his audience to live-action feature production, which he sensed would have to come sometime if he was to maintain a steady flow of films and not have to place all his bets on the relatively small number of animated features he could turn out. "I had to grow with them," he said later. "I couldn't make a live-action feature until I had experience."

After *Saludos Amigos* was launched, he began planning another South American feature, this one to combine live and animated characters in the same sequences. Meantime, he fell prey to the influence of Major Alexander de Seversky, the great proponent of and author of *Victory Through Air Power*, by which De Seversky meant strategic as opposed to tactical (or support) bombing. Disney decided that the major's message was so important that he should finance the film himself, however heavy the further strains it would impose upon his budget and the flack he would encounter from the battleship-oriented navy brass with whom he was also doing business at the time. The curious appeal of strategic air power to people of rightist political leanings has never been analyzed, though it is perhaps not amiss to note that any philosophy that views the human aggre-

gate as a mob incapable of choosing its own destiny and therefore in need of totalitarian leadership can easily be stretched to
accommodate a certain indifference to massive, unselective destruction of that inconvenient mob. Strategic bombing has, possibly, a special appeal to people of a midwestern background,
for whom it may be the reverse coin of the region's traditional
isolationism. Peremptory aggressiveness at long range and in a
manner that spares one the sight of the suffering it causes is a
way of "getting the boys back home" quickly, perhaps even enabling them never to leave. That, of course, is the highest value,
and after all, those who suffer from the strategy are only for-
eigners, not "human beings"—to again borrow the Cheyenne
phrase. In the case of Disney there was, in addition, an appealingly novel technological vision in De Seversky's ideas. Air
power was, to him, efficient power—and, as we have seen, Disney loved efficiency. War fought by planes would, De Seversky
argued, be economically inexpensive compared to the creation
and supply of huge land armies. Best of all, it would save more
lives than it would cost—a dangerous speculation that is, of
course, still accepted as revealed truth by many people, despite
the well-known air force studies of the strategic bombing of
Germany that tend to prove it is the most wildly inefficient form
of mass destruction yet devised.

At any rate, Disney pushed the film out in a hurry, even setting aside his distrust of limited animation under the impress of
urgency. There was a certain massive power in the studio's rendering of sky-blackening flights of planes moving across the
screen and in its loving treatment of machinery of all sorts in
action. But Agee began his review by hoping "Major de Seversky and Walt Disney know what they are talking about, for I
suspect an awful lot of people who see *Victory Through Air
Power* are going to think they do. . . . I had the feeling I was
sold something under pretty high pressure, which I don't enjoy,
and I am staggered by the ease with which such self-confidence,
on matters of such importance, can be blared all over the nation,

without cross-questioning." Beyond this general *caveat*, the critic had some specific reservations, having to do with the film's occasional attempts to be poetic, cute and funny about such a serious subject, in particular "the gay dreams of holocaust at the end."

Agee added: "I noticed, uneasily, that there were no suffering and dying enemy civilians under all those proud promises of bombs; no civilians at all, in fact. Elsewhere, the death-reducing virtues of De Seversky's scheme—if he is right—are mentioned; but that does not solve the problem. It was necessary here either (1) to show bombed civilians in such a manner as to enhance the argument, (2) to omit them entirely, or (3) to show them honestly, which might have complicated an otherwise unhappy sales talk. I am glad method (1) was not used, and of method (3) I realize that animated cartoons so weak—at least as Disney uses them—in the whole human world would be particularly inadequate to human terror, suffering, and death. Even so, I cannot contentedly accept the antiseptic white lies of method (2). The sexless sexiness of Disney's creations have always seemed to me queasy, perhaps in an all-American sense; in strict descent from it is this victory-in-a-vacuum which is so morally simple a matter . . . of machine-eat-machine."

Of the film one could at least say that Disney was, by his own lights, trying to be true to himself and to a belief he held at least strongly enough to back at considerable cost to himself. *The Three Caballeros*, the last of his wartime features, released in January, 1945, did not have even this rudimentary integrity. Agee found, after seeing it, that "a streak of cruelty which I have for years noticed in Walt Disney's productions is now certifiable." Otis L. Guernsey in the New York *Herald Tribune* found it no better than "a variety show with the accent on trick photography and oddities of line and color." There was a certain novelty value in the combination of live actors and cartoon characters in the same scenes, he said, but he found it "difficult to see what Disney has gained in the way of entertainment from this development," particularly since "there is artistic self-consciousness about almost every individual sequence in the film." Even Disney's best critical friend, Bosley Crowther, was somewhat put off by the film. It "dazzles and numbs the senses," he said, "without making any tangible sense."

It is fair to say that the film reflected Disney's own mood. Nothing made sense to him. He had gone, in a decade, from threatened poverty to success of the sort he had dreamed of for many years, then back to a poverty that seemed to promise very little. He now had a large studio, a large payroll and a basic product that was increasingly expensive to create and increasingly dubious as a marketing proposition. He also had stockholders to worry about. Said Walt Disney, "We had to start all over again." Said Roy Disney, "When you go public, it changes your life. Where you were free to do things, you are bound by a lot of conventions—bound to other owners."

"We're through with caviar," Walt Disney declared. "From now on it mashed potatoes and gravy." "His first four post-war features . . . looked like mashed potatoes all right," one magazine commented, "but they didn't bring in much gravy." All were, in one way or another, "musicals," folksy and folkish in a sham sort of way and all contained, as Agee said of the first of them, *Make Mine Music*, "enough genuine charm and imagination and humor . . . to make up perhaps one good average Disney short." The second, *Song of the South*, contained some pleasant animated sequences devoted to Joel Chandler Harris' tales of life in the briar patch, plus a finale in which the darkies gather 'round the big plantation to sing one of Massah's children back to health—a scene sickening both in its patronizing racial sentiment and its sentimentality. Of it, Crowther declared, "More and more, Walt Disney's craftsmen have been loading their feature films with so-called 'live-action' in place of their animated whimsies of the past and by just those proportions has the magic . . . decreased . . . approximately two to one [is] the ratio of its mediocrity to its charm. If he doesn't beware, a huge Tarbaby will snarl his talents worse than poor B'rer Rabbit's limbs." Crowther was undoubtedly unaware of just how snarled Disney was at this moment, but his proportion of mediocrity to charm held for the next two releases, *Fun and Fancy Free* and *Melody Time*, also anthologies of short sequences in which live action and animation were mixed. It was now clear that the tradition that had produced the folk song and story somehow could not be used to vitalize popular art, as many admirers of Disney—and other purveyors of mass art—had hoped might happen. As early as 1944, Louise Bogan, the poet, declared that the folk tradition "has become thoroughly bourgeoisified. At present there is no way for the artist to get at it, for it has been dragged into a region where nothing living or nutritious for its purpose exists." Disney had certainly been one of the bourgeoizifiers and since he had never really known what he was doing culturally, he, particularly, could not find his roots. Between him and his past he had erected a screen on which were projected only his own old movies, the moods and styles of which he mindlessly sought to recapture at cut rates in the bastard cinematic form of the half-animated, half-live-action film.

It must be stated that in the Forties and throughout the Fifties most of the entrepreneurs of mass culture who had any pretentions to the higher things were caught in the same Sargasso Sea, however more or less successful they were than Disney in navigating it. The war years and the postwar years were, preeminently, the years of what came to be called the "middle-brow," and the middle-brow style, which attempted to blend the best elements of folk culture and high culture, nearly always succeeded in meshing their worst elements. These were the years of *Oklahoma!* and *Carousel*, of *Death of a Salesman* and *The Best Years of our Lives*, of "A Ballad for Americans" and the Katherine Dunham dancers, an era in which the rough edges of common speech and experience were poeticized to the advantage of neither our prose nor our poetry. It was an era when our popular writers and performing artists—and many others—groped, with varying degrees of honesty, for what was authentic in the vernacular tradition, but they could not seem to resist smoothing it down, slicking it over, making it just a little more palatable to polite company, never realizing that such ministrations were bound to spoil it and spoil as well the higher forms into which they willy-nilly sought to cram this intractable and essentially formless stuff.

It seemed, one supposes, a patriotic thing to do. And one can say this much for the whole dreary process; it awakened for a few in the audience an awareness that there were any number of precious things in our common heritage. If a few people were led back from the various adaptations of folk material to the original sources, then the business may possibly have been worthwhile. It is also beginning to seem clear that the forced marriage between high culture and low was not quite the calamity that some observers thought it was (and still think it is). The bastardized products continue to roll off the various assembly lines, and many of them continue to achieve an eminence and a prosperity out of all proportion to their merits. But it is becoming increasingly clear that mass popular culture is not necessarily a hybrid form, that it can create forms of its own in its own good time. This is particularly true of movies. The western, the detective story, comedies of certain sorts, even an occasional musical on the order of *Singin' in the Rain*, can transcend whatever backgrounds originally nourished them and become preeminently screen forms, which cannot be rendered as well in any other medium. Similarly, the film has attained, over the comparatively short span of its history, a critical language uniquely its own, one that can be compared only invidiously, in the techniques and effects it describes, to the other arts. A film by an Antonioni, a Truffaut, a Resnais, even a Stanley Kubrick, owes nothing to anything but the history of the cinema. A great deal of the excitement that has stirred our culture in recent years—the McLuhan fad, for example, or the rediscovery of the great silent comedians, even such cultish affairs as the deification of Bogart or the campy delight taken in old Busby Berkeley musicals—testify to this. Whether a mechanized culture can produce works of the lasting value of either the folk tradition it obliterated and now, in fact, succeeds, or of the traditional culture with which it uneasily coexists and may possibly obliterate in its turn, is a serious and open question.

What can certainly be said is that for a brief moment, in the early Thirties, Disney had the opportunity to contribute to the emerging tradition of mechanized, popular culture and that he did indeed make sizable contributions to it when he was working with the characters he and his employees created. It may even be argued, though with a little less certainty, that his feature-length animated adaptations of folk and children's stories were so strongly cinematic in their values that they, too, transcended any sensible comparison with their sources and reached toward a state of pure cinema, at least in their highest moments.

The fact remains, though, that Disney was an untutored man with, as we have seen, a fatal attraction toward the intellectual community in this period. Their regard clearly meant something to him, and prior to announcing for "meat and potatoes," he had tried to satisfy them as well as the simpler demands of his audience and his own primitive taste. He was led astray by them—or more properly by people who posed as intellectuals—in several ways. To begin with, those who might have sprung the mote from his eye—a James Agee, for example—were not available to him. Instead, he mistook someone like Deems Taylor for the genuine intellectual article. Second, he fell prey to the depressing tendency of the time to downgrade the film as film and to think that its elevation as an art form depended on its being ever more tightly tied, through adaptation, to the literary forms—a tendency by no means dead in Hollywood, especially since it has become clear that a hit play or a best-selling novel has a "pre-sold" audience. This blend of cultural insecurity and practical economics has been one of the great hindrances to the development of a more flexible American motion picture style, and Disney, surely, was one of its earliest victims.

At least as important as these practical, immediate factors in the growing estrangement between Disney and the intellectual community was the general intellectual climate of the century. As the English critic Martin Green has summarized it, this climate has grown out of a dialectic between two sensibilities. On the one hand, there is "a spirit of broad general knowledge, national and international planning, optimism about (or at least cheerful businesslike engagement with) the powers of contemporary science and technology, and a philistinism about the more esoteric manifestations of art and religion." Ranged against this possibly majoritarian view of the world is another that "insists on narrow intense knowledge (insights), on the need for personal freedom within the best-planned society, on the dangers of modern science and technology, on the irreducibility of artistic and religious modes." Disney, clearly, held with the first group, the most significant members of the artistic and intellectual community with the second. Looking back, it seems a miracle that they could find common ground for as long as they did. It seems likely that their brief embrace was greatly facilitated by the general interest in science and technology that "scientific" Marxism generated among the intellectuals as well as the rather self-conscious egalitarianism of this group as it attempted to relate itself to the masses, among whom the idea of progress was most widely construed in materialist terms. In any event, this deviation from the true faith was a brief one for the intellectuals, and by the beginning of the postwar era they had returned to their customary suspicion of the values treasured by people like Disney. Disneyland would become a pure expression of his basic faith; their disgusted response to it, a pure expression of theirs. Disney, with his sure grasp of the popular mind, had almost no sense of how the cultivated mind worked. He was dismayed and disgusted by its inability to share his vision and could only bluster at its criticism.

From Disney's point of view, it is fair to say he was unceremoniously dropped by the intellectuals at the very moment he could have most used their help. From being an object of veneration he passed with blinding speed to being an object of scorn, and if, in his later years, he was particularly unpleasant about intellectuals, he may truly be said to have had his good reasons. It was they, not he, who declared his early work to be art; they who informed him that his more self-conscious attempts, as well as the work of his last years, were symbols of all they came to be alienated from in American life. Undoubtedly Disney misunderstood them, but it is equally true that they misunderstood Disney—and never more so than when they most adored his work. This is not an unfamiliar phenomenon; their praise spoiled the great silent comedian Harry Langdon and turned the head of Charles Chaplin, not to mention dozens of other less well-known film makers who had the misfortune to turn out a praiseworthy work or two and the weakness of character to believe their notices. Disney was in a great tradition of mutual misunderstanding.

28 *A winner never quits,
a quitter never wins.*
—Old American saying

IN THE FORTIES, it seemed that everyone had deserted Disney—the intellectual audience and the mass audience. So he paused to grope. It was a long pause. Visiting the Disney Studio in this period, Bosley Crowther gathered the impression that Disney was preparing to withdraw from active participation in his business, make his brother caretaker of such assets as it had and "live . . . happily ever after on television residuals."

Added Crowther: "He seemed totally disinterested in movies and wholly, almost weirdly concerned with the building of a miniature railroad engine and a string of cars in the workshops of the studio. All of his zest for invention, for creating fantasies, seemed to be going into this plaything. I came away feeling sad."

There was no need for sorrow, as Crowther himself later came to realize. What he witnessed was not a man preparing to give up but rather a man gathering strength and ideas for another great leap forward. "The late forties," says a veteran of that period in the studio, as he attempted recently to summarize Disney's mood, "was the time when Walt Disney discovered Walt Disney." One of the ideas he was toying with was, for the first time, hiring established movie stars to appear in his films. "We kept trying to tell him that he himself was a bigger star, a bigger name, than any he could hire, but he had trouble believing us." Fortunately for him, Disney had an equal amount of trouble bringing himself to pay star salaries and granting star billing since, until then, his was the only name that had ever appeared above the title of any of his films. In the end, he did begin to hire well-known names to do the voices for his cartoon features, but that was as far as he went, at least at first. (After live-action features worked out so well for him, he began to use slightly bigger names in them but under a policy that was cruelly, if accurately, summarized by the industry in the phrase, "Disney gets them on the way up or on the way down.")

At the end of his long period of brooding, Disney emerged with a plan that called both for a return to first principles and for diversification. For a start, he determined not to abandon animation but to concentrate the studio's efforts in that area of production on one fully animated feature every three or four years. There would be no more mixture of live action and animation in vaguely focused anthology presentations, though animation might be used occasionally to enhance an essentially live-action feature (as it was in *Mary Poppins*) or there might be live-action sequences in essentially animated films. But films of both sorts would concentrate on telling a single story: there would be no more anthologies. As for the live-action films, they would appear on a much more frequent basis than the animated films, their cost would be carefully controlled, at least in the beginning, they would not be contemporaneous in setting or subject matter, thereby protecting them from dating and thus insuring their rerelease value. As far as short subjects were concerned, work on new cartoons would be phased out, the old ones rereleased (as of 1966 the average Disney color cartoon had been reissued sixteen times, and they have, all told, grossed seventy million dollars. If animated features were risky, short animated films were impossible to make profitably, at least in the full animation technique to which Disney was committed. Replacing them on the current production schedule would be the short nature films on which he had long planned to experiment.

Then there was television. "When the industry was cussing television and trying to ignore it," Roy Disney said later, "Walt moved in and worked with it and made it work for him." This took time, and precise plans crystalized slowly over more than a half-decade. The same may be said of an idea that was, at the time of Disney's retreat into himself, no more than another long-held dream, Disneyland. But its development, now moving again to the forefront of Disney's mind, ultimately hinged, according to Disney himself, on the development of an effective television strategy.

Sometime in the late forties, Disney had it out with his brother on the subject of their future in general and of animated features in particular. Roy Disney was frankly fearful of committing the studio to the risky expense of a full-scale animation

283

project of the kind they had done before the war and was happy to hold on to the modest profits that were beginning to accrue again. Walt Disney, however, was adamant on the need for progress. As he remembered his speech to Roy, it went this way: "If we try to coast, we'll go backward. Let's get back into business or sell out." He demanded financing for what amounted to a five-year production plan, including three new animated features and the schedule of nature shorts. Somehow, Roy managed to find the money, principally by denying the stockholders anything but minimal profits and by plowing the slightly expanding grosses of the late forties back into the business. This was undoubtedly one of the periods Roy Disney had in mind when he said to a reporter: "I just try to keep up with him—and make it pay. I'm afraid if I'd been running this place we would have stopped several times *en route* because of the problems. Walt has the stick-to-itiveness."

In any event, Walt, as usual, got his way. And three animated films were soon on the boards—*Cinderella*, *Alice in Wonderland* and *Peter Pan*. He also had another opportunity to prove his stick-to-itiveness. The exact date on which Walt Disney wandered into the little camera store that a man named Al Milotte was running in Alaska is unrecorded, but Milotte and his wife, Elma, who was a schoolteacher, were enthusiastic semiprofessional movie photographers and apparently Disney had heard of their work. "How would you like to make some pictures for me up here?" Disney inquired, as Milotte recalled later. "I said, 'What kind of pictures?' He said vaguely, 'I don't know—just pictures. Movies. You know—mining, fishing, building roads, the development of Alaska. I guess it will be a documentary or something—you know.' "

Milotte did not, but he went to work anyway. He was soon flooding the studio with film and receiving enigmatic wires in return: "Too many mines. Too many roads. More animals. More Eskimos." More footage was ground out. Then Milotte decided to try an idea he had long harbored, which was to visit the Pribilof Islands, to which fur seals by the thousands mysteriously migrate year after year to fight, mate, bear their children and, from which, when their convention ends, they disappear as mysteriously as they arrived. He explained the notion and received one more wire from Disney. "Shoot fur seals," it read.

He did—for a year—during part of which he lived in igloos with the local Eskimos. Periodically he would ship his footage off to Hollywood, and periodically he would get a wire in return saying, "More seals." In the end he shot miles of film, and in the end Disney emerged with a thirty-minute short he called *Seal Island*.

There are two versions of what happened next, though there is basic agreement that no exhibitor would touch the film. The official version was told by Disney: "My brother Roy phoned me, heartbroken, from New York," he said, " 'Nobody wants to buy it. They all say, "Who wants to look at seals playing house on a bare rock?" ' I said, 'Come back out here, Roy; the sun is shining.' " There is also agreement on what happened next. In 1948 the Disneys got a Pasadena theater owner to play the film, where it attracted good audiences and where, more important, it qualified for a 1949 Academy Award nomination (a film must play a week in the Los Angeles area within the year preceding the awarding of the Oscars). When the film won the prize as the best two-reel short subject of 1948 the exhibitors naturally clamored for bookings—and for more nature films. The difference between the official version and the one told by old studio hands is, in the latters' memories, that Roy Disney agreed with the exhibitors in seeing no future in the project. They say that the morning after Disney won the Academy Award, he trotted around to his brother's office, opened the door and flung the Oscar at the wall above his head.

Whichever story of the beginnings of the nature series is true, it is obvious that Roy Disney quickly began to appreciate the virtues of the series. By ordinary Hollywood standards nature photographers are low-paid craftsmen, and so the short films they turned out were ridiculously inexpensive to shoot, even though the studio had to pay field expenses for as much as a year in order to get enough usable footage to make one short film. And if Disney did not pay the photographers very much, he did provide them with the opportunities and the equipment to pursue their difficult craft in a manner to which they were not ordinarily accustomed. The Milottes, for example, were given a specially reinforced truck in which they could live and from which they could safely photograph wild African animals at ranges closer than anyone ever had before. At one point the Milottes stayed in the truck for sixty days without ever leaving it. An elephant charged it on one occasion and might easily have overturned it had he not been distracted by something at the last moment. On the other hand, at least one pride of lions grew so used to the strange vehicle that they even allowed it to accompany them on nocturnal safaris, on which they were photographed by the light of searchlights—something no one had ever accomplished before. Other photographers were provided with telephoto lenses that could photograph subjects over a mile away or with high-powered arrangements of lenses, automatic cameras and strobe lights that could stop action up to 1/100,-000 second and fill the screen with a shot of a beetle so small that fifty of its breed could hitch a ride on a honey bee's leg.

The tales of the patience and the courage of the cameramen are endless. The Milottes, for example, waited six weeks beside an alligator's egg in order to photograph it hatching. Another time they watched herons for forty days in order to photograph one of them catching a fish within camera range. On yet a third occasion Milotte spent five months stalking a mountain lion to get the footage he wanted. (Even he had his limits, however. Working on *Beaver Valley* he waited weeks to get a close-up of a beaver gnawing down a tree, but as he put it, "Contrary to popular notion, beavers are not always busy. Most of the time they just horse around. I was cold and wet and tired after weeks of watching these clowns and ready to give up when I looked out and saw what I'd been waiting for. I grabbed my camera—and it wasn't loaded." He was so angry he dashed out of his blind, grabbed the sapling, jabbed it back in the ground and ordered the astonished beaver "to do that again, you punk." By the time he had his camera loaded, the beaver was obligingly sawing away at the tree.) Another Disney photographer resorted to the old Indian trick of dressing in a buffalo skin in order to crawl among the herd to get close-ups. He reported some curious sniffings from wiser heads among the animals, but no aggressive behavior. One of his colleagues reported a herd of the great beasts thundered when they moved, just as the cliché had it, "But what I had never heard of was the sibilant, silken swish which accompanies the stampeding buffalo. It was even more terrifying than the thunder."

Disney's policy with the nature photographers was, essentially, the same one he had employed with his animators. He gave them the best equipment, all the time they needed (the ratio between footage shot and footage used in the finished film was about 30 to one), and as he had with animation, he insisted on tight storytelling and, of course, anthropomorphism. Said a writer who worked on the series, "Any time we saw an animal doing something with style or personality—say, a bear scratching its back—we were quick to capitalize on it. Or otters sliding down a riverbank—humorous details to build personality. This anthropomorphism is resented by some people—they say we're putting people into animal suits. But we've always tried to stay within the framework of the real scene. Bears do scratch their backs and otters are playful."

The success of the series of animal shorts led Disney, in the early Fifties, on to another series dealing with "People and Places" and, at last, to the generally well-regarded documentary features, *The Living Desert* and *The Vanishing Prairie*, of 1953 and 1954 respectively. Working on them, Disney had two criteria he always insisted upon. He wanted facts and more facts in the narration. How much does the baby elephant weigh? How old is he? How many animals in the herd?—these were questions of the kind he constantly asked as he screened finished sequences. On the framework of this factuality, however, he insisted upon erecting dramatic structures sometimes whimsical, sometimes terrifying. A sampling of his comments on *The Living Desert* was preserved by the studio and set down by Robert De Roos in his 1963 profile of the man:

"In sequence where tortoises are courting . . .: They look like knights in armor, old knights in battle. Give the audience a music cue, a tongue-in-cheek fanfare. The winner will claim his lady fair . . .

"*Pepsis* wasp and tarantula sequence: Our heavy is the tarantula. Odd that the wasp is decreed by nature to conquer the tarantula. When her time comes to lay eggs she must go out and find a tarantula. Not strength but skill helps her beat Mr. Tarantula.

". . . Our other heavy is the snake. . . . With wasp and tarantula it's a ballet—or more like a couple of wrestlers. The hawk should follow. Tarantula gets his and then Mr. Snake gets his. . . . Should be ballet music. Hawk uses force and violence. One could follow the other and have a different musical theme as contrast."

And so on. *Time* saw what Disney was getting at—"the sense that the camera can take an onlooker into the interior of a vital event, indeed into the pulse of the life-process itself," then added: "Thus far, Disney seems afraid to trust the strength of his material. He primps it with cute comment and dabs at it with flashy cosmetical touches of music. But no matter how hard he tries he can't make mother nature look like what he thinks the public wants: a Hollywood glamor girl. 'Disney has a perverse way,' sighs one observer, 'of finding glorious pearls and then using them for marbles.'"

Reviewing *The Living Desert*, Bosley Crowther was even more severe. He decried the "playful disposition to edit and arrange . . . so that it appears the wild life . . . is behaving in human and civilized ways . . . all very humorous and beguiling. But it isn't true to life." He also detected another current, running alongside the cuteness, which he described as a "repetition of incidents of violence and death" that tended eventually "to stun the keyed-up senses" in such a way that his accumulated impression of the film was one of "a sort of zoological morbidity."

The nature films indeed present one of the most difficult problems of critical evaluation in the entire Disney history. On the one hand, no one can doubt that Disney's photographers did bring back the pearls and that they were displayed in a variety and profusion previously unknown on the theater screens of the world. The short documentary has not had a very distinguished history in the commercial cinema: the Pete Smith specialties and the Fitzpatrick travelogues were the rule rather than the exception. In their sheer technical virtuosity, in their ability to put on the screen rarities and oddities from the natural world, the Disney films were so far above their competition as to deserve a category all to themselves. In them he satisfied the simplest, most basic demand of film making: he gave us a chance to see things we might not otherwise have ever seen. And yet he falsified this material in precisely the ways his critics suggested. The charge that he excessively emphasized the violence of nature does not stand up nearly so well as the charge that he prettified it. Nature is, after all, violent, and all one can say about his handling of its life and death struggles is that it is quite wrong to make a tarantula or a snake into a "heavy," even by implication. There is no moral hierarchy among the species, and the business of "cuing" response through music, narration or film editing that leads to this sort of ranking by the spectator is reprehensible. Just as bad is the business of reducing to a joke a mating ritual, or a young bird's attempts to master flight or a young animal's first experience of the hunt. None of these matters, to put it simply, is funny to the participants, and they would not seem funny to us if we were to observe them unedited, with our own eyes, in the field. They become jokes only when the creatures are anthropomorphized for us by the film maker. The business of individuating animals not only falsifies our understanding of them; in the last analysis, it cheapens experience, substituting patronization for the sense of awe that the truly sensitive observer feels in the presence of nature's enigmas. "Nature," said Henry Beston, one of the most sensitive of contemporary writers on the subject, "is a part of our humanity, and without some awareness and experience of that divine mystery man ceases to be man." In the work of the great naturalists, the more knowledge one gains, the greater one's sense of the ultimate mystery contained in the subject. But in Disney's work a little knowledge becomes a truly dangerous thing, shutting down the subject instead of opening it up, either compartmentalizing it by emphasizing its believe-it-or-not freakishness or cheapening it by making it seem that animals are comically trying to imitate, in their little ways, man's mastery of his environment. The tone of a Disney nature film is nearly always patronizing. It is nearly always summoning us to see how very nicely the humble creatures do, considering that they lack our sophistication and know-how. This attitude does no credit to our humanity as Beston uses the word, and certainly it explains away the necessary, endlessly entrancing mystery far too easily. In any case, anthropomorphism is, literally, child's play. Seeking explanations for phenomena that he cannot comprehend, a child, with his innocent egoism, always invests the objects of his play and observation with the only qualities he knows— those of his own personality. As he grows older he learns that there are other forces in the world beyond his own personality, and education rightly conceived is the process by which he learns to value those forces, mastering and turning to his own uses those that he can, respecting those he cannot. Disney never could seem to learn this simple distinction, and confronted with things that were inexplicable to him, he either turned away in disgust or willfully falsified them by reshaping them in terms that he understood and approved. Much the same thing, had happened in his animated films in which all material was re shaped to suit the limited artistic style he insisted upon, how ever incongruous that style might be to the subject matter.

It can be argued that without this kind of reductionism the series would not have been successful and we would therefore have been denied access to many of the treasures it did contain. This, of course, is always the argument of the popularizer; it is a difficult one to deny, however much one disapproves of it What one can say is that we will never really know its truth until someone actually does an unpatronizing set of nature films for popular consumption (just as until someone tries we will never know if there is an audience for a genuinely serious set of television dramas). At this point all we know for certain is that Disney preempted the field in such a way that it will probably be a long time before anyone tries again and that, if they do try, they will undoubtedly be tempted to imitate his proven formula.

It seems worthwhile to observe that Disney's pattern with the nature series exactly followed the one he had previously established in the cartoon field. Beginning with the relatively modest and unpretentious first efforts, he moved quickly to a greater sophistication of technique and to a more crowded production schedule that had the effect of dominating the market through saturation. Then came the move to features and then, finally, to bastardization. What followed the documentaries were semi-documentaries, the first of which was *Perri*, the biography of a squirrel, in which the animal "stars" had names and virtually human relations with one another. After that came such works as *The Legend of Lobo*, in which a seemingly wild animal was trained by handlers to do tricks that he could not and would not normally do in his wild state but that, of course, the audience did not know were unnatural to him. However entertaining some of these stories were, at the most childlike level, they were fundamentally dishonest—the more so since they partook of the

True-Life Adventure series' reputation for not containing any faked footage.

In any case, the nature films did help Disney to reestablish himself and his studio. They brought him back into the public's consciousness, and they made money. The first two features, for example, cost $300,000 and $400,000 respectively and grossed in their first domestic releases upwards of five million and four million apiece. Along with the five other nature features, they stayed in release for years, continuing to play here and there, now and then, almost constantly and without need of any elaborate or expensive promotion and advertising budget as a True-Life Adventure Film Festival.

The year after he won his Academy Award for *Seal Island* Disney at last made his first complete live-action fictional feature, following Roy's suggestion that he use funds that had been blocked in England. The film was *Treasure Island*, and it featured Robert Newton's superbly funny, scenery-chewing performance as Long John Silver. For it, Disney received the best set of notices he had got since *Pinocchio*, and best of all, he brought it in at a cost low enough to insure a high margin of profit. He returned to England each summer for the next three years to supervise personally the production of sequels—*Robin Hood, The Sword and the Rose*, and *Rob Roy*. As *Time* said "They were all amazingly good in the same way. Each struck exactly the right note of wonder and make-believe. The mood of them all was lithesome, modest. Nobody was trying to make a great picture. The settings in the English countryside were lovely, wide swards and sleepy old castles and glens full of light. Best of all, Disney was careful to choose his principals— Richard Todd, Glynis Johns, Joan Rice, Bobby Driscoll—not for their box-office rating or sexual decibel, but rather as friends are chosen, for their good, human faces and pleasant ways. As a result each of the pictures was just what a children's classic is supposed to be, a breath of healthy air blown in from the meadows of far away and long ago." Indeed, it is possible to say that because of the modesty of their aims these pictures came closer to fulfilling their intentions than any films Disney ever did. Feeling no impetus toward afflatus and, indeed, having every reason to control himself, Disney kept the pictures tight in structure, simple in development. There was nothing to tempt him, as there was in animation, toward the frightening or the fantastic. On the other hand, realism here was simple to achieve—being merely a matter of costuming and set decoration —instead of an essentially insoluble problem in illusion making. In all, there was an air of ease and comfort about the films that was most refreshing.

Undoubtedly the atmosphere of their creation was considerably lightened because the last three were made in a period when it was clear that the trend in the studio was, at long last, an upward one. By the summer of 1950, when *Treasure Island* was released and *Rob Roy* was in production, the potential of the nature series was clearly established and, even more comforting, the studio was in the midst of what Roy Disney later called "our *Cinderella* year." By that he meant that the release of that film had untapped the greatest flow of coin into the box offices since *Snow White*. Indeed, the $4.247 million gross it achieved in its first run actually topped the mark set by Disney's first feature in its first domestic run by some $55,000. Over the years its domestic gross has reached $25.5 million. There were a good many critical reservations about the film, talk of its "full-blown and flowery animation," and its "glamorous style of illustration" toward which "the more esthetic may take some degree of offense." Again, there was dubiousness about the ability of the animators to capture human movement in a satisfying way. But *Cinderella* is, of course, the most famous of all fairy tales, and perhaps more important, the generation that had been enraptured by *Snow White* thirteen years before was now anxious to provide their children with a similar thrill of discovery. In that year, after two years in the red, the company showed a profit and the Disney sales chart began its long upward trend, a trend that, just five years later, was to take it past the ten-million-dollar mark in revenues for the first time and that was to provide it with the funds it needed to lay the groundwork for the truly fantastic growth that was to come in the ten years that followed. The long era of trouble was finally over. For the first time in a decade Walt Disney could definitely say that the worst was past and begin to claim the rewards of survival.

PART TEN

Disney's Land

29 *The moment of* survival *is the moment of power.*
—Elias Canetti, *Crowds and Power*

IT IS A MEASURE of how well things were going for Walt Disney in the early 1950s that the failure of his next animated feature, *Alice in Wonderland*, was not reflected in a downward dip on the gross sales chart of his organization or in a failure to register profits in that year. He personally did not like the film very much, retrospectively grumbling that it "was filled with weird characters." The more he worked with it, the more he came to think of Alice herself as a prim and prissy little person, lacking in humor and entirely too passive in her role in the story. Audiences, he felt, could not identify with her and he could not blame them much: neither could he. He made a little money on *Alice*'s successor, *Peter Pan*, which grossed $24.4 million over the years, though it was no better received critically than *Alice*. In both instances, he later said, he felt trapped by the literary reputations of the works, unable to Disnify them as freely as he could a fairy tale. In both cases the styles in which the tales had been originally told were at least as memorable as the characters or the stories. These three elements were intertwined so tightly that the studio could not successfully substitute its standard style for those of the originals without altering their basic patterns beyond recognition. Somehow, the Disney artists were never able to set the gentle wistfulness of *Peter Pan* on film, somehow they were never able to convey the free, fantastical parody of conventional logic which is the reason for *Alice's* existence and which makes it a work of art. Occasionally the sheer speed of the action in the encounters with Captain Hook, for instance, or the broad humor of the Disney version of the Mad Hatter's tea party, could sweep away—temporarily— one's objections, but the fact is that by this time the studio style was so inflexibly realistic, so harsh and so obviously the product of a factory system, that it was incapable of catching more than the broad outlines of these classics. It simply could not come to grips with their essences, and without those essences, there was very little point either to making the movies or to seeing them.

Indeed, there was something arrogant about the way the studio took over these works. Grist for a mighty mill, they were, in the ineffable Hollywood term, "properties" to do with as the proprietor of the machine would. You could throw jarring popular songs into the brew, you could gag them up, you could sentimentalize them. You had, in short, no obligation to the originals or to the cultural tradition they represented. In fact, when it came to billing, J. M. Barrie's *Peter Pan* somehow became Walt Disney's *Peter Pan*, and Lewis Carroll's *Alice* became Walt Disney's *Alice*. It could be argued that this was a true reflection of what happened to the works in the process of getting to the screen, but the egotism that insists on making another man's work your own through wanton tampering and by advertising claim is not an attractive form of egotism, however it is rationalized. And this kind of annexation was to be a constant in the later life of Disney. The only defense one can enter for him is that of invincible ignorance: he really didn't see what he was doing, didn't know how some people could be offended by it, and certainly could not see that what was basically at fault was his insistence that there was only one true style for the animated film—his style. If he had earlier learned that there are many ways to draw and that some are better suited to a given story than others, then he would not have been forced to jigger every project into a shape his style could handle. Similarly, if he had had some taste for comedy other than the folksy or emotions other than the bathetic, he would not have had to twist stories so radically to fit them for his Procrustean bed. Had he been a more flexible entrepreneur of animation in these later years, he might have fared better with animated features at the box office in the 1950s.

As it was, returns slipped until they reached the nadir in *Sleeping Beauty*, not only the most serious financial failure the organization suffered in this period but the most disastrous artistic failure as well. Paul V. Beckley, writing in the *Herald Tribune*, said that it was "Disney imitating Disney" and "it is not necessarily the best qualities of Disney's earlier work that is [sic] being imitated. . . . The stress is . . . on soft cuteness. Goodness gets itself defined as a form of bumbling innocence with a perky tail-twitching, simpering quality, just as badness becomes unvaryingly sinister, black, slinky, sinuous and grotesque." In short, even returning to the fairy tale form, with which he had been most successful and in which there were few detailed or subtle conventions of literary form to bother him, could not rescue him. Facility had surely grown, but it was a narrow facility and somehow choked off the capacity to feel and the ability—never the strongest element in the studio's work— to express these feelings graphically. In all the later animated products there were plenty of effects but there was little emotional impact.

Of them all, the best was the last that Disney personally had a hand in supervising—his version of *The Jungle Books* of Rudyard Kipling. It is not, of course, for purists. It is based on a selection of stories contained in the original collection, and those stories are compressed and radically rearranged to form a tight, cohesive story. Again, there is no attempt to find a filmic equivalent for the marvelous tone imparted to the original work by Kipling's splendid style (in which mystery and simplicity were blended in a way that never condescended to the child). The jungle animals of India are, in the film, turned into familiar American types making familiar American jokes and singing songs intended for the top of the pop charts. But in terms of the Disney tradition, rather than any literary tradition, the film is remarkably successful. Just 64 minutes long, full of inventive sight gags and innocent high spirits, *The Jungle Books* has a gaiety and a lack of pretentiousness absent from Disney animated features since *Dumbo*. There is almost no striving for effects of high visual art and no attempts—so often disastrous in Disney studio work—to realize any mythic or literary overtones. There aren't even any scary effects of the type parents objected to in the past. It is as if Disney and his craftsmen had finally abandoned the last of their aspirations to make a statement in cultural traditions fundamentally alien to them. In effect, and despite the fact that their starting point was, indeed, a classic of children's literature, they returned here to first principles—they were, like the earliest Disney artists, making just another cartoon.

The performance of the animated features in the Fifties and Sixties seemed to confirm what Disney had suspected before launching them—that their potential return might not be worth the risk. Just five animated features emerged from the Disney studio in the years 1953–68, while in the same period over fifty live-action features were released. To be sure, all five of the animated features appear on *Variety*'s list of the all-time box office champs, but sixteen live-action films from the same period also appear there. What is more significant is that only two of the animated films of this time grossed more than $8 million (*Cinderella*, with $9.25 million in three releases and *Lady and the Tramp*—a 1955 release that was replayed once—with

$8.3 million), he could not forsee that ultimately they would gross as well as his earlier animated features. He could see, though that no less than eight of the live-action films, all made at far less cost made better than $8 million in domestic release. *Sleeping Beauty*, moreover, which grossed $5.3 million in 1960, actually lost so much money that it sent the company into the red that year—the only time that unfashionable color had appeared in the Disney ledgers since 1949. Meantime, live-action features that most people scarcely remember —films like *The Shaggy Dog, The Parent Trap, The Absent-Minded Professor, 20,000 Leagues Under the Sea, Old Yeller, Swiss Family Robinson, Lt. Robin Crusoe, USN, Son of Flubber* and *The Ugly Dachshund*—all performed spectacularly and at virtually no risk. And, of course, *Mary Poppins*, which most people will remember for a long time to come, became Disney's greatest hit, ultimately grossing $45 in the U.S. and Canada alone.

There is really very little point in discussing these movies critically. They are about equally divided between animal stories, children's classics and originals that put a heavy stress on personal inventiveness and family togetherness. *The Shaggy Dog*, released in 1959, has some significance in the Disney canon because it was his first venture into live-action comedy. "I got to thinking," he said later, "'When it comes to comedy, we're the ones'; so we did *The Shaggy Dog*." In its first release it earned nine times its cost of slightly more than one million dollars, a figure that should be compared to the money-losing *Sleeping Beauty* to see why Disney's production schedule changed so radically in the 1950s. The genesis of films like *The Absent-Minded Professor* and its sequel, *Son of Flubber*, was equally simple as Disney told it. "We've always made things fly and defy gravity," he told an interviewer. "Now we've just gone on to flying flivvers, floating football players and bouncing basketball players." Indeed, both of these films, which starred Fred MacMurray, who is to the Disney studio of the 1950s and 1960s what Mickey Mouse was to it in the 1930s (and to whom Disney was devoted as to no other actor since The Mouse), were a little bit better than his average. The hero, an impractically practical, small-town, backyard inventor, is an authentic American folk figure, the sort of person Disney himself admired and may occasionally have thought he was himself, and so there is a little more feeling in the pictures—despite their descent into aimless farcicality and folksiness—than was customary in most of the studio's live-action films. Moreover, the plot line of *The Absent-Minded Professor* is very reminiscent of Disney's own wartime experience with Secretary Morgenthau—the hasty night flight to Washington by the simple, rustic inventor who comes bearing a creation of priceless worth to his government; the rebuff of man and work by uncomprehending bureaucrats, and finally the triumphant moment when the true value of his creation is incontrovertibly proved and the former skeptics tumble over themselves to do him honor. In fact, the entire film might be seen as a symbolic vision of Disney's career as seen from his vantage point.

There were a handful of other reasonably good films in the live-action group. *20,000 Leagues Under the Sea*, for instance, was a superior and, for Disney, quite lavishly produced adventure, with James Mason superbly cast as the mad inventor, Captain Nemo, whose submarine, complete with pipe organ and marvelously plush fittings that combined twentieth-century functionalism with nineteenth-century elegance, was a triumph of the set designer and decorator's art. Nemo was also something of a projection, albeit a dark one, of Disney himself—a lonely man in love with vanished graces and future technology. *Davy Crockett*, a paste-up of three television shows that started one of the great juvenile fads of the decade, turned out to be a pleasantly exuberant adventure story when it reached the theater screens—simple, solid kid stuff—while *The Great Locomotive Chase* was a bit better than that. Based on a true Civil War adventure, in which northern raiders sneaked behind southern lines and made off with a train, it looked to *Herald Tribune* critic William K. Zinsser as if "everybody obviously had a fine time making the movie"—which, given Disney's love of trains, was probably true. Certainly the film had a zestful inventiveness about it, as well as a drive and a tension that one did not often find in the Disney product of this time—possibly because there was no time to pause over the antics of children and animals as so many of his other pictures did.

All these films, however, stood a little bit outside the Disney mainstream. Or Main Street. The place where he operated most comfortably in the late Fifties and early Sixties was the American small town and in the country surrounding it. Admittedly, this locale, as he pictured it, was not unattractive. It was always verdant, and the old houses, with their wide verandas and big front lawns, sitting complacently on their quiet streets, formed an irresistible setting for the little romances and comedies and animal stories that unfolded there at a leisurely pace and in a warm, chuckly tone. Even when he used this setting for a crime story, as he did in *That Darn Cat*, it completely lacked menace. Or modern reality. The small town is today as subject to blight as any other American place: the neon signs blink on and off; cars circle endlessly in search of parking places, causing small-scale traffic jams in the process; the big old houses are converted into apartment buildings or offices for group medical practices; the blare of television and the gunning of hot-rod motors drown out the chirp of crickets in the evening hours. Only in Disney films has it remained unchanged.

Equally unchanged are the characters that inhabit it: the flinty old shopkeeper; the rich, eccentric widow up on the hill; the comically bumbling, heavily impractical, often inventive or idealistic leading man, with his sensible, patient wife or girl friend and their pleasantly bubbling teen-age relatives—children or siblings—who may be prankish but are never delinquent. In these films time has stopped and character has become conventionalized. We feel, when we enter this world, a certain nostalgia and, more than that, a certain comfort. Nothing will surprise us or hurt us or unduly stir our emotions. Comedy is a canoe overturned in the midst of a romantic outing, tragedy is a lost dog, love is a song cue, and villainy is an overpunctilious banker (Disney never tired of satirizing the type).

Disney no more invented the basic situations of the standard situation comedy then he invented animation, but he did take it over as if to the manner born, which, in fact, he was. Indeed, most Americans are. The tradition begins, so far as film is concerned, in the 1930s, with comedies of the sort that Disney's friend, Frank Capra, frequently made—well tooled and tending to demonstrate that you did not have to be as zany or grotesque as the silent comedians and their direct heirs, the Marx Brothers and W. C. Fields, were in order to be funny. Perfectly nice, seemingly normal people could get laughs when they were placed in odd situations. These films were particularly well suited to carrying a light, liberal message about the virtues of the common man—very useful in the depression decade as well as during the war years, when demonstrations of the qualities we were fighting to preserve were in order. Capra's work had the virtue of freshness, while Preston Sturges, the greatest of the directors to work in this tradition, added a note of mordant blackness to it. Other sources also contributed to the conventions of the form—the Andy Hardy pictures, for example, and such excellent radio programs as *Fibber McGee and Molly* and *The Great Gildersleeve*. Within two decades there were few stereotypes left to be cast, few new situations left to be explored. One laughed—if one still attended at all—not in surprise but in recognition of old friends up to their old, familiar tricks once again. Of recent years, shows in this tradition—*The Donna Reed Show, Leave It to Beaver, Dennis the Menace, Hazel*— have even worn out their welcome on television (though the reruns roll on in the daytime and Disney's favorite actor, Fred MacMurray, perseveres in prime time with *My Three Sons*).

The form is kept alive with gimmicks: families that used to be found on Main Street are now *Lost in Space* or they have a son with the second identity of *Mr. Terrific.* This is essentially what Disney did with the form in the movies. The small-town locale, was preserved and many of the subsidiary characters stayed on in it unchanged, but there was usually a gimmick of some sort to enliven things: The Absent-Minded Professor invents Flubber in his garage and thereafter his Model T, fueled on the stuff, can fly; Hollywood's idea of a typical teen-age boy is turned into a shaggy dog; a Siamese cat becomes a detective, and so on. Juvenile fantasies all—but superficially original, "imaginative," as the untutored audience understands that term. And all taking place against a reassuringly ordinary, completely familiar, indeed well-loved, background.

The search for novelty was not always successful. Disney sent his typical American family to Paris in *Bon Voyage* for a change of scene and there Pop (MacMurray) got innocently involved with a prostitute. Somehow Disney let the sequence pass, but it was a disaster: his audience couldn't understand what was happening, he later claimed, and neither could he. The shock to their expectation was simply too rude, and Disney vowed never again to deal in such racy material. Without an enlivening gimmick, however, the films were unbearable instead of merely innocuous—for example, the film released a few days before Disney died, *Follow Me, Boys!* The story of a man who spends some forty years as a small-town scoutmaster though denied children of his own, it is an orgy of sentiment unparalleled in our day and age. The plot is no more than a loose string of incidents; the characters, so bland as to be fully explained the minute they appear on screen. There is nothing to do therefore but exploit the almost saintly goodness of the scoutmaster, his wife and the generations of splendidly upstanding lads he helps to mold. It is incredible, it is smug, it is without any relationship even to historical, let alone contempo-

303

rary, reality. It is, in short, a travesty—unintentional camp and the *reductio ad absurdum* of Disney's strange need to ingratiate himself with the least common denominator of his audience.

In addition to the intrinsic weaknesses of its plot and characterizations, *Follow Me, Boys!* suffered from the effort to puff it up into a major release for the Christmas trade. What might have been barely bearable at the length of an hour and a half was simply excruciating when spread over better than two hours. The film was not quite an imitation *Mary Poppins*, but it was no longer in the mold of, say, *The Absent-Minded Professor.* To see just how the Disney product could suffer from a fully conscious attempt to have, as Roy Disney put it in 1967, "at least one *Mary Poppins* every year," viewers had to wait until the following Yuletide season when *The Happiest Millionaire* came crashing down on them. Based on Kyle Crichton's modest little play of the same title (which was, in turn, based on the reminiscences of her father that Cordelia Biddle Duke wrote with Crichton's aid), the film was a nightmarish blending of dull songs, flat family comedy, fraudulent period charm and insipid juvenile romance, directed by Norman Tokar—a contract craftsman at the studio—as if twenty years of movie history had never happened. Fred MacMurray, a modestly gifted *farceur* in the romantic comedies of his youth, an amiable enough presence in more middle-class surroundings, was unable to capture the Wodehousian nuttiness of an aristocratic eccentric and received precious little help in the attempt from either direction or script (both of which had been supervised by Disney). Greer Garson played his wife as a curious blend of Mrs. Miniver and Mrs. Roosevelt, Tommy Steele's unquestioned talent and energy were not effectively governed in the role of a supposedly comic butler, and Lesley Ann Warren and John Davidson were simply blah as the young lovers. In short, this would have been a badly blighted product in the best of circumstances, but as a major production—again well over two hours long—which for a time the studio had hoped to release as a hard-ticket, road-show attraction, it became positively offensive. Here, perhaps more than in *Mary Poppins*, Disney and his people could be faulted for rounding off the principal character's eccentricities until he was reduced to a veritable nubbin of ordinariness. Worse, they put before their public something quite rare for the studio—a truly dishonorable failure. In the past, at least, it could be said that films like *Fantasia*, or the nature films failed, despite at least partially honorable intentions because the studio lacked the intellectual sophistication to realize all the values inherent in their subjects, or that the little live-action comedies failed for lack of ambition. But *The Happiest Millionaire* failed for the most cynical of all reasons—it was a wretched attempt to imitate merely the success—not the spirit—of a previous hit.

Again, as in the case of MacMurray's scoutmaster in *Follow Me, Boys!*, the film's chief interest lay in its projection of an aspect of Disney's own character in one of the leading parts. This time we had a vision of Disney as a young man (John Davidson's juvenile lead) monomaniacally pursuing a new technological breakthrough. This youth's dream was not the advancement of the animated cartoon but the automobile, and like the historical Disney, he was capable of ignoring even the girl he loved when a new idea—an innovative braking or carbureting system, for example—suddenly occurred to him. He even had a ghastly song, an unbeat hymn to "Detroit" ("you can hear it humming, you can feel it coming") with which to express his faith in the future. The last shot in the film is, indeed, of the young couple putt-putting along in their car with the towers of the Motor City rising out of the smog in front of them and a great orange sun rising above the pollution. To Americans of 1967, for whom the car has turned from a wonder to a maiming, environment-destroying nightmare, the scene is incredible in its naïveté. Disney films are usually out of touch with reality, but rarely as directly opposed to it as this one was.

Most of his live-action films were not so actively offensive as

The Happiest Millionaire. But they were all, one way or an·other, too cozy, too bland, too comfortable and comforting. In the best American culture, high and low, there is always expressed, one way or another, a wild surmise. Sometimes it is, as music critic Wilfrid Mellers expressed it, "a Whitmanesque energy and comprehensiveness, an ubiquitous love of humanity and of every facet of the visible and tactile world." Sometimes the American creator "is a solitary, alone with Nature, seeking a transcendental order within the flux of reality." Whichever direction he turns, however, the effect is the same. One senses in his work the vast spaces of the land, the loneliness of the individual lost in that space and trying to find meaning in his isolation. True, Disney was only an entrepreneur of low-level popular art, of family entertainment. But one catches a glimpse, an overtone, a perhaps unthinking hint of the American nightmare in all kinds of popular work no more elevated in its intentions than his—in the good westerns and in the adventures of the private eyes, in the surreal comedies of the Marx Brothers, in the vicious parodies of bourgeois longing that W. C. Fields used to make, surely in the wanderings of Chaplin's Tramp. How was it that Disney could never bring himself—or at least allow his employees—to allude to these great and constant themes of our culture? Why did he, by preference, huddle in the small town or on the farm, forted up, as it were, against wild beasts and the skulking Indians of the American imagination? The answer is, perhaps, clear by this time, and it is, of course, the clue to his popularity as purveyor of entertainment as well as to his ultimate failure as an artist after the decent promise of his beginning. He was heir, of course, to the puritan spirit, defined by William Carlos Williams as "a tough littleness to carry them through the cold" and as a religious zeal—"not a thrust upward to the sun, but a stroke in: the confinement of the tomb." In short, he feared man as he feared nature. As he sought to deny the mystery of the latter by anthropomorphism—that is, by relating it to the more familiar patterns of human behavior—so he denied the former its infinite possibilities by reducing it to comic clichés, by imitating old imitations of life. And so he passed, at last, beyond—or beneath—criticism. In the last decade and a half, the success or failure of a Disney film in no way depended upon reviews or upon the magic or lack of magic of some combination of stars and story. It existed quite outside such factors, which normally weigh so heavily upon the heads of the film industry's chieftains in these parlous times. Pressed by a reporter to explain what he thought might be the deciding factor in the success or failure of a Disney film, E. Cardon Walker, the tough-minded Disney vice president in charge of merchandising, confessed that he had no easy answers. Titles, he thought, had something to do with it. *Savage Sam*, for example, was a perfectly good dog story of the sort the studio had previously done well with, but it flopped. Walker thought people probably were misled into thinking that it might not be quite the warm, whimsical, wonderful sort of a tale about a pooch they liked to see. Even the Disney name could not pull it over the top. Similarly in the case of *The Moonspinners*, the adventure-mystery sounded unlike Disney's customary concoction, so they skipped it. *Pollyanna*, on the other hand, has come to have an unfortunately oversticky connotation, and all the studio's efforts to convince people that its version of the old story was nothing like the image they had in their heads were to no avail. (Nor indeed did the studio convince the star, Hayley Mills, who played the title role and recalled recently, in a New York *Times* interview, that she enjoyed working for Disney in five films "but those films were very restricting. Conveyor belt jobs. So goody-good, you know? And there was this image I created which was hideous. I wasn't supposed to be seen drinking or buying cigarettes or smoking in public. The reasoning was that the audiences for the Disney films were very young and if they saw me smoking eight cigars a day, why shouldn't they?") Walker was inclined to be philosophical about all this. So long as he has a strong film for Christmas release, usually one that has what are known in the trade as "production values" —*i.e.*, an expensive look—and a film that has a solid appeal to teen-agers for the summer drive-in trade, he can be reasonably sure of having a good year. Around these, the studio tends to tuck one animated "classic," a double feature bill composed of rereleases of the more successful live-action films and one or two minor new pictures done on very tight budgets (often one of these will be a two-or three-part television project that looks strong enough for theatrical release and can always be placed on the TV show a couple of years later anyway).

That this pattern worked was because it was a pattern, a predictable schedule of films on a fairly narrow range of subjects and directed at two well-defined movie markets—the so-called family market, which was essentially a youthful one, still taking its young children to the movies rather than sending them off alone, and the teen-age market, which in these still simple days demanded only broad farce and sanitized romance conducted by actors who looked to be the audiences' contemporaries. Such audiences responsive to gimmicks and twists but not to excessively novel or challenging material—a posture that suited Disney very well. If one of his films flopped in these markets, the loss was not high and the chances were that later in the year something else, for its own somewhat mysterious reasons, would recoup the modest failure that preceded it. From 1950 through 1966 no less than twenty-one Disney features grossed more than four million dollars apiece, an average of slightly more than one a year. It is as risk-free a way of making movies as anyone ever devised.

It did not, however, spring into being overnight. And it is doubtful if it would have become as successful as it did without several developments that occured in 1953 and 1954. The first of these was the formation of Disney's own distribution subsidiary, Buena Vista, named after the street on which the studio's main gate is situated. The company was largely Roy Disney's invention, and he was motivated largely by the reluctance of

Disney's long-time distributor, RKO Radio, to get behind *The Living Desert* with suitable enthusiasm and by a similar lack of interest among RKO's competitors. In addition, the Disneys had long chafed under the heavy percentage of their grosses that went to their distributors, even though the 30 percent RKO was getting was close to rock bottom in the industry. By setting up the lean Buena Vista operation, the Disney people cut distribution costs to 15 percent of the gross and, equally important, gained direct control over the handling of their films in the market. They could keep them off double-feature bills where they might be paired with products deemed unsuitable to them, and they could begin to package entire programs, consisting, for example, of a feature, a cartoon and a nature film, which usually ran a bit longer than the usual short subject and was thus often hard to wedge into other people's programs. Compared to the other events of this decade in Disney's land, the founding of Buena Vista was not very glamorous or exciting, but it did represent, for the Disneys, the final step in gaining complete control of their own destiny, complete freedom from interference by outsiders in the creation and exploitation of their products. It also, of course, symbolized their rise out of the ranks of the independents to a status in every way coequal with the major Hollywood production companies, which had all along had their own distribution arms. Most important of all, the studio was able to time the release of its films so that they could most effectively be coordinated with ancillary activities (*i.e.*, the big film is released in a period where television-viewing is at a peak, and more people are likely to see the commercials for it). The studio also gained a very valuable form of self-protection: no one will ever be able to sell out a Disney product at a discount or in a hurry merely to improve the distributor's cash flow, a problem that constantly besets the independent producer.

The other important development of 1954 was Disney's entrance into television. Unlike other Hollywood producers, he was quite unafraid of the new medium. It was, after all, only a new technology applied to the business of entertaining large numbers of people, and new technologies in this area had never been anything but good for Walter E. Disney. His immediate goal, however, was not the exploitation of his movies but of what one observer called "the world's biggest toy for the world's biggest boy"—an amusement park of a quality and a dimension no one but Disney and a few associates could quite envision.

Through the years he had continued to nourish his notion of a new kind of amusement park, and in the outwardly fallow postwar period he had begun to doodle plans for what his brother continued to regard as another of "Walt's screwy ideas," principally because Disney, as usual, had trouble in logically articulating just what he had in mind and just how his amusement park would be different from all other amusement parks. All he knew for certain was that he did not want to imitate the existing pattern because, as he had discovered when visiting them with his daughters years before, they were "dirty, phoney places, run by tough-looking people." There was, he said, "a need for something new, but I didn't know what it was."

By 1952 he had some ideas roughed out, and using ten thousand dollars of the studio's money—all, apparently, that Roy would give him—and such money as he could raise on his life insurance, he had commissioned "plans, drawings, designs and models" for a park, which he had already christened "Disneyland." In that same year he set up WED Enterprises and recruited for it a small staff of designers, quickly, and with a typically Disneyian disregard for the niceties of language, dubbed "Imagineers." In that same year the Stanford Research Institute was commissioned to conduct an analysis of the sites available for the park within the Los Angeles area. Among the criteria it drew up to aid in its search, the most important was that the parcel be large enough to accommodate a preexisting ground plan, without crowding. In addition, the Stanford people were told to study the desirability of the neighborhood, the price of the land, available utilities, topography, population trends, freeway patterns, summer and winter temperatures, tax rates, zoning and even the number of days per year when the smog might settle so heavily on the magic kingdom as to rob it of its magic (Pacific Ocean Park, the largest traditional amusement park in Los Angeles, lost far too many profitable nights of operation, in Disney's opinion, because of smog).

The Stanford study ruled out anything within the more densely populated areas of Los Angeles because land costs were too high, and the San Fernando Valley was climatically all wrong—too hot too much of the time. That left Orange County, south of the main population center, as the best bet. Land was still cheap there—it was given over mostly to orange groves—and the maps of the highway planners showed the half-completed, half-projected Santa Ana Freeway reaching out in the right direction and, indeed, passing along one of the borders of a site the researchers thought met most of their other criteria reasonably well. This was a parcel of small orange groves near Anaheim, a town that owed its limited fame to nightly mention in the frost warnings broadcast on local radio stations for the benefit of fruit ranchers and to Jack Benny's radio writers who made a national gag out of an imaginary train route running through the heart of the citrus country—"Anaheim, Azuza and Cucamonga." The advantage of the site was that it would be no more than twenty-seven minutes from the Los Angeles city hall once the freeway was finished. Its disadvantage was that the 160 acres it encompassed—it has since grown to 185 acres—were owned by no less than twenty families.

Negotiations with them consumed the better part of two years, and as is customary in assembling properties piecemeal, the asking prices of the owners immediately shot far above what was customary in the neighborhood. One family even struck a unique deal with Disney, demanding as a condition of sale that he preserve in perpetuity two stately palm trees of sentimental value to them. (Luckily they stood in an area designated for "Adventureland" and so form part of the tropical background for the well-known African riverboat ride there.) Another family home, a pleasant example of the Spanish mission style of architecture, was also preserved and became an administration building for the park.

But even as the land was being purchased, Disney was running into other problems. Early in 1954, the year he had scheduled for the beginning of building, Disney sent four staffers off on an around-the-country tour looking for ideas at established amusement parks and the firms that manufactured equipment for them. The only idea on which they found general agreement was that Disney was crazy. You could not, their informants said, have an amusement park without a roller coaster, a ferris wheel or barkers to shill the customers into the various attractions. Nor were they optimistic about Disney's plan to bar outdoor hot-dog stands and the sale of beer just because he did not like the smells these enterprises created on hot, still days. The equipment manufacturers were especially frustrating, according to one of the surveyors. They wanted to sell Disney their standard-model thrill machines and were totally indifferent to the Disney group's pleas for something new. "I can remember only two or three of the long-time amusement operators who offered any encouragement at all," one member of the team said later.

That was two or three more visionaries than Disney encountered in the financial community. Everywhere he went in search of the minimum of seventeen million dollars he needed to start building, he was reminded that, if anything, the outdoor amusement business was a cultural anachronism that had already declined into senility. Even with his plans laid before them, the bankers could not see what Disney was talking about. Once again, in his phrase, "they stepped on my neck."

Some funds were acquired by a unique leasing arrangement with concessionaires. Thirty-two firms, among them some of the great names in American industry as well as some of the best-known purveyors of food and drink, expressed a willingness to open exhibitions and restaurants in the projected park, which proved again Henry Ford's dictum that managers have a sense of imagination infinitely more venturesome than that of the financial community. Disney insisted that they sign five-year leases and pay the first and fifth year's rent in advance. This provided him with some ready cash, and he found it easy to get more by turning the unpaid but safely anchored portions of the leases over to the banks as collateral for loans.

This was still not enough, however, to begin construction. And that was where television entered the picture. "I saw that if I was ever going to have my park," he told an interviewer, "here, at last, was a way to tell millions of people about it—with TV." It was perhaps a little more complicated than that. What happened was that he concluded a deal with American Broadcasting Company–Paramount Theatres, Inc., under which he agreed to produce, for seven years, a weekly one-hour television program, to be called "Disneyland," on which he would be free to promote liberally not only his amusement park but his films. Distinctly the third network at the time, ABC desperately needed Disney's name and skills, so much so that as an obvious *quid pro quo*, but under an entirely separate arrangement, ABC–Paramount agreed to purchase 34.48 percent of the shares of Disneyland, Inc., a new firm chartered in 1951. Western Printing and Lithographing, the large firm that has published almost all the books and comic books bearing the Disney imprimatur since the 1930s, took 13.8 percent of the new firm's stock, and by this time, Walt Disney Productions was rich enough to be able to afford 34.48 percent. Disney himself retained the twenty-four hundred shares that had been, in 1953, the entire outstanding stock of Disneyland. They had a par value of $100, represented 16.55 percent of the new firm and were considered recompense for his independent work in developing the concept of Disneyland. Another one hundred shares went to WED Enterprises in return for that holding company's license to use the Disney name on the park and the TV show.

Even in this tight spot, the Disneys drove a hard bargain. Both ABC–Paramount and Western Printing had to give Productions an option to buy their shares at par value plus 5 percent per year, an option that Productions began to exercise in 1957, just two years after the park's official opening. The last of ABC-Paramount's holdings were bought out in 1961, but at the considerably higher price of $1,500 a share. Meantime, the ABC network quickly discovered it had two hits on its hands— its newly acquired stock and its new television program. When *Disneyland* went on the network in the fall of 1954 it quickly climbed into the top ten of the Nielsen ratings, and it and its successor on NBC, *Walt Disney's Wonderful World of Color*, have stayed there, or close to it, ever since. In his first year on television, Disney won an Emmy for *Underseas Adventure*, hardly more than a promotion piece for his most expensive live-action film to date, *20,000 Leagues Under the Sea*, describing the process and problems of underwater photography. By no means coincidentally the film became the biggest grosser to that time of any of Disney's live-action features, totalling $6.815 million in its first release and adding another $5 million or so in various releases. As for Disneyland itself, after a full season of promotion on television, followed by an opening day that was also televised nationally, it was almost instantly a success. Very quickly it came to be regarded as one of the wonders of the modern world, both by visitors to the premises who have included, according to its publicity department, which is maniacal about such matters, eleven kings and queens, twenty-four heads of democratic states and twenty-seven royal princes and princesses—and by the once-indifferent financial community, which is impressed by properties capable of grossing $195 million in ten years, as Disneyland did, and capable of financing, out of its own pocket, $33 million worth of expansion in the same period. Grosses and similarly financed expansions in the same amounts are projected for the five-year period ending in 1971.

There are many humorous stories about the opening of Disneyland—of how the toy Dumbos that were supposed to fly on wires over the park weighed a skein-snapping 700 pounds apiece when they were delivered; of how the rivers snaking endlessly through the park ran dry immediately after the water was pumped in and had to be rebottomed with clay to hold the moisture, of how extra crews had to be worked around the clock in the two weeks before the park opened in order to have it ready on time and of how concrete was still being poured as the TV cameras were set up to record the great day (there were thirty thousand invited guests in the park for it). So it must have been a fretful Disney who stepped before the microphones and cameras on July 18, 1955, to promise that "Disneyland will never be completed, as long as there is imagination left in the world."

Still, one can also imagine a deeper satisfaction underlying whatever minor impatiences and disappointments he felt that day. For he was opening something that was far more than a whimsy or a modest sideline to his other endeavors. Disneyland, to him, was a living monument to himself and his ideas of what constituted the good, true and beautiful in this world. It was a projection, on a gigantic scale, of his personality. If not quite an extension of man, in the McLuhanesque sense of the term, then surely an extension of *a* man in the way that the pleasant grounds of Versailles were an extension of The Sun King. It has none of the discreet impersonality of, say, Rockefeller Center. It was, and is, a statement containing, in general and in particular, conscious expressions of everything that was important to Disney, unconscious expressions of everything that had shaped his personality and of a good many things that had, for good and ill, shaped all of us who are Americans born of this century.

Very simply, it was, in every sense, the capstone of a career and a life. Very possibly it is the capstone of a time and a place as well.

30 *Shows there will certainly be in great variety in the modern civilization ahead, very wonderful blendings of thought, music and vision; but except by way of archeological revival, I can see no footlights, proscenium, prompter's box, playwright and painted players there.*

—H. G. Wells,
A Modern Utopia (1905)

THE CAPSTONE OF A career very quickly became the cornerstone of an empire. In the first six months of its existence in 1955 slightly more than a million people visited Disneyland, and Productions that year grossed over $25 million for the first time in its history. In 1956, Disneyland's first full year, about three million people passed through its gates, producing gross revenues of $10 million, its share of which helped send Walt Disney Productions past the $30-million mark in revenues for the first time. Thereafter, word of mouth and the publicity machinery spread the news of the glories of Disneyland, and with the park itself generating the capital to finance a vast expansion (abetted by tax laws that encourage fast depreciation), the curves on all the charts shot upward. By 1959, Productions was trending close to the $60-million line in its grosses. Every time the park expanded its capacity, revenues increased more than proportionately to the added capital.

The figures were undoubtedly gratifying to Walt Disney— an omen of a stability he had not known before. But they were, it seems, of no consequence in comparison to the joys he found in the park itself. Stephen Birmingham, the novelist, captured

316

Disney's feeling for the park very well when he wrote: "Walt feels about Disneyland the way a young mother feels about her first baby. He coddles it, pampers it, fusses at it, bathes it, dresses it, undresses it, peers at it from all directions—and boasts of its latest accomplishments to anyone who will listen. He has even fitted himself out with a tiny apartment in Disneyland—above the fire house on Main Street—decorated it like a jewel box in red plush and velours and furnished it with gaslight era antiques, just so, if necessary, he can be near Disneyland when it sleeps. He keeps his own twin-engine plane and pilot and as often as twice a week, flies over Disneyland to check on his darling from the sky."

The stories of his compulsion to keep the place perfectly groomed at all times are legion. All day long sanitation men dressed in costumes appropriate to their assigned area prowl the streets, picking up litter, so that the slovenly habits of the "guests" (who are never called customers) will not be apparent. Every night every street and walkway is thoroughly hosed down, and crews armed with putty knives get down on hands and knees to scrape up carelessly discarded chewing gum. Even the targets in the shooting galleries, dulled by the previous days shots, are repainted. Every year some 800,000 plants are replaced because Disney refused to put up signs asking his "guests" not to trample them. All of this cuts profit margins as a cost accountant normally calculates them, but it adds immeasurably to the appeal of the place and undoubtedly contributes to the astonishing fact that 50 percent of the people who enter the gates are returnees.

The staff is as well scrubbed as the grounds and is so polite and well mannered that by the end of the day a visitor's face muscles begin to ache from the effort of returning so many smiles and murmuring so many return pleasantries. There are twenty-three hundred permanent employees; in the peak summer months that figure doubles. Known in the ineffable jargon of the park as "people specialists," all must spend a few hard days in the "University of Disneyland," which trains them in the modern American arts forms—pioneered by the airlines—of the frozen smile and the canned answer delivered with enough spontaneity to make it seem unprogramed. Many of the summer people are college and high school students who bring a certain natural exuberance to their work and whose salary expectations are no higher than were those of the apprentices in Disney's old studio art school. All are carefully schooled in good grooming and good manners, as defined by local custom, and crammed full of the facts, figures and folksy anecdotes that comprise the lore of the place. Some measure of the prevailing institutional tone may be gathered from the university's textbook: "We love to entertain kings and queens, but the vital thing to remember is this: *Every* guest receives the VIP treatment." Or, "Disneyland is a first name place. The only 'Mr.' here is 'Mr. Toad.' . . . It's not just important to be friendly and courteous to the public, it's essential." Or, in a more philosophical vein: "Show business is fun and fulfilling and rewarding. But it is also an exacting endeavor which requires the toughest form of personal discipline. . . .

"At Disneyland we get tired, but never bored, and even if it is a rough day, we appear happy. You've got to have an honest smile. It's got to come from within. And to accomplish this you've got to develop a sense of humor and a genuine interest in people. If nothing else helps, remember that you get paid for smiling. . . ."

The Disneyland staff has a place for every human variety except the traditional carnie type, but as its director of personnel told one visiting reporter, every effort is made to scrub the rough edges off: "No bright nail polish, no bouffants. No heavy perfume or jewelry, no unshined shoes, no low spirits. No corny raffishness, yet the ability to call the boss by his first name without flinching. That's a natural look that doesn't grow quite as naturally as everybody thinks."

As a result, the people specialists tend to present a rather standardized appearance. The girls are generally blonde, blue-eyed and self-effacing, all looking as if they stepped out of an ad for California sportswear and are heading for suburban motherhood. The boys, who pilot vehicles and help you on and off rides, are outdoorsy, All-American types, the kind of vacuously pleasant lad your mother was always telling you to imitate. If the interviews and the personality tests every Disneyland job applicant must undergo suggest that a young man is more than usually outgoing—more of a ham—then he may get a job as a talker on one of the rides like the jungle boat ride, on which the spiel both enhances the drama of the occasion and also, because it has an ironic twist to it, constantly reminds the overimpressionable that all is artifice. Even the cops at Disneyland are a new breed—generally moonlighting schoolteachers, with physical-education instructors predominant among them.

Disney himself once commented: "The first year I leased out the parking concession, brought in the usual security guards —things like that. But I soon realized my mistake. I couldn't have outside help and still get over my idea of hospitality. So now we recruit and train every one of our employees. I tell the security officers, for instance, that they are never to consider themselves cops. They are there to help people. . . . It's like a fine restaurant. Once you get the policy going, it grows."

The aim of the staff is to keep everyone in a spending mood without ever once overtly suggesting that Disneyland is, in the last analysis, hardly a charitable enterprise. The trick is not to harass the visitor into spending but rather to relax him to the point where the inner guardians of his frugality are lulled into semiconsciousness. It works; the average expenditure is $6.50 per person per visit—making a day at Disneyland no cheap excursion for the family. The spending process is eased by books of discount tickets that are effectively and extensively promoted. Priced at various levels, they are available at the entrance and all contain tickets of different denominations that may be evenly exchanged for rides and attractions.

Thus, money, well known to be dirty stuff, is not exchanged every time the family decides to embark on a new adventure, and Dad is freed of the gathering annoyance of repeatedly groping for his hip pocket. Indeed, quite the opposite effect is created. The family feels an impetus to get the full benefit of its bargain by using all its tickets before leaving the park. Officials say that the only consistent complaint they receive comes from those whose spirits are willing but whose flesh weakens before they have used up their tickets. But that, of course, is their problem, not Disneyland's. Since they have received an automatic 20 percent discount by buying the ticket books and they probably have fewer than 20 percent of their tickets left at the end of the day, the chances are that they have come out a little bit ahead anyway. The unspent tickets, in any case, remain redeemable throughout the year.

The park's general design further enhances one's willingness to contribute to its economic well-being. There are plenty of shade trees and much greenery and, psychologically most important of all, lots of cool water in ponds and lakes and rivers, all of which are man-made. As many rides as possible move on water. As a result, one is never oppressed by heat or by the dust and dirt that inhabit most amusement parks. Equally pleasant, all the walks are wide enough to accommodate large numbers of people without any sense of crowding or jostling, and there is little anxiety, therefore, that a small child may be lost or hurt in the press of people. The walks curve gently under the trees and beside the waters, encouraging a strolling pace, a sense of ease and well-being that is utterly unique in the context of an amusement park. The layout also encourages a sense of discovery that, in turn, encourages impulse buying. One is forever turning a corner and coming upon some previously unnoticed marvel that cries out for investigation.

Once committed to such an investigation, the visitor will generally find that the line at the entrance is far shorter than he is used to finding in public places of amusement. The "imagineers" have broken the usual single line into many short lines by an arrangement of railings that neatly, and without a word needing to be spoken, divide the patrons into small groups who are then kept moving through a sort of maze until they reach their destination. If it is a ride, they will discover that the vehicle, instead of having one or two entrances, has one for each row of seats and that the rows exactly match the number of exits from the waiting maze. An attendant gives you a firm hand into the vehicle, which helps prevent accidents, seems a polite thing to do and, incidentally, speeds the loading process. The whole thing is a marvel of technology applied to mass psychology. People simply feel better if the line they are in is short and if it is constantly moving. And the management increases turnover, and therefore its take, with no need to resort to the depressing advice to step lively, keep moving, don't push, that so often marks the effort to find recreation in these overcrowded times. Disneyland is, on this basic level, one of the most intelligently conceived pieces of architecture in America and one well worth the study of anybody faced with the problem of creating structures to serve large numbers of people comfortably but with no loss of efficient revenue production.

But one has come to expect nothing less than the best from Disney in technical matters. Once one yields to the rage for order, however, it is difficult to know when its demands become excessive. This is particularly true in the case of Disneyland, where the audience is an integral part of the show and where the proprietor has gone to extraordinary efforts to provide for its convenience. The next logical step is some sort of visa control at the frontier of the magic kingdom, assuring that visitors meet the same standards of dress and decorum that the staff maintains. A small start in this direction has been made on those nights when the park remains open after its normal closing hour to serve as the host for all-night high school graduation parties. A way of turning idle hours to profit, and also providing youngsters with a safe, supervised environment for their revels, the idea has added to the park's revenues and has been gratefully received by parents. But boys are required to wear coats and ties on these occasions, and anyone eccentrically dressed is turned away at the gates. The young men are also frisked to see that they are carrying neither weapons nor liquor into the Magic Kingdom. One understands the problem facing the management and yet one resents its solution. Why should the innocent majority be subjected to this humiliation, however briefly and discreetly it is carried out, because of excessive corporate fear of a group it acknowledges is a distinct minority in the teen-age subculture? Why, indeed, is the American middle class so preoccupied by the current fantasy of mass juvenile delinquency? Why does it insist upon alienating the law-abiding majority of youngsters by treating them as if they, too, are potential revolutionaries? Why this excessive concern with such superficialities as hair style and dress when the creation of genuine understanding and sympathy between the generations receives so little concern? These questions are beyond the scope of this book, but the unthinking embrace of the conventional wisdom about youth by Disneyland is further evidence of its almost maniacal desire to keep the eccentricities of individualized expression—right down to the details of dress and verbal expression by its staff—away from its door. If it could, one suspects that it would try to force all its visitors into patterns its founder regarded as suitably nice.

The contents of the park present a more difficult critical problem than its style of hospitality. Though Disneyland is a circle divided into five sections, each representing an area of thought or fantasy of great significance to Walt Disney, there is only one entrance to the park, and its location compels the visitor to pass through a turn-of-the-century American Main Street, an idealized vision of Disney's boyhood environment. Beyond it is a central plaza with main avenues leading to four lands. Tomorrowland is, of course, a monument to Disney's delight in technological progress. Fantasyland allows one to step into the environments made familiar by Disney's animated films and which, like them, remind one that, imaginatively, Disney has remained always something of a child. Adventureland is, of all the areas, the one least closely tied to Disney's own psychology and creations, but it nevertheless represents an ageless and universal dream of exploration. Finally, Frontierland, with its western street and its river, not only captures the standard American nostalgia for free land and a free life but also contains two attractions that are obviously derived from Disney's boyhood fantasies in Missouri. One is a river steamer, setting of *Steamboat Willie*, and, of course, a dream of grandeur shared by many midwestern boys and often movingly expressed by the writer after whom Disney named his large scale model, Mark Twain. The *Twain*, along with some Indian war canoes, some "Mike Fink" keelboats, some "Tom Sawyer" rafts and the strangely out-of-place model of the *circa* 1790 sailing ship *Columbia*, circumnavigates (on tracks hidden under the water) "Tom Sawyer's Island." This, according to employees, is the only attraction in the park that Disney designed completely by himself. Everything on it—a play fort, log cabins, a string of pack mules you can ride—is free. "I put in all the things I wanted to do as a kid—and couldn't," Disney once told a reporter. "Including getting into something free."

Throughout the park there is, as Aubrey Menen, the Anglo-Indian novelist, observed, a masterful matching of scales and proportions to the psychological content of the fantasy environments. For example, Main Street. "It's not apparent at a casual glance that this street is only a scale model," Disney said once. "We had every brick and shingle and gas lamp made five-eighths true size. This costs more, but made the street a toy, and the imagination can play more freely with a toy. Besides, people like to think their world is somehow more grown up than Papa's was." Menen noted that there was even more subtlety to Main Street's design than this simple reduction in scale. A trick was played with proportions as well. "Everything on the first

323

floor was as it should be. . . . But above them were windows that were too small; above them, again, were gables that were smaller still. The reduction in size as one's eye traveled upward was so beautifully done that it was almost imperceptible."

Moving on through Frontierland and Fantasyland, he observed a similar sensitivity to the uses of proportion in different ways. The bears and the Indians on Tom Sawyer's Island are, he noted, full size; the fairytale creations in Fantasyland are on the tiniest possible scale. He comments: "There are two kinds of legends: with one sort we can get inside them; with the other we are all spectators. I suppose there can be no American male who's not, at some time in his life, found himself alone in the countryside and explored Tom Sawyer's Island or fought Indians or crept on his belly up to a paleface fort. But nobody, I think, at any age plays water rat and toad, or goes in a mole's house, or plays Prince Charming or Cinderella (unless driven to it by sentimental elders). These stories are too complete to have room for the outsider. We should know what to say to Pinocchio if we met him, or the Three Ugly Sisters. But we do not imagine ourselves as being these people. A lesser man than Disney would not realize this. But here Tom Sawyer's island is big enough for children to play on; and Pinocchio's village is so small there is not even room in its street to put one's foot. Once again Disney shows himself a master of the use of proportion."

It must not be assumed that the pleasures of Disneyland are only a matter of such artifices. The bobsled run around and through the scale model Matterhorn (which is big enough to contain in its bowels a basketball court for the use of off-duty employees) is as thrilling a ride as anyone is ever likely to take in an amusement park, a vast improvement on the rollercoaster, which is strictly an up-and-down thing. The Matterhorn ride produces not only dips and rises but hairpin turns as well. The submarine ride in Tomorrowland gives a generally satisfactory impression of a trip underwater: a giant squid and an octopus fight it out just beyond the portholes, the ship scrapes along beneath a polar ice cap and past a sunken pirate treasure ship and even rocks alarmingly when a squall comes up suddenly. Throughout there is realistic-sounding dialogue between captain and crew on the intercom; the oily smell of machinery at close quarters pervades the air, and there is a deliciously claustrophobic quality to the experience—not enough to frighten you, but just enough to jerk you out of the attempt to remain a detached, nonparticipant observer of the fantasy.

It is possible, in a single day in Disneyland, for the visitor not just to see but to enter into time and experience past and time and experience future, to recapitulate not only his own memories and fantasies but those of the race as well. He can visit, impressionistically, every continent of the globe, its mountain heights and ocean depths as well as almost any historical epoch, including the prehistoric. In the revised Tomorrowland he can now even gain an impression of interstellar travel on a ride that simulates such astronautical experiences as weightlessness. It is therefore sometimes possible to feel that Disneyland is best summarized as a model of the "global village" Marshall McLuhan is always talking about, a place where one can literally touch, smell and see, in an instant, and almost as easily as turning around, some representation of the thoughts and experiences that have made us what we are, some representation of the thoughts, traditions and styles that made our fellow villagers.

If that is too fanciful a description of the place or too weighty a one, it is certainly possible to see in Disneyland one of the best mixed-media shows ever devised, an unconscious—and, of course, simplified—vision based on the tradition that, in the higher arts, has been known as modernism. In this tradition, as Arnold Hauser puts it, "The dream becomes the paradigm of the whole world-picture, in which reality and unreality, logic and fantasy, the banality and sublimation of existence, form an indissoluble and inexplicable unity. . . . Art is seized by a real mania for totality. It seems possible to bring everything into relationship with everything else, everything seems to include within itself the law of the whole. . . . The accent is now on the simultaneity of the contents of consciousness, the immanence of the past in the present, the constant flowing together of the different periods of time . . . the impossibility of differentiating and defining the media in which the mind moves."

Disney surely wanted Disneyland to be perceived as a work of art. He was very careful to protect it from intrusions by the outside world. He threw an earthen bank fifteen feet high around it so that nothing of its surroundings could be seen from inside; he spent fourteen thousand dollars removing telephone poles from sight and burying the lines. He even found himself temporarily dismayed by the free-enterprise system as a result of his insistence on keeping the world out. He had originally planned to buy power for the park from the local, municipally owned power plant, but then he was approached by a utilities magnate who observed that Disney ought to be true to his economic principles, avoid the taint of socialism and buy his electricity from a privately owned firm. Disney agreed and the company began bringing in lines from a considerable distance. To his horror Disney discovered that they were mounted on huge, ugly poles that seemed to be marching, marching, marching down upon his art object. "I stood in the middle of *my* park and all I could see were high tension lines," he recalled. "It was awful." The company refused to bury the lines unless Disney paid the cost, which he naturally did.

To Disney, Disneyland was the greatest of all his statements, and he could never let it rest until the end of his life, because it was his. His. His. In the first decade of the park's existence he spent thirty-six million dollars over and above the initial investment, and there were plans to spend another forty-five million dollars over the next five years. By 1966 the number of major attractions at Disneyland had risen from twenty-two to forty-eight, and the end was not yet in sight. "For twenty years I've wanted something of my own," Disney said in 1963. "I worry about my pictures, but if anything goes wrong in the park, I just tear it down and put it right."

It is perhaps a measure of his unfamiliarity with the ways of the artist that Disney took this attitude toward his great work. The drive of the artist must always be toward completion, toward an end to the agony of creation. It is impossible, psychologically, to sustain creativity endlessly. But Disney, obsessed with the perfection of this peculiar vision of his, could not help but go on and on trying to improve it. Indeed, in his mind, the great virtue of Disneyland might have been that it could be ever improved. Unlike his movies, which perforce he had to let go out into the world regretfully, Disneyland was pinned down in time and place and could not avoid his endless ministrations, any more than he could avoid being reminded of its existence. It could not avoid him, he could not avoid it. The dream was thus a nightmare. Indeed, it was worse than a nightmare, the effects of which the light of day can sometimes dispel and the passage of time can surely blunt. So he huddled over the thing, changing it, expanding it, improving it, if not absolutely, then in his own eyes. As a result, what was genuinely good about it was somewhat advanced, but what was bad about it grew more and more obvious.

From the start there had been occasional critiques of the place from wandering literary minds who, as usual, saw the place darkly, through the glasses of their attitudes, and therefore quite lost their balance. For example, Julian Halévy's 1958 piece in *The Nation* correctly summarized the elements in the park that must make any objective observer a little queasy, then noted:

"As in the Disney movies, the whole world, the universe, and all man's striving for dominion over self and nature, have been reduced to a sickening blend of cheap formulas packaged to sell. Romance, Adventure, Fantasy, Science are ballyhooed and marketed: life is bright colored, clean, cute, titivating, safe, mediocre, inoffensive to the lowest common denominator, and somehow poignantly inhuman. The mythology glorified in TV and Hollywood's B films has been given too solid flesh. By some Gresham's law of bad art driving out good, the whole of Southern California and the nation indivisibly is affected. The invitation and challenge of real living is abandoned. It doesn't sell tickets. It's dangerous and offensive. Give 'em mumbo-jumbo. One feels our whole mass culture heading up the dark river to the source—that heart of darkness where Mr. Disney traffics in pastel-trinketed evil for gold and ivory.

"But the overwhelming feeling that one carries away is sadness for the empty lives which accept such tawdry substitutes. On the river boat, I heard a woman exclaim glowingly to her husband, 'What imagination they have!' He nodded, and the pathetic gladness that illuminated his face as a papier-maché crocodile sank beneath the muddy surface of the ditch was a grim indictment of the way of life for which this feeble sham represented escape and adventure."

There is truth in these observations, but it is not a carefully observed truth. It is important to note that the alligator is, technologically far advanced over papier-maché—it is a very, very good imitation of the real thing, and one can respond, legitimately, to the quality of its craftsmanship. Nor is the ditch muddy. It is sparkling clean—and that represents progress over Coney Island. Nor can one blame Disney for the impoverishment of our national mental life. It is indeed sad that we generally do not have the time, money and courage to venture up the real Amazon in search of authentic experience, but what age has? Finally, it is an absolute error to impute cynicism to Disney in the creation and operation of his empire. He always wanted to make money with anything he did. But he always gave fair value, so far as he could see, in return. Indeed, to many the best part of his success was precisely that he did make money without seeming to compromise his vision. It proved, to these impressionable souls that there was something magical in the American air causing art and commerce to blend most wonderfully.

DISNEY'S LAND

In a later piece in *The Nation* John Bright caught perfectly the secret of Disney's success with mass man. "To call him a genius, as his sycophants do, is not only absurd; it is unenlightening. I think the man's unique success can be understood only by reference to his personal non-uniqueness. Of all the activists of public diversion, Uncle Walt was the one most precisely in the American midstream—in taste and morality, attitudes and opinions, prides and prejudices. The revealing clue is his familiar (and utterly sincere) statement that he never made a picture he didn't want his family to see. His competitors made pictures they thought, or guessed, the public wanted to see. Disney operated through maximal *identification* with John Doe; the others seek to discover what John Doe is like in order to cater to him.

"The celebrated Disney inventiveness is the x-factor in the success story. The key to this might be found in his immaturity, or not realized maturity—not used here in the pejorative sense. Walt, growing from infant to child to youngster, to adult, to uncle, and granduncle, never abandoned the delights and preoccupations of each stage of development, as most of us have done, at least in part. That was his 'genius.' Disneyland could have been created only a by a man-child who never tired of toys or shed the belief that animals and insects have human attributes."

Time once put this curious case of psychological arrest, and its results, in a good metaphor: "He has no mind or time for the niggling refinements of taste. There is too much to be seen and done, too many wonderful things in the world. . . . Away he rushes with his intellectual pockets full of toads and baby bunnies and thousand leggers, and plunges eagerly into every new thicket of ideas he comes across. Often enough he emerges in radiant triumph, bearing the aesthetic equivalent of a rusty beer can or an old suspender. They are treasures to Walt and somehow his wonder and delight in the things he discovers make them treasures to millions who know how dearly come by are such things as wonder and delight."

329

The point is that he had the courage to proclaim the childlike quality of his imagination for all the world to see, and that, frankly, was more than his audience ever did. They hide their happiness over the opportunity he provided for controlled regression behind middle-class styles and attitudes and thus avoid damaging admissions about the true nature of the Disneyland experience. The lady that Halévy overheard praising the "imagination" of the jungle ride's alligator was using a favorite method of disguising the truth of what she felt. There is nothing at all imaginative about the ride itself: we have all seen it in a hundred movies and television shows, fictional and documentary. The ride gives us nothing deeper intellectually or emotionally than we get from either the big or the tiny screen. To go beyond that Disney and his "imagineers" would have had to create, in three dimensions, an objective correlative to the mood of terror Conrad invokes, through means that are in the last analysis inexplicable and therefore inimitable, in *Heart of Darkness*. Not only is art of that quality unreproduceable technologically, it is also quite unwanted by most people.

When the lady on the boat ride spoke of imagination she meant something quite different from what a literary critic does. She meant that the technical imitation, the piece of machinery, if you will, is "imaginatively" put together—which it is (all home craftsmen and backyard tinkerers purely love Disneyland for precisely this reason). She does not mean by the word an intensification, through art, of experience, either inner or worldly, to an exciting and therefore agitating level. What the average, middle-class American wants and has always wanted of art and of the objects he mistakes for art, is the fake alligator that thrills but never threatens, that may be appreciated for the cleverness with which it approximates the real thing but that carries no psychological or poetic overtones. "By golly, that Disney—he sure could have fooled me," chuckles Dad as the boatman-guide blasts the steel and plastic thing with a blank cartridge and they all head for Schweitzer Falls just

330

around the bend, where a few passengers will be lightly touched by spray that is at least created out of real water. It's all over in a minute, just the way the scary part in the movie is, and you carry away not some dark phantom that may rise up someday to haunt you but an appreciation of the special-effects man's skill.

At that simple level Disneyland is as harmless as any other amusement available in the country (whether we have entirely too many amusements available is another question entirely). What is frustrating about it is that it is not better than it is, that just when something has about captured you, caused you willingly to suspend disbelief, the "imagineers" rudely nudge you awake and whisper, "Just kidding, folks." On the submarine ride, for example, all is going reasonably realistically, when the ship suddenly glides past a mermaid and the trip is spoiled by the intrusion of this obviously fictional creature. (One cannot help but notice also that though she is bare-breasted, she lacks nipples.) Another example: there is a train ride—an adaptation of the New York World's Fair "Magic Skyway"—that takes you past extremely artful dioramas, showing various geological ages. When the age of the dinosaurs is reached, there are excellent moving models of the great creatures, far more artfully done than any you are likely to encounter in a museum. But then you notice the baby tyrannosaurs represented as just breaking out of their eggs, and, wonder of wonders, they are cuddly and adorable. The dear round bottom of one is wiggling comically as he shakes off his shell. The message, apparently, is that cuteness existed as an ideal in nature long before man appeared.

The word "dream" is often associated with Disneyland, particularly by its promotion and publicity people. It is, as they have it, "Walt's Dream" and a place that awakens the desire to dream in the visitor. But the quality of the dreams it represents is most peculiar—no sex and no violence, no release of inhibitions, no relief from real stresses and tensions through their symbolic statement, and therefore no therapeutic effect. It is all pure escapism, offering momentary thrills, laughs and nostalgic pleasures for the impressionable; guaranteed safety for that broad spectrum of humanity whose mental health is predicated on denying that there is any such thing as mental ill health or, indeed, a mental life of any significance beneath the conscious level; guaranteed interest for the technologically inclined; guaranteed delight for those who like to prove their superiority to the mass of men by making fun of their sports.

These levels of enjoyment remain available at Disneyland, but since 1963 there has been something else there, Walt Disney's last great advance in animation, a last mighty thrust toward the ability to simulate physical reality technologically. And this grotesquery, which he called Audio-Animatronics, threatens to change the essentially harmless character of the place.

The story of Audio-Animatronics begins at least as early as 1945 when one of his New York-based executives visited the studio and found Disney "all wrapped up in something mysterious that he was doing with Buddy Ebsen, who in those days was a fine dancer. He had Buddy doing a dance number and there were men in the room punching holes in what seemed to be a mechanical roll. Then I saw Walt playing with little Buddy Ebsen dolls which were attached by electric wires to a huge console-type machine. The men would feed the piano rolls into the console like a continuous IBM card and the little Buddy Ebsen dolls would repeat the dance steps I had seen Ebsen himself do. It didn't work because those were the days before transistors and the equipment was too cumbersome, so Walt put the whole thing aside. But now it is nineteen years later and I go to the World's Fair and I see Walt's Lincoln and fighting dinosaurs and dancing children. It's been refined by electronics but it's the Buddy Ebsen idea all over again. He carried it around with him all of those years until, finally, he was able to make it work."

In fact, Disney did more than carry the idea around with

him: he obsessively fought for its development. By 1955 WED engineers began making 1½-inch model figures that had cam and lever joints. In a short while an electronic-hydraulic-pneumatic approach to the problem of movement was added to the cam-lever devices, and the simple movements required, for example, of that alligator in the jungle ride were made possible. Then came the big breakthrough—the activation, through sound impulses, of pneumatic and hydraulic valves within a performing figure. These impulses, recorded on a magnetic tape, can activate anything in a figure from a simple, gross arm movement to a facial tic and can coordinate them in patterns of amazingly lifelike subtlety. By recording these impulses—as many as 438 of them at any given second—on a thirty-two-channel magnetic tape, they can be perfectly synchronized with music, dialogue, sound and light effects to present an entire show at the touch of a button, a show that, barring a breakdown in the machinery, will never suffer from a human error: no light or sound cue can ever be missed, no actor will ever blow his lines.

There is a certain irony in the development of Audio-Animatronics in that the sophisticated tape technique that forms the basis for its highest development was first perfected as a means of controlling the launching of space rockets. But there is no record that Disney, the Goldwater Republican, hesitated to use such government-sponsored research for his own ends any more than he hesitated to use tax advantages to his own ends. If anything, he probably saw it as some sort of compensation for the spiritual discomfort big government caused him. Certainly, the irony of putting space-age technology to use in an amusement park is not much stressed by Disney's people. Indeed, to them there is a certain implicit fitness about this meeting and mingling of the great forces of the age, Disneyism and electronic scientism, in the former orange groves of Anaheim.

The new Audio-Animatronics system was introduced discreetly in a Disneyland attraction known as "The Enchanted Tiki Room," where audiences group themselves around a bunch of handsomely feathered birds that perch in a small jungle setting and sing and tell jokes. It's a fantasy and the question of how it works is really quite insignificant, since the effect is not an especially arresting one. The same may be said of the use of Audio-Animatronics to give life to three of the exhibits WED ran up for the New York World's Fair of 1964–65. Pepsi-Cola's It's a Small World had a nightmarishly insistent theme song, sung by dolls in all the tongues of the world, but the dolls which seem to sing it are, after all, only toys. The Magic Skyway in which Ford cars moved riders past glimpses of the world in various epochs was morally neutral as was the General Electric Progressland. One was free to enjoy, or not enjoy, according to taste, their applications of Disney's latest technological marvel. Even his use of the technique to create mechanical men to serve as guides to exhibitions was somehow acceptable. They were only a little more disconcerting than a human guide who has been brainwashed and programed by a corporate training program and whose manner and response to stimuli is therefore almost as routinized as that of a robot. But as George Orwell once observed, "so long as a machine *is there*, one is under an obligation to use it." And so Disney's "imagineers" could not resist taking the logical next step.

Which was Great Moments with Mr. Lincoln, the Illinois Pavilion's prime attraction, in which the outer aspects of a man, a man who once lived and walked the earth and who had a unique personality—a soul if you wish—was mechanically reproduced with astonishing fidelity to his known physical dimensions and mannerisms. To Disney, as to most of his audience, Lincoln was the greatest of our folk heroes, the common man raised to the highest level of achievement, both worldly and spiritual. To place his wonderful new machinery in the worshipful service of this mythic figure was, for Disney, an unparalleled opportunity. His love for the Lincoln Legend knew few bounds—he could quote long passages from his speeches—and as for Audio-Animatronics, he thought it was an art comparable in stature to Lincoln's stature as a human being. Says a WED press release: "Walt has often described 'Audio-Animatronics' as the grand combination of all the arts. This technique includes the three-dimensional realism of fine sculpture, the vitality of a great painting, the drama and personal rapport of the theater, and the artistic versatility and consistency of the motion picture." Obviously so great an achievement must not be wastefully confined to the representation of tropical birds and prehistoric monsters.

So Disney labored over Mr. Lincoln as he had not labored to bring forth his Mouse. "Imagination had to be tempered with authenticity," he told a reporter. "Drama must intertwine with serenity. Fantasy would be entirely abandoned, since its presence would defeat our purpose. Reserve was demanded but would have to take the form of subdued excitement. And dignity would have to be the constantly sounded keynote." Thus was the sixteenth president, martyr, hero and summary of the virtues of democratic man turned into a living doll, "capable of forty-eight separate body actions as well as seventeen head motions and facial expressions" (at least in 1965: there was a new, improved model a year later). Disney, caught in the grip of his technical mania and protected by his awesome innocence about aesthetic and philosophical matters, had brought forth a monster of wretched taste which, for all the phony reverence and pomposity surrounding its presentation, leaves one in a state of troubled tension. Are we really supposed to revere this ridiculous contraption, this weird agglomeration of wires and plastic, transferring to it, in the process, whatever genuine emotions we may have toward Lincoln in particular, toward mankind in general? If so, we are being asked to abjure the Biblical injunction against graven images and, quite literally, we are worshipping a machine that is no less a machine for having the aspect of a man. Perhaps, then, it is a form of art? But art is not imitation; its strength lies precisely in the art object's inability to speak or to move and the transcending compensations the artist makes for his inability. Take, for crude example, the Lincoln Memorial in Washington. The huge size of the figure, so often described as brooding, overpoweringly reminds the visitor of his own puniness of size and that Lincoln's spirit was alleged to have been similarly outsized in comparison to the ordinary. The silence of that massive figure encourages one's own reflections on the enigma of greatness. Surely, the atmosphere cues a quasi-religious response, but it does not force a choice between the varieties of religious experience on the spectator as the Disneyland show attempts to do with its effects of lighting and music. Disney's Lincoln, for all its mechanical sophistication, reminds us that Lincoln was only a man; Daniel Chester French's Lincoln suggests that he might have been something more. But perhaps modern man is made uncomfortable by such suggestions. It is easier for him to live with the smaller "uneasiness" Ortega described some years ago when writing about the dummies at Madame Tussaud's. "The origin of this uneasiness lies," he wrote, "in the provoking ambiguity with which wax figures defeat any attempt at adopting a clear and consistent attitude toward them. Treat them as living beings, and they will sniggeringly reveal their waxen secret. Take them for dolls, and they seem to breathe in irritated protest. They will not be reduced to mere objects. Looking at them we suddenly feel a misgiving: should it not be they who are looking at us? Till in the end we are sick and tired of those hired corpses. . . ." He adds: "The mob has always been delighted by that gruesome waxen hoax."

He should only have lived to see Abraham Lincoln rise up from his chair to mouth his carefully selected platitudes, with gestures—and is that a tear glistening in his eye as a mighty chorus of "The Battle Hymn of the Republic" swells behind him? Ortega would have been interested to hear of the curious fact the "imagineers" discovered, quite by accident, about the plastic Mr. Lincoln's skin is made out of; after a while it excretes oils just as the human skin does and so "takes makeup wonderfully," as the press agent eagerly informs you. He would also like to know of the interesting protection afforded Mr. Lincoln's electronic guts down in the basement. Should a fire break out, huge metal doors clang irrevocably shut in thirty seconds and the temperature drops instantly to thirty degrees below zero. A man tending the machinery could get killed, but the dummy would live—or exist, or whatever it does.

What can be said of Mr. Lincoln and of all the other human simulacra that are following him into Disneyland (not far away a group of pirates loots a town and rapes its women, who enjoy the process because, it is explained, they're all old maids) is that he stirs the observer to thought in a way that nothing else in the Magic Kingdom does. Here *is* the dehumanization of art in its final extremity, paradoxically achieved by an ignorant man who was actually, and in good conscience, seeking its humanization and who had, indeed, arrived at this dreadful solution, after a lifetime search for a perfect means of reproducing the reality of human life. At this point the Magic Kingdom becomes a dark land, the innocent dream becomes a nightmare, and the amusement park itself becomes a demonstration not of the wondrous possibilities of technological progress, as its founder hoped, but of its possibilities for horror.

PART ELEVEN

A Final Balance

31 *Sometimes I feel there is a conspiracy to seduce and ruin our youth. I'm sick of sick pictures, offensive sex and bad taste. . . . The movies these days seem more interested in turning your stomach than in warming your heart. And over and over again: What's going to happen now that Walt Disney is dead?*

—Lenore Hershey, quoting responses to a poll of readers in "What Women Think of the Movies," *McCall's*, May, 1967

HE WAS MR. CLEAN NOW. All reference to him as a serious film artist had long since ceased and in a period when traditional middle-class values— indeed, the traditional middle class itself—were being questioned as they had not been since the 1920s, Walt Disney became, in the minds of his public, something more than a purveyor of entertainment. He became a kind of rallying point for the subliterates of our society, the chosen leader for the desultory—and ambiguous—rear-guard action they were trying to fight against a rapidly changing cultural climate. At the very outset of this book it was noted that the period of Disney's greatest economic advance coincided with the years of the greatest economic trials among his competitors.

His solution to their common problem was based primarily not, as some simple souls believed, on the moral uprightness of his films but rather on his ability to convert his operation from a narrow base to a broad one, drawing its revenues not merely from films but from all the other areas he penetrated—right down to a glorified bowling alley, known as the Celebrity Sports Center, in Denver. Just before he died, still greater diversification was in the works: the Mineral King project in northern California was to be not merely a place of entertainment but a place of recreation. The best solution offered by his competitors to the problem of the vanishing audiences in the crisis years was a greater daring in subject matter and a greater frankness in the way they treated love, sex, social problems, language and, indeed, the human form in its unclothed and semiclothed states. The age of what the industry proudly called "the adult film" thus finally arrived

And it did succeed in drawing audiences. But it also confused them. For the age of the adult film was also an age of sensationalism, and not only in the movies, and so it became difficult for ordinary and untutored people to tell the difference between honest realism and dishonest titillation. (A curious instance: in the *McCall's* poll, cited above, the good ladies managed somehow to choose *Who's Afraid of Virginia Woolf?* as both their least favored film and their fourth most favored one. As usual, the mass audience is a hypocritical one, buying tickets to entertainments they later pretend to despise.)

In any case, one of the first casualties of the new Hollywood was the old program feature aimed at the family market—modest situation comedies, chaste adventure films, romances, animal pictures and so on. Products in this vein could be seen any night on television. By default, whatever movie-theater market was left for this sort of thing was left to Disney. And that meant that the confused middle class expected him not merely to cater to their values but to articulate them as well.

It might have been hard for him at first. He had a broad

streak of vulgarity in him: one screen writer quit the studio for a brief time because Disney kept trying to slip bathroom jokes into her scripts, and he insisted on calling a one-time associate and latter-day competitor, "I. P. Freely"—an eight-year-old's crude pun on the man's name. But Disney soon learned the value of the public figure that had been foisted on him. He could hide behind it. He gave freely of his opinions on contemporary screen morality to interviewers, a topic that gave him a ready-made theme for public appearances. His exalted standing thus diverted attention from matters that were of infinitely more interest to him—like converting prosperity into certifiable tycoonship. It has been observed that practical joking, to which Disney had once been addicted, is a last, despairing effort by the fundamentally shy person to establish communication. But the creation of a public personality, behind which the insecure individual can hide and that ultimately may subsume the poor, stunted, incomplete private self, is an even better solution for some people. And so it was for Walt Disney.

This book began with a set of figures, for somehow figures more accurately summarize Disney's achievements than any other data about him can. Along the way, the bench marks of his career have been set forth in statistics about box-office grosses, stock prices, cost figures and so on, for those were the measures he and his associates applied when they spoke most frankly of his progress. As the end of his life approached, the figures piled up higher and higher, and they almost completely obscured the private man. We are left, in the end, not with an individual to try to summarize but with a celebrity, which is quite a different thing.

Even his closest associates found Disney more enigmatic, more difficult to describe or to communicate with in the 1960s. No one spoke of him any more as a father figure. Instead, he was known almost universally to those who worked for him—but always behind his back—as "Uncle Walt." There is a considerable difference between a father and an uncle; one of the prime characteristics of the latter is that he tends to be a rather distant and emotionally neutral figure. As late as the mid-Fifties, associates reported that Disney sat on the lawn near his office after lunch, chatting amiably with employees; he was not observed in public in so relaxed a posture afterward, though strenuous efforts were made to maintain the old down-to-earth image that had served him so well for so long. "Before I met him," Aubrey Menen reports, "every effort was made by his aides to impress me that Walt Disney was, in fact, avuncular. He was open and affable, they said, and easy to talk to. Instead, I met a tall, somber man who appeared to be under the lash of some private demon . . . I remember him smiling only once and he is not at ease." The slender, smooth-faced young man of the 1930s with the thin, retail clerk's mustache and the slick hair that formed a widow's peak had become a portly, somewhat rumpled figure in later life. His face was pouchy, the mustache, like the waistline, had thickened; the smile, when it was offered, flashed too briefly and often seemed to involve only a baring of the teeth; the eyes remained almost hidden beneath the heavy-hooded lids. Listening, Disney had a way of seeming to stare through visitors as if fascinated, as one associate observed, by the sight of "something very small and very ugly at the back of your skull."

The mood of the studio, though outwardly serene, had a certain tension about it. One visiting journalist recalled being warned by a secretary to be sure to accept the glass of tomato juice Disney habitually offered his luncheon guests in his office before taking them over to the commissary, where he, of course, had a corner table commanding a view of the whole dining room where stars and executives eat (there is a cafeteria for the others). The man inquired what would happen if he turned down the proffered refreshment. "I suggest you just take the tomato juice," the girl said with cool finality. The same visitor detected a distinct change in the atmosphere when Disney entered the dining room a little while later. "Everyone's voice shot up about two octaves," he recalled. "All the women began sounding like Minnie Mouse, all the guys started sounding like Porky Pig." He may have exaggerated, but only slightly. For when Uncle Walt came around, anxiety came with him, and like army privates who feel the eyes of the sergeant upon them, his people tended to get very, very busy, very, very preoccupied, hoping they would not be singled out for his attention.

Among the countless stories of his forays into the lower depths of his organization, there is one about the time he set up on a sound stage for one last inspection prior to shipment, all the exhibits WED did for the New York World's Fair. He watched silently as Mr. Lincoln did his turn, then said mildly that he thought it would be wonderful if the effigy could be programed to take one step forward before beginning his spiel. This necessitated, of course, an enormous—and highly complex —effort at electronic revision against a deadline. But Walt's whim was his employees' command, and the task, not strictly necessary to the success of the enterprise, was undertaken. On another occasion Disney dropped in at the Tahitian Terrace in Disneyland, the chief feature of which is an enormous tree placed in the center of the room, where it shelters both spectators and South-Seas-style dancers. Disney took a seat in the top tier and found that the tree's branches partially obscured his view of the floor show. The tree was forthwith ordered pruned, but its proportions were destroyed. So new branches were installed to restore its symmetry. Another time, a visiting magazine editor, allowed to see Lincoln before his public debut, made an innocent inquiry about exactly how precisely the figure's lip movements, when he spoke, matched those of a human being saying the same phrases. Disney immediately ordered an underling to hire a lip reader as a consultant—to assure accuracy in this matter and, perhaps, to reassure himself of his power. No detail was to small for Disney to catch. He ordered Annette Funicello the one-time star of the Mickey Mouse Club who had matured into adolescent roles, never to wear low-cut dresses in order to preserve the modesty of her image—and his. He was forever telling Disneyland guides who erred on the side of formality to be sure to call him Walt. Once at the park he took the jungle-boat ride and to his dismay found that the trip only lasted five minutes. "It should take seven," he told the man in charge. "Do you know how much those hippos and elephants cost? I hardly saw them." Needless to say, the ride was slowed down.

This incessant tinkering with the machinery of his empire was, naturally, costly. But Disney compensated for it by extraordinary stinginess in other matters. In particular, he was notorious for the bargains he and his organization drove with outsiders—actors and, above all, the authors of material on which screenplays and television shows might be based. As strangers, they could claim none of the prerogatives of citizenship in the Magic Kingdom, where, though salaries were low by Hollywood standards, there was security that was unavailable at competing studios (Disney had a sentimental regard for those who had demonstrated their loyalty despite temptations from outside and could scarcely bear to retire them, let alone fire them.) These old retainers, of course, became virtual unemployables elsewhere in Hollywood and so grew each year more dependent on him. The free-lancers, naturally, had no opportunity to build up a symbiotic relationship with Uncle Walt, and to them the studio was often cavalier. Actors got nothing like the top Hollywood salaries, and a participation deal on a Disney film was unheard of. The stars of a Disney movie are utterly interchangeable with others of their types. It was his name, and now, in his absence, it is the studio's name that draws the people. As for the original authors of the stories filmed by Walt Disney Productions, they were often caught in a curious bind. Few other studios were interested in acquiring stories about children or animals, and so there was no one to bid up the prices for them as there often is when a hot best seller goes on the Hollywood market. Running the only game in town,

Disney could often obtain worldwide film rights to a children's book for as little as one thousand dollars, and his alert story department often found short stories and magazine articles that everyone else had passed but that could serve as the basis of a Disney picture and for only a few hundred dollars. Almost never did the original authors get a cut of the merchandising bonanza the studio habitually generated when the story finally reached the screen. (Irony of ironies, some booksellers reported Disney versions of *Mary Poppins* outselling the original Travers novels by 5 to one.) It was Disney's frugal habit to acquire low-cost literary properties in job lots, then put his staff of writers to work Disnifying them. If this could not be done, the loss was small, and no grudge was held against the local talent who bought the works in the first place or failed to translate them into acceptable scripts. There were always plenty of stories where they came from—literature's bargain basement.

On the Disney lot, the only strong personality was Uncle Walt's. He rarely hired a forceful director, a man who would place a strongly individual stamp on a film. He liked men who could work efficiently within the house style—which is why the Disney films tended to look alike in an age when independent production had erased the stylistic trademarks by which one used to be able to tell the difference between a Warner film, for instance, and one from Fox.

Disney's tinkerings were not, of course, confined to Disneyland or his movies. He occasionally toyed with people, too. He used to tell the story of how he had got exactly the revisions he wanted on a script from a writer by dangling before him the opportunity of directing the finished product, a breakthrough the man was particularly anxious to make. Even in Disney's telling, the story had a faintly sadistic ring, however joking Uncle Walt's tone. He also made little attempts to improve, by his lights, relationships between his workers. One executive reported that on his first day at the Disney studio he hollered out his window to ask a gardener to stop mowing the lawn, since it was interfering with his concentration. An hour later, the executive got a call from one of Disney's secretaries, telling him to report to the boss's office immediately. The man rushed to answer the summons and was told, "You spoke harshly to that man. He's been with me for twenty years. I don't want it to happen again." The executive managed a contrite, if startled, "Yes, sir." To which Disney responded, "And there's another thing I want you to remember. There's only one s.o.b. at this studio—and that's me."

So it must have seemed to his employees at times. They always tried to place in the best light his sudden, generally unpremeditated intrusions into their routines. If not seen as the harmless foibles of a genius, they were regarded as evidence of that genius's infinite capacity to take pains with its work. But one must wonder. The incidents described here are all clustered at the end of Disney's life, when his power and his fame were at their height, when, in fact, there were left no real threats to his economic survival. One imagines that all of them were manifestations of a new form of anxiety, the anxiety of absolute command. Elias Canetti points out that "the satisfaction which follows a successful command is deceptive and covers a great deal else. There is always some sensation of a recoil behind it, for a command marks not only its victim, but also its giver. An accumulation of such recoils engenders a special kind of anxiety. . . ." The ultimate sanction of command is, of course, the threat of death, if not physically, then—as in Disney's case—in terms of one's professional life. All commands leave their victims with the memory of this threat, the commander knows this and sees, growing up around him, an ever-increasing number of people who he knows nurture this memory in common; there is always the possibility of revolt should they unite against him. He has no choice but to do "everything he can to make such a reversal impossible."

If this seems a somewhat melodramatic description to apply to an entrepreneur of entertainment, it should be remembered that Disney did everything possible to build a closed world, an empire masquerading as a Magic Kingdom. The construction of such a place represents, of course, a recognition that in the larger world a man's power is necessarily limited, that even absolute dictators cannot control everything or have everything their hearts desire. At the opening of one of Disneyland's newest attractions, a New Orleans square, the mayor of the real New Orleans thought to compliment the creator of the imitation by saying, "It looks just like home." To which the imitator replied, with more than a trace of self-satisfaction, "Well, I'd say it's a lot cleaner." That was, to him, the insuperable advantage his little world had over the great world. He could order it precisely as he wanted to. Compared to the mayor of a modern city, who must feel his way through the traps set for him by what one municipal executive calls "the power brokers," ruling Disney's land—or at least its outer aspects—was easy.

Not that citizenship in the Magic Kingdom was an easy matter. Where could you go to discharge those accumulated memories of threat? They naturally tended to pile up around the master of the domain. That is, perhaps, the reason why Disney always resisted giving the appearance of being a mogul in the more familiar Hollywood style. It was as if he was aware of—and afraid of—just the situation in which he found himself at the end. The informality of his working habits in the beginning, his attempts at creating a family atmosphere, his dream of the utopian studio—were these manifestations of his desire to avoid the anxiety of command while enjoying its privileges? The insistence on carrying over at least some of the forms of the old days—the first naming, the lack of conspicuous consumption in dress, food and style of living, the reams of careful publicity about the creativity of his "team"—were these attempts to mask the "endless, torturing awareness of danger" implicit in the assumption of absolute power such as Disney held in his last years?

Perhaps. Certainly he seemed to fear that suddenly his organization—always in his eyes an extension of himself—might have grown too large for him to control personally as he always had in the old days. This undoubtedly accounts for his insistence on involving himself in the most minute details of script revision, in his attendance at the daily rushes of footage from films in progress, in his fretful fussings over each detail of the construction of new attractions for Disneyland. Everything had to funnel through his office, but even so, things got away from him, things were done without his approval, and worst of all, he was convinced that there were things going on in his world, and in the great world beyond it, about which he knew nothing but that conceivably would harm him and his works.

Talking for public consumption, Disney liked to cite "the four Cs" as the secret of his success—"curiosity, confidence, courage and constancy." But to these surely a fifth must be added—the compulsion to control. The word was constantly on his lips. "We must have control," he would say in discussing a project. Or he would reply to a suggestion, "Oh, no, we'd never do that—we couldn't control it." The writer heard him use the word no less then twenty-five times in the course of one half-hour briefing session with some journalists. Perhaps his morbid fear of death was a manifestation of this need for control—for what is death but the ultimate loss of control over one's destiny? Surely, his stubborn intransigence toward outside financial interests was still another manifestation of this compulsion. At the end, with his organization prospering as never before, he maintained a policy of extremely low dividends—40 cents per share and a 3 percent stock increment—even though the company's earnings per share were the highest in the industry and even though far less profitable entertainment concerns were paying out anywhere from 80 cents to $1.20 per share on stocks selling at lower prices. Apparently, he still resented giving up control of "his" money to stockholders, and also apparently, he feared being caught short as he had been in the past. Said one of his executives, "Everything Walt does today is conditioned by his past problems. When he makes one of his tough deals, he negotiates like he's afraid someone might take another Oswald the Rabbit away from him."

There should be no mistake on this matter. Disney in his last years was capable not only of the small, nervous sadisms that marked his tours of his plant but of larger cruelties as well. The sensitive writer of the book on which Disney based one of his most popular recent films recently said in correspondence that any public discussion of the adaptation was impossible, "for I fear and feel distaste for the streak of brutality that is in him and the ferocity with which he wields the power the contract gives him."

Perhaps he would not have used that power; it is hard to see *how* he might have used it. Anyway, Disney had an image to protect, and the harassment of essentially undefended individuals would not have suited it very well. But it is true that in the last years there was no one to say him nay (which makes his anxieties all the more ironic). His films had passed beyond serious comment by critics, and our social critics had little that was relevant to say about his amusement park or his merchandise or his television program. The only serious criticism of Disney came from that small band of specialists who concern themselves with literature for children. They are not, themselves, always as venturesome as they might be in their critical standards, but they could see just what a perversion the Disney literary product was. The lady who emerged as their leader was Frances Clarke Sayers, gray-haired, semiretired, one-time director of children's services for the New York Public Library, latterly a lecturer in library science at U.C.L.A. The instrument of her emergence was the incredible Dr. Max Rafferty, the right-wing Superintendent of Public Instruction in California, who also writes a weekly newspaper column in Los Angeles. One day in 1965 Rafferty was moved to do a piece extolling Disney as "the greatest educator of this century—greater than John Dewey or James Conant or all the rest of us put together." To

Rafferty Mickey Mouse and his gang were merely the spring-board "from which he [Disney] launched into something unprecedented on this or any other continent—compensatory education for a whole generation of America's children. The classics written by the towering geniuses out of the past who had loved children enough to write immortal stories for them to begin to live and breathe again in the midst of a cynical, sin-seeking society which had allowed them to pass almost completely into the limbo of the forgotten." There was more in this dubious vein, including praise for the Disney live-action films as "lone sanctuaries of decency and health in the jungle of sex and sadism created by the Hollywood producers of pornography," an observation that "beatniks and degenerates" find Disney "square," and a wish that *Mary Poppins* makes $100 million for Disney, so that others would see the profitability of cleanliness, and a peroration as delicious as one could ever hope to find in columnar journalism: "Many, many years from now —decades, I hope—when this magical Pied Piper of our time wanders from this imperfect world which he has done so much to brighten and adorn, millions of laughing shouting little ghosts will follow in his train—the children that you and I once were, so long ago, when first a gentle magician showed us wonderland."

It was all too much for Mrs. Sayers, who fired off a letter to the editor that briskly summarized the case against Disney as follows:

> Mr. Disney has his own special genius. It has little to do with education, or with the cultivation of sensitivity, taste or perception in the minds of children.
>
> He has, to be sure, distributed some splendid films on science and nature, but he has also been a shameless nature faker in his fictionalized animal stories.
>
> I call him to account for his debasement of the traditional literature of childhood, in films and in the books he publishes.

He shows scant respect for the integrity of the original creations of authors, manipulating and vulgarizing everything to his own ends.

His treatment of folklore is without regard for its anthropological, spiritual or psychological truths. Every story is sacrificed to the "gimmick" (Dr. Rafferty's word) of animation.

The acerbity of Mary Poppins, unpredictable, full of wonder and mystery, becomes, with Mr. Disney's treatment, one great, marshmallow covered cream-puff. He made a young tough of Peter Pan, and transformed Pinocchio into a slap-stick, sadistic revel!

Not content with the films, he fixes these mutilated versions in books which are cut to a fraction of their original forms, illustrates them with garish pictures, in which every prince looks like a badly drawn portrait of Cary Grant, every princess a sex symbol.

The mystical Fairy with the Blue Hair of the Pinocchio turns out to be Marilyn Monroe, blonde hair and all.

As for the cliche-ridden texts, they are laughable. "Meanwhile, back at the castle . . ."

Dr. Rafferty finds all this "lone sanctuaries of decency and health." I find genuine feeling ignored, the imagination of children bludgeoned with mediocrity, and much of it overcast by vulgarity. Look at that wretched sprite with the wand and the over-sized buttocks which announces every Disney program on TV. She is a vulgar little thing, who has been too long at the sugar bowls.

Mrs. Sayers extended her remarks in an interview picked up by several publications, and it drew an interesting response. About half her correspondents, a sort of informal anti-Disney underground of parents, educators and librarians praised her for taking a stand on a matter that had long troubled them but that, in the general atmosphere of idolatry surrounding Disney, they had been unable to articulate; the other half reacted with an emotional intensity that was startling. The lines of these correspondents tended to be remarkably similar. "God bless Walt Disney," one of them cried, "in this day of misguided educators . . . and the peddlers of smut and obscenity to whom his artists are repugnant." "In my estimation," chimed in another, "he [Disney] stands for 'Decency—U.S.A.,' " while a third just said, "NUTS."

Disney himself never entered the fray, nor did his studio take any position in the Rafferty-Sayers controversy. In truth, Mrs. Sayers said nothing, in her letter or in the interview that followed, that had not been said before, though few had said it with such delightful acerbity. What is interesting is the intensity of the response she garnered and the fact that even Rafferty had little to say about the artistic quality of Disney's work. He, as well as Disney's other defenders, rested their case entirely on the crudest of moral grounds, and these, in turn, rested on the distinctly unprovable assumption that the nation has entered upon a period of prolonged moral decline. This is not the place to rehearse the arguments for honestly portraying, in works of art, the potential difficulties and pleasures of the sexual encounter or for the unblinking portrayal of the broad streak of violence that exists in American life. It is worth suggesting, however, that in an era of radical change such as we are now experiencing, the most dangerous immorality is to ignore these matters. Nor does it seem necessary to labor the point that Disney's defenders are hopelessly blind to the content of his work, which contained a fairly high quotient of violence—as has been pointed out by his critics from the beginning of his career—and that his work also has a strong, though displaced, sexual element. So far as his audience was concerned, out of sight was out of mind.

None of the foregoing should be construed as an indictment of Disney for not venturing out of the realm of escapist film making in his later years. Few American producers do. What is interesting is that by the end of his career, such argument as

Disney's work excited was carried on strictly in terms that he and his organization had chosen. Vulnerable on aesthetic grounds, they emphasized the wholesomeness of the Disney product and found a ready response to this emphasis among the untutored. One of the most depressing aspects of American life is that nine-tenths of what should be an aesthetic discussion ends up as a totally inapposite moral argument. There can be no serious discussion of the quality of popular culture until there is a general recognition that the significant moral issues it raises are far more subtle than questions of décolletage.

Disney, in short, was fundamentally uninterested in the issues Mrs. Sayers raised. Of all the many states of his realm, literature—or more properly, subliterature—had the smallest claim on his attention. Though he was an avid, even scholarly, reader of screen treatments and scripts, he rarely read the original works on which they were based. As for the reductions of children's classics that went out unobserved by Disney to dimestore and drugstore book racks, he seemed to care nothing about them so long as someone in the organization saw to it that they were clean and decent: these works were merely part of the "total marketing" concept of which the organization was very proud when it was talking to its stockholders or its fellow tradesmen. The books helped create the three billion "impressions" in all media for which the company estimated it achieved through its marketing techniques when it was releasing, for example, its double feature of *The Ugly Dachsund* and *Winnie the Pooh*. Indeed, the nineteen Disney books based on these subjects were rather less important than the tie-in that was engineered with the Kal-Kan dog food company for the same films. Peter and Dorothy Bart, who wrote on Disney and literature, suggested it was possible that "a flowering of Disney books might take place were Walt Disney himself to emerge from his award-lined office and take a more direct and active interest." But, they added, it seemed unlikely that he would, since "the big money is in film and the big gimmickry is in Disneyland, and money and gimmickry have always exerted a spell over Walt Disney."

If there is any consolation for the bookish in all this, it may lie in the Disney organization's not taking a more serious interest in literature. As it is, there is some reason to believe that most of the reading matter it causes to be produced is irrelevant to children. If it is not the positive force it might be, it is probably not quite the disaster many of his critics thought it was. New York schoolmaster Donald Barr summed up this view when he wrote that in a typical Disney book "what has vanished is motive and temperament, all the pulse of life under the skin of events, all the wild hope of someday understanding. Disney's world is not a child's world at all, for a child is a human reading for his future; it is an oldster's world, for an oldster is a human relaxing into his past." Indeed, Barr's words are applicable to almost all Disney's works in the 1950s and 60s.

Disney agreed as to intent, if not as to valuation. "I don't make films exclusively for children," he said. "I make them to suit myself, hoping they will also suit the audience. . . . I've proved, at least to myself and our stockholders, that we can make money, lots of money, by turning out wholesome entertainment. My belief is that there are more people in America who want to smile than those who want to be artistically depressed." He admitted that the works of Tennessee Williams, for example, might be great art, though they were not for him. Sometimes he could even be funny about his prudery, as when pressed for an exact description of the relationship between Mary Poppins and Bart, her street-artist companion, he replied, "They're just good friends." Often, however, he was extremely emotional on the subject. "I don't like depressing pictures," he growled to another reporter. "I don't like pestholes. I don't like pictures that are dirty. I don't ever go out and pay money for studies in abnormality. I don't have depressed moods and I don't want to have any. I'm happy, just very, very happy."

354

Does one detect in the last statement a note of hysteria creeping into the tone? Perhaps. But a note of hysteria tends to creep into this subject, whoever is discussing it. However enlightened some people seem to be on the subject of sexuality, however clear it is that titillating as well as honestly stated examinations of the subject often do extremely well at the box office, it is also clear that while the screen as well as our literature has grown more frank in its treatment of the once forbidden topic, this hysteria has grown. Does it represent the view of an alarmed majority seeing its numbers beginning to shrink? Or does it represent a minority growing increasingly paranoid as it sees its "islands of decency" going under? It is impossible to say. But the tone of the discussion is increasingly shrill.

Disney never addressed himself to this subject, for example, until the 1960s, when it appeared to offer some publicity mileage and when, of course, it suited his new role of elder statesman. One does not deny the sincerity of his beliefs on the matter: they fit too well with the other aspects of his personality. One notes them, finally, as yet another example of his uncanny and unstudied identification with his audience. Indeed, had he not at the same time been so avidly concerned to keep on expanding his empire, one might be tempted to believe that this sudden readiness to take every available opportunity to speak out about morality in art was evidence that he was himself "relaxing into his past."

The public man spent a good deal of time in public-relations activities, from squiring VIP guests around his domain (they always got a signed photo of themselves and Disney, with the wrinkles in Disney's face carefully smoothed by the retoucher's air brush) to accepting spurious awards (a cub scout pack, for instance, made him a replica of the Great Seal of the United States out of forty-five pounds of beans, rice, mustard and sunflower seeds, millet, peas, barley and popcorn kernels). He even received some worthwhile awards, among them the President's Medal of Freedom, the citation for which read "Artist and impresario, in the course of entertaining an age, he has created an American folklore." (When the President pinned the medal on him in 1964, Disney wore a small Goldwater button under his lapel, where Mr. Johnson could not miss it, and he had to be talked out of wearing one big enough to show in news photos.) At the time of his death, a small, informal but worldwide group was promoting—with the covert assistance of his publicity department—his nomination for the Nobel Peace Prize.

But for all these diversions, he continued to work at his customary pace—arriving early and staying late at the studio. In 1964 he ventured away from small-risk film production for the first time in many years, turning out *Mary Poppins* and receiving for it awards and rewards beyond the dreams of avarice. We have seen that Mrs. Sayers, among others, objected to Disney's treatment of the beloved Nanny, but it must be said that, for all the studio's tampering with her character, all its attempts to explain her magic in rationally comprehensible terms, the picture had a charm of its own. The fresh-scrubbed, youthful good looks of Julie Andrews in the title role might have been offensive to *Poppins* purists, but they were welcome to others. If she was not quite the deep-dyed, very English eccentric that P. L. Travers originally portrayed, she was hardly the cream puff that Mrs. Sayers described, either. She had, in the film, a spunky independence to which any child could respond, and she remained acceptably nonconformist in her ways and views and therefore a useful model for children to contemplate. It should be remembered, moreover, that good as the Travers novels are, they are a long way from being literary achievements on the level of *Alice in Wonderland* or the Grimms' fairy tales in the version those strange savants originally set down. They have, at times, a queasy, old-maidish patronization in their writing, and at the most basic structural level, the original books present a serious problem for the adapter in that they are essentially collections of loosely related short stories. They have little cumulative narrative strength (though they have a cumulative emotional attractiveness, which is a different matter). Disney's adapters did quite an artful job in maintaining the major incidents of Miss Travers' first book yet weaving them into a sensible, reasonably suspenseful story. The original books, to be sure, are generally painted in pastel hues, while the Disney film has a bright, sharp-edged definition. But some of what is lost from the original—that sense of wonder and mystery that Mrs. Sayers spoke of—is more than compensated for by the energy and high spirits of the film. In short, it is a likable piece of entertainment, and in its musical numbers, especially the picnic that takes place inside Dick Van Dyke's sidewalk painting and the chimney-sweep dance, it is rather more than merely likable. Indeed, these sequences have a cinematic excitement entirely missing from most film musicals of recent years and far in advance—as the whole film is—of something like *The Sound of Music*, to which it is superior musically, directorially, thespically and even intellectually. It is difficult to explain how, after years of routine production, the Disney organization accomplished this breakthrough. Obviously the willingness to gamble on relatively heavy production expenses has something to do with it; clearly the intrinsic quality of the basic literary material does, too. But it has a sense of style, often lacking in the live-action films, a lack of corniness and sentiment all too often excessively present in the other Disney pictures that sets it apart. The film may have been too sweet for some devotees of the Travers stories, but compared to other Disney work it was a tartly flavorsome venture, with some of the good nostalgic quality he achieved in his early live-action adventures made in England.

It should not be imagined that Disney had no setbacks in this period. As noted, the studio never recovered its early lead in animation, some of its live-action films performed feebly at the box office as well as critically, and the expensive effort to develop a projection system that could entirely surround the viewer—introduced at the Brussels World's Fair in 1959 and also visible at Disneyland and at Expo 67—was a failure. Technologically it worked fine, but there was no way of telling a story or even making a coherent documentary production utilizing a 360-degree screen. Again possessed by his desire to encompass all reality with a quasi-art form, Disney exceeded sensible limits. One can see views—living, superpostcards in the special theater required for this device—one can even be briefly entranced by the sheer marvel of the thing. But it is only a novelty, rather like 3-D movies, not a genuine breakthrough, though one can imagine its being used more imaginatively than Disney's people have, perhaps by some purveyor of mixed-media environments or by an exponent of synthetic psychedelic experience.

All of these setbacks were, however, minor compared to realms of glory opened up by the profitability of *Mary Poppins* and of Disneyland. With the latter able to finance almost unlimited expansion out of its own funds, Disney rushed ahead with even more grandiose real estate ventures. He resented that he had not been able to protect Disneyland from the fast-buck operators who clustered around it, and he would have liked to have a piece of the action obtained by motel and restaurant owners whose business boomed after the park opened. In ten years a quarter of the nation's population had made its way to Disneyland, and the number of available hotel rooms in Anaheim rose from 100 to 4,300; some 250 new businesses located in the area; new sports and convention facilities arose, and the tourist business of this one county is claimed by the locals to exceed that of every other state in the union as well as that of all California's other counties combined. Of the riches that poured in, $273 million went to Disneyland, but another $555 million was spent outside its gates—just outside them.

Disney vowed to rectify that error. And so the organization quietly began buying up land near Orlando, Florida, 27,500 acres of it—twice the size of Manhattan island. He called his new project Disneyworld, and he explained that he needed all that land "to create an environment around the project which would be in keeping with its character and purpose." In short, he would have complete control of it. At its center would be an amusement park, which he originally planned to place under a great dome so that the weather inside could also be controlled. Nearby would be EPCOT (experimental prototype community of tomorrow), housing Disneyworld's employees and any industry that cared to locate north, south, west or east of Eden. The telegram inviting editors to the press conference at which the project was formally announced called it the most significant event in the state's history since its discovery by Ponce de León. Since the organization estimated the capital expenses involved in developing a tract twice the size of Manhattan at perhaps $100 million—who could say the press agent was wrong?

Meantime, Disney pressed ahead with his Mineral King project in northern California—a year-round outdoor resort in a mountain valley, where the "imagineers" were toying with the idea of placing, among other amenities, a restaurant on the top of each of four surrounding peaks. The project's launching was delayed and ultimately killed by a coalition of conservationists after Disney died. And after several millions had been spent on acquiring and planning the site. But that was only one of Disney's latter-day projects.

Before he died he had given land from the studio ranch to serve as the site of a new university, to be devoted to the arts and familiarly known as Cal Arts (he had rejected the idea of putting his name on the place on the ground that students and potential faculty members might be put off by its nonscholarly associations). According to those who worked with him on this project, he was planning for it as he had planned for his commercial ventures—shrewdly purposefully, eagerly. It was, on a grand scale, his old dream of an artist's utopia reconstituted; it was the old studio art classes grown up. A good share of Disney's estate went to this, his last monument, which he saw as a place where all the arts might mingle and stimulate one another, as he had once hoped they might in his movies and as he fondly believed they did in Audio-Animatronics.

In all his last projects one sees clearly "the real mania for totality" so characteristic of our age. One senses also that in these projects Disney was reaching toward a kind of satisfaction he had never found in his motion pictures enterprises. Not long before he died, he told one of his writers that he was no longer interested in "little pictures," that in the future he wanted to concentrate on potential blockbusters of the *Mary Poppins* variety, and given the scale of his operations in late years, this was reasonable. He could afford to risk more now, and there was no need to hedge his bets as he had in the past with movies. Somewhat more saddening was his remark, upon seeing some rushes for *The Jungle Book* which displeased him: "I don't know, fellows, I guess I'm getting too old for animation." In sum, he was leaving behind him—emotionally at least —two careers that would have been enough for most men and beginning to reach out for yet a third.

32 *I count my blessings.*
—Walt Disney, on numerous occasions

IN EMBARKING on that third career, it seems that once again Walt Disney had intuitively sensed the shift of his audience's tastes. Indeed, it is pointless to undertake a book-length investigation of Walt Disney if the author does not believe that, in his link with his audience, Disney was something more than a mere teller of childish stories, a mere maker of childish tricks. To see him as merely the proprietor of a mouse factory is to miss entirely his significance as a primary force in the expression and formation of the American mass consciousness. One must, at last, take him seriously, because whatever the literary content of his works, however immature his conscious vision of his own motives and achievements was, there was undeniably some almost mystic bond between himself and the moods and styles and attitudes of this people. He could not help but reflect and summarize these things in his almost every action. We have lately been taught to understand that the medium is the message, and it seems indubitable that there was a message in each of the media that Disney conquered, a message that transcended whatever he thought—or we thought—he was saying. When we seemed to demand an optimistic myth he gave us the unconquerable Mouse. When we seemed to demand the sense of continuity implicit in reminders of our past, he gave us fairy tales in a form we could easily accept. When we demanded neutral, objective factuality, he gave us the nature films. When, in a time of deep inner stress, we demanded another kind of unifying vision, he gave us a simplified and rosy-hued version of the small town and rural America that may have formed our institutions and our heritage but no longer forms us as individuals. When we demanded, at last, not formal statements but simply environments in which to lose ourselves, he gave us those in the amusement park built and the amusement parks still to come.

His statements were often vulgar. They were often tasteless, and they often exalted the merely technological over the sensitively humane. They were often crassly commercial, sickeningly sentimental, crudely comic. They were easy ones to criticize, and, over-all, they had little appeal to anyone of even rudimentary cultivation. But the flaws in the Disney version of the American vision were hardly unique to him. They are flaws that have crept into it over decades, and they are the flaws almost universally shared by the masses of the nation's citizens.

Balanced against them must be the virtues he shared with his countrymen as well—his individualism, his pragmatism, his will to survive, his appreciation of the possibilities inherent in technological progress, despite the bad odor it often gives off today. Above all, there was the ability to build and build and build—never stopping, never looking back, never finishing—the institution that bears his name. There is creativity of a kind in this, and it is a creativity that is not necessarily of a lesser order than artistic creativity. "The American mechanizes as freely as an old Greek sculpted, as the Venetian painted," a nineteenth-century English observer of our life once said, and it is sheer attitudinizing not to see in our mechanized institutions one of the highest expressions of this peculiar genius of ours. These industrial institutions may ultimately be our undoing, but it is being blind to history not to see that they were our making as well. It is culturally blind not to see that Disney was a forceful and, in his special way, imaginative worker in this, our only great tradition. The only fitting honor to be paid him is to associate him firmly with it and not with some artistic tradition that was fundamentally alien to him and invoked standards inappropriate to the evaluation of of his accomplishments. The industrial and entrepreneurial tradition that both moved and sheltered him was neither more nor less flawed than he was.

And so there is a certain appropriateness about his last works. Film is, after all, a transitory thing, as all works of art are in comparison to that thing that every American knows to abide—the land. Or as we prefer to think of it, real estate. At heart, Disneyland is the very stuff of the American Dream—improved land, land with buildings and machinery on it, land that is increasing in value day by day, thanks to its shrewd development. With its success Disney realized the dream that had been denied his father and that had driven Disney as it drives so many of us. The day before he died, he lay in his hospital bed, staring at the ceiling, envisioning the squares of acoustical tile as a grid map of Disneyworld in Florida, saying things like, "This is where we'll put the monorail. And we'll run the highway right here." Truly, he had found The Magic Kingdom.

Typically, this was a secret he kept to himself. To be sure, he told anyone who bothered to inquire that he was not a producer of children's entertainment, that in fact he had never made a film or a television show or an exhibit at Disneyland that did not have, as its primary criterion of success, its ability to please him. And he often admitted that his great pleasure was the *business* he had built, not the products it created. But he—and most especially his organization—did nothing to discourage the misunderstanding of his work and his motives. And so much did we want to believe that he was a kind of Pied Piper whose principal delight was speaking, for altruistic and sentimental reasons, the allegedly universal language of childhood, so much did we *need* an essentially false picture of him, that the public clung to this myth almost as tightly as an eager Wall Street hugged to its gray flannel bosom the delightful reports on the recent economic performance of Walt Disney Productions. The commercial statistics were powerful enough to send the price of the stock to the highest levels in history *after* Disney died, even though the only foreboding its analysts expressed about it in the 1960s was based precisely on the fear of the founder's death and the inability of his executives to carry on in the great tradition. The myth of the Disney personality became similarly inflated after his passing. It was well expressed by the correspondent of *Paris Match* who, in an obituary cover story (Mickey was displayed in full color, crying), reached an un-precedented—and quite possibly fictive—mawkishness, with his description of the scene at the hospital on the day of Disney's death:

"At St. Joseph's Christmas party, the delighted children were applauding the trained dog act and singing 'Oh, Tannenbaum.'

"The hospital chaplain stepped out of the room where the successful life of Walt Disney had just come to an end.

" 'Lying there, he looks like Gulliver with his dream menagerie gathered around him,' he whispered."

One likes to think that, however pleased Disney might have

been by the sentiment, there was a secret recess of his mind where he kept a rather precise accounting of who he was and what he was. Ray Bradbury, the writer, once conceived the notion of having Disney run for mayor of Los Angeles on the not completely unreasonable ground that he was the only man with enough technological imagination to rationalize the sprawling mess the megapolis had become. He journeyed out to the studio to put the idea to Disney, who was flattered but declined the opportunity. "Ray," he asked, "why should I run for mayor when I'm already king?"

And so he even managed to speak his own best epitaph, the one he always feared someone would speak for him. Like all his other works it seemed fanciful only at first glance. At heart, it was completely realistic.

Acknowledgments

IT IS A PLEASURE to thank the people—many of them strangers—who helped me gather the material on which this book is based. It is a frustration not to be able to acknowledge publicly the assistance of an almost equal number of people, connected in one way or another with the Disney studio, who were generous with their reminiscences and opinions but whom I can best serve by preserving their anonymity. I have no firm reason to suppose that the organization would take reprisals against them, but late in 1966, well after I had begun my research and shortly before Mr. Disney died, I was given to understand that the studio did not approve of this study, and I have no wish to compromise those who spoke to me, many of them before this opposition was formally stated.

I must, however, extend my gratitude to Walt Disney Productions for generously allowing me to join a group of journalists who were given a week-long tour of the studio, WED and Disneyland and who were extended every courtesy, allowed to ask any question and to obtain detailed answers to all of them. I am sorry only that the mood of that trip did not extend a little bit farther, and I remain somewhat mystified by the sudden closing of the studio's doors, particularly after I had already been made privy to so much of what goes on behind them. I feel obligated, moreover, to report to my readers that no pictures of Disney's creations are in this book because the studio denied my request for permission to include such copyrighted material. But I do want to thank all the very kind people who made my trip so pleasant and so deeply informative.

ACKNOWLEDGMENTS

As to those people whose cooperation I can acknowledge, I really do not have words to express my gratitude adequately. All are busy people, but many found time to spend several hours being interviewed. Still others responded with alacrity to queries, dug into their files or memories to supply me with missing facts and, in the process, often volunteered valuable information that I did not know existed. Among them were a group of animators—Arthur Babbitt, Stephen Bosustow, James Culhane, William Hertz, John Hubley, Lou Keller—who conducted a short course in their art with patience, wit and insight. The following people provided me with anecdotes, theories, introductions, references and other passports to The Magic Kingdom: Ray Bradbury, Robert Crichton, Josette Frank, Arthur Knight, Joe Morgenstern, Carol Morton, Harold Rand, Maurice Rapf, Frances Clarke Sayers, Willard G. Triest and William K. Zinsser. Willard Van Dyke kindly arranged for me to screen the Disney short subjects in the collection of the Museum of Modern Art. Mary De Marzo undertook the jobs of researcher and typist and handled both with intelligence and dispatch far above the usual call of those duties.

My editor, Richard Kluger, undertook the lengthy task of encouraging me to attempt this book, fretted with me over its problems and then, having got me into it, had the grace to get me out again, relatively unscathed, by the application of a firm yet sensitive editorial pencil.

I am grateful for the care, concern and interest of two editors, Ruth Kozody of Simon and Schuster and Colin Webb of Pavilion Books.

R.S.

Bibliographical Note

THE FOLLOWING is by no means a complete listing of the books and articles consulted in the preparation of this book. It does, however, name all the works from which direct quotations were taken—with one exception. I have not given citations here for the reviews of individual Disney films. My method regarding reviews was to sample the relatively small number of American newspapers and periodicals that have a tradition of reliable movie reviewing and to select for quotation in the text those reviews that seemed to me most representative of the general critical response to a particular film or the ones that were especially interesting in their own right. All told, a couple of hundred reviews were thus checked, and to list all of them would unnecessarily burden this bibliography. For the record, the publications consulted were: *The Nation, The New Republic, Newsweek, The New York Times*, The New York *Herald Tribune* and *Time*. Also excluded from this listing are a handful of short news items, many of them anonymously written, culled from a file of clippings placed at my disposal by the Disney organization. Though useful to me, I doubt if they would be of interest to the general reader. In any case, my primary purpose here is to acknowledge —with gratitude—my largest debts and to suggest to that handful of readers who may be interested in pursuing this subject still further the directions in which they might most sensibly head. In furtherance of this last objective I have annotated the bibliography with a few critical comments that may prove helpful.

1. Books About Disney or Containing Substantial References to Him

AGEE, JAMES. *Agee on Film.* McDowell, Obolensky, 1958.
BECKER, STEPHEN. *Comic Art in America.* Simon and Schuster,

1959. Contains a short chapter on film animation, with some useful material on the early days of the art.

FEILD, R. D. *The Art of Walt Disney.* Macmillan, 1942. Concentrates heavily on the technical aspects of production at the Disney studio, and is decidedly uncritical in its approach. Nevertheless, it contains some material unobtainable without the cooperation of the Disney Studio, which the author had.

HALAS, JOHN, AND ROGER MANVELL. *Design in Motion.* Visual Communications Books–Hastings House. 1962. An illustrated survey of animation around the world which helps to put Disney's achievements in a wider-than-usual perspective.

JACOBS, LEWIS. *Introduction to the Art of the Movies.* Noonday, 1960. Contains Gilbert Seldes' first review of Disney's short subjects, "Disney and Others," written for *The New Republic* in 1932.

JACOBS, LEWIS. *The Rise of the American Film.* Harcourt, Brace. Now outdated, this survey remains a model of sound historical writing about the period it covers, and its chapter on Disney is an excellent reflection of the esteem in which he was held in the late 1930s.

KNIGHT, ARTHUR. *The Liveliest Art.* Macmillan, 1957. The best of the more recent historical surveys.

LINDSAY, CYNTHIA. *The Natives Are Restless.* Lippincott, 1960. An informal, witty survey of manners and morals in Southern California in the period of Disneyland's rise.

MILLER, DIANE DISNEY (AS TOLD TO PETE MARTIN). *The Story of Walt Disney.* Holt, 1957. An admittedly prejudiced, daughter's eye-view of the man but still the most complete firsthand record of his life and works that we have.

STRAVINSKY, IGOR, AND ROBERT CRAFT. *Expositions and Developments.* Doubleday, 1962. The composer's version of his quarrel with Disney is included.

TAYLOR, DEEMS. *Walt Disney's Fantasia.* Simon and Schuster, 1940. An early example of the nonbook, but it does contain a few useful anecdotes as well as a convenient summary of the film.

TALBOT, DANIEL. *Film: An Anthology.* Simon and Schuster, 1959. Includes Irwin Panofsky's "Style and Medium in the Motion Pictures," originally written in 1934 and later revised. It contains an extremely interesting note on Disney's work.

THOMAS, BOB. *The Art of Animation.* Golden, 1958. Undertaken at the behest of the Disney Studio and therefore somewhat narrow in its viewpoint, the book is nonetheless clearly written, generously illustrated and full of anecdotes about the creative life in Disney's shop.

368

BIBLIOGRAPHICAL NOTE

II. Magazine and Newspaper Articles About Disney and His Works

ALEXANDER, JACK. "The Amazing Story of Walt Disney." *The Saturday Evening Post*, Oct. 31, Nov. 7, 1953. Approving, anecdotal, superficial.

ALPERT, HOLLIS. "The Wonderful World of Walt Disney." *Woman's Day*, Oct., 1962.

BARR, DONALD. "The Winnowing of Pooh." *Book Week*, Fall Children's Issue, Oct. 31, 1965. A short, sharp, sensible critique of Disney's reduction of the Milne classic to fit mass tastes.

BART, PETER AND DOROTHY. "As Told and Sold by Disney." *The New York Times Book Review*, Children's Book Section, May 9, 1965.

BIRMINGHAM, STEPHEN. "The Greatest One Man Show on Earth." *McCall's*, July, 1964. A solid profile in the slick magazine vein.

BREWER, ROY. "Walt Disney, RIP." *National Review*. Jan. 10, 1967. A eulogy in the form of a letter from a determinedly antileftist union leader.

BRIGHT, JOHN. "Disney's Fantasy Empire." *The Nation*. Mar. 6, 1967. An intelligent attempt at a balanced survey of the man's career and his place in our cultural history.

Business Week. "Disney's Live-Action Profile." July 24, 1965.

CHURCHILL, DOUGLAS. "Disney's Philosophy." *The New York Times Magazine*, Mar. 6, 1938. An interview with the master at the height of his acclaim over *Snow White*.

————. "Now Mickey Mouse Enters Art's Temple." *The New York Times Magazine*, June 3, 1934. More about the how of animation than the why of Disney's success with it.

CORLISS, RICHARD. "The New Generation Comes of Age." *Time*, July 20, 1981.

COMPTON, NEIL. "TV While the Sun Shines." *Commentary*, October, 1966. A discussion of animated films for children on television, a very useful appraisal of the current state of the art.

CROWTHER, BOSLEY. "The Dream Merchant." *The New York Times*, Dec. 16, 1966. A good, short appraisal of Disney's career, appearing in the same edition as that publication's extensive and useful obituary.

DAVIDSON, BILL. "The Fantastic Walt Disney." *The Saturday Evening Post*, Nov. 7, 1964.

DAVIS, SALLY OGLE. "Wishing Upon a Falling Star at Disney." *The New York Times Magazine*, Nov. 16, 1980.

DE ROOS, ROBERT. "The Magic Worlds of Walt Disney." *National*

Geographic, August, 1963. An extraordinarily complete trip through The Magic Kingdom, conducted by a coolly admiring guide.

DISNEY, LILLIAN (WITH ISABELLA TAVES). "I Live with a Genius." *McCall's*, February, 1953. Mrs. Disney's only extensive public reminiscence of her life with Walt Disney.

DISNEY, WALT. "The Cartoon's Contribution to Children." *Overland Monthly*, October, 1933. Obviously ghost-written but still an interesting insight into the young Disney's mentality.

——. "The Life Story of Mickey Mouse." *Windsor* (London), January, 1934. Another useful curiosity.

FARLEY, ELLEN. "Disney Heirs' Stock May Be Key." *Los Angeles Times*, April 1, 1984.

FERGUSON, OTIS. "Walt Disney's Grimm Reality." *The New Republic*, Jan. 26, 1938. A sizable essay on *Snow White*, marked by fine taste and perception.

Forbes. "Disney Without Walt . . ." July 1, 1967.

FORSTER, E. M. "Mickey and Minnie." *The Spectator* (London), Jan. 19, 1934. Mr. Forster in his lightest, most charming mood.

Fortune. "The Big Bad Wolf." November, 1934. Anonymous but marvelously complete study of Disney's artistic and financial techniques of the time.

HALÉVY, JULIAN. "Disneyland and Las Vegas." *The Nation*, June 7, 1958. An annoyingly attitudinizing piece.

HARRIS, KATHRYN. "Takeover Talk Adds Pressure as Disney Tries to Snap Back." *Los Angeles Times*, April 1, 1984.

HAYES, THOMAS C. "The Troubled World of Disney." *The New York Times*, Sept. 25, 1984.

——. "Trouble Stalks the Magic Kingdom." *The New York Times*, June 17, 1984.

——. "Disney's Chief is Forced Out." *The New York Times*, Sept. 8, 1984.

HERSHEY, LENORE. "What Women Think of the Movies." *McCall's*, May, 1967.

JOHNSTON, ALVA. "Mickey Mouse." *Woman's Home Companion*, July, 1934. Old-fashioned, slick journalism by a reporter better than his medium.

LOW, DAVID. "Leonardo da Disney." *The New Republic*, Jan. 5, 1942. An expression of enthusiasm by the great British cartoonist.

MCDONALD, JOHN. "Now the Bankers Come to Disney." *Fortune*, May, 1966. Perhaps the best single piece about the total Disney operation—certainly the best of recent years.

BIBLIOGRAPHICAL NOTE

McEvoy, J. P. "Of Mouse and Man." *This Week*, July 5, 1942.

———. "McEvoy in Disneyland." *The Reader's Digest*. February, 1955. Concentrates on the nature films.

Magnet, Myron. "No More Mickey Mouse at Disney." *Fortune*, Dec. 10, 1984. The best single source on recent Disney doings.

Main, Jeremy. "The Kempers of Kansas City." *Fortune*, April, 1967. Contains interesting materials on the city as Disney knew it as a young man.

Mano, D. Keith. "A Real Mickey Mouse Operation." *Playboy*, Dec., 1973.

Marlow, David. "Working for Mickey Mouse." *New York*, April 6, 1973.

Menen, Aubrey. "Dazzled in Disneyland." *Holiday*, July, 1963. Perhaps the best single piece about Disneyland.

Miller, Jonathan. "Another Wonderland." *The New York Times Book Review*, Children's Book Section, May 7, 1967. A fine piece on the art of adaptation.

Morgenstern, Joseph. "Walt Disney (1901–1966): Imagineer of Fun." *Newsweek*, Dec. 23, 1966. A sensitive obituary.

———. "What the Kids Should See." *Newsweek*, Sept. 18, 1967.

Nathan, Paul. "Rights and Permissions." *Publishers' Weekly*, Jan. 2, 1967. Anecdotes about Disney's dealings with the literary world.

Newsweek. "Fifty Million Customers." Mar. 14, 1955. A comprehensive report on the studio in midpassage.

Paris Match. "Farewell to Walt Disney." Dec. 24, 1966. A tearjerker.

Rafferty, Max. "The Greatest Pedagogue of All." *Los Angeles Times*, Apr. 18, 1967.

Reddy, John. "The Living Legacy of Walt Disney." *The Reader's Digest*, June, 1967.

Ross, Irwin. "Disney Gambles on Tomorrow." *Fortune*, Oct. 4, 1982.

Rouse, James. "Rouse on Problems and Wifely Help." *Life*, Feb. 24, 1967.

Russel, Herbert. "Of L'Affaire Mickey Mouse." *The New York Times Magazine*, Dec. 26, 1937. A summary of the varmint's worldwide impact when he was at the height of his fame.

Santora, Phil. "Disney: Modern Merlin." New York *Daily News*, Sept. 29, 30, Oct. 1, 2, 1964. An anecdotal newspaper series.

Sayers, Frances Clarke. "Letters to the *Times*." Los Angeles *Times*. April 25, 1965.

SCHICKEL, RICHARD. "In Computerland with TRON." *Time*, July 5, 1981.

————. "The Great Era of Walt Disney." *Time*, July 20, 1981.

SELDES, GILBERT. "No Art, Mr. Disney?" *Esquire*, September, 1937. The best critical statement about the short cartoons ever written —thorough, sympathetic, sensibly critical.

SHEARER, LLOYD. "What Kind of Motion Pictures Do You Really Want?" *Parade*, Jan. 7, 1962. Contains a long statement from Disney on the need for clean and uplifting films.

VAN DOREN, MARK. "Fairy Tale in Five Acts." *The Nation*, Jan. 22, 1938. Less interesting for what it says than for who is saying it.

Time. "Father Goose." Dec. 17, 1954. A cover story that really covered its subject—critically, sociologically, financially. In all, a superior piece of journalism, ranking with the best treatments of Disney ever written.

————. "Mouse and Man." Dec. 27, 1937. Cover story on the occasion of *Snow White*'s release.

————. "Walt Disney: Images of Innocence." Dec. 23, 1966. An obituary.

TAYLOR, JOHN. "Project Fantasy." *Manhattan, inc.*, Nov., 1984.

WALLACE, KEVIN. "Onward and Upward with the Arts. The Engineering of Ease." *The New Yorker*, Sept. 7, 1963. A piece concentrating on the creature comforts of Disneyland.

WOLFERT, IRA. "Walt Disney's Magic Kingdom." *The Reader's Digest*, April, 1960.

WOLTERS, LARRY. "The Wonderful World of Walt Disney." *Today's Health*, April, 1962.

Variety. "All-Time Boxoffice Champs." Jan. 4, 1967; Jan. 16, 1985.

Other Books Consulted

ARNHEIM, RUDOLF. *Film as Art*. University of California, 1957. Contains several chapters from his earlier *Film* (1933), in which he made the most coherent summary of his theoretical views.

BENDINER, ROBERT. *Just Around the Corner*. Harper & Row, 1967. An excellent short social history of the 1930s, concentrating heavily on the quality of ordinary, day-to-day experience in the depression decade.

CAMPBELL, JOSEPH. *The Masks of God: Primitive Mythology*. Viking, 1959. The first volume of his monumental study of world mythology, the opening chapters contain an excellent summary of this great scholar's theories on the subject.

CERAM, C. W. *Archeology of the Cinema.* Harcourt, Brace & World, 1965. The best study of the inventions that preceded the development of the motion picture camera and projector as we now know them.

CANETTI, ELIAS. *Crowds and Power.* Viking, 1963. Idiosyncratic, insightful study of the will to dominate and the urge to be dominated.

CROWTHER, BOSLEY. *The Lion's Share.* Dutton, 1957. A history of M-G-M, invaluable to any student of Hollywood's greatest age of power.

Disneyland. Arnoldo Mondadori Editore. No date.

ERIKSON, ERIK H. *Young Man Luther.* Norton, 1958. Indispensable to anyone wishing to understand the Protestant mind in any age.

GALBRAITH, JOHN KENNETH. *The Great Crash.* Houghton Mifflin, 1955. Social history at its wittiest and most incisive.

Grimm's Fairy Tales. Pantheon, 1944. The folkloristic edition, with an excellent afterword by Campbell.

HARPER, RALPH. *Nostalgia.* Western Reserve, 1966. A fine little essay on a subject often discussed, rarely studied.

HAUSER, ARNOLD. *The Social History of Art* (Vol. 4. *Naturalism, Impressionism, The Film Age*). Vintage, 1958.

HILLEGAS, MARK R. *The Future as Nightmare: H. G. Wells and the Anti-Utopians.* Oxford, 1967.

HOFFER, ERIC. *The Ordeal of Change.* Harper & Row, 1963.

———. *The Temper of Our Time.* Harper & Row, 1967. Mr. Hoffer's essay on "The Juvenile Temperament" could have been written with Disney and his audience in mind.

HOFFMAN, FREDERICK J. *The Twenties.* Viking, 1955. Literary and social history of the highest order.

HUGHES, JONATHAN. *The Vital Few.* Bantam, 1965. Short studies in the American tradition of entrepreneurship, excellent for placing Disney in the industrial context.

JONES, ERNEST. *Papers on Psychoanalysis.* Beacon, 1961. Contains his classic study of anality.

KAYSER, WOLFGANG. *The Grotesque in Art and Literature.* Indiana University, 1963.

KEMPTON, MURRAY. *Part of Our Time.* Simon & Schuster, 1955. Has a good chapter on the Hollywood leftists of the 1930s and 40s.

LEWIS, C. S. *Of Other Worlds.* Harcourt, Brace & World, 1966. Contains several excellent essays on juvenile taste, on writing for children and on the fairy tale as an art form.

McLUHAN, MARSHALL. *Understanding Media.* McGraw-Hill, 1964.

BIBLIOGRAPHICAL NOTE

MELLERS, WILFRID. *Music in a New Found Land*. Knopf, 1964. Though the metaphor is modern American music, this is a profound study in national character as well.

MENNINGER, KARL. *A Psychiatrist's World*. Viking, 1959. The Kansas doctor includes in this huge collection of articles several bearing directly on the country and society that shaped Disney's personality.

ORTEGA Y GASSET, JOSÉ. *The Dehumanization of Art and Other Essays*. Princeton University Press, 1948.

ORWELL, GEORGE. *The Road to Wigan Pier*. Harcourt, Brace, 1958. Has some of his most interesting reflections on the mass mind in an industrial age.

SCHLESINGER, ARTHUR M., JR. *The Age of Roosevelt* (Vol. 1. *The Crisis of the Old Order*). Houghton Mifflin, 1957.

VEBLEN, THORSTEIN. *Absentee Ownership*. Beacon, 1967. The chapter on the country town is a great essay in descriptive sociology and invaluable to an understanding of a little-studied force in our culture—and certainly in Disney's.

WHALEN, RICHARD J. *The Founding Father*. New American, 1964. Good on film finance.

WILSON, EDMUND. *The Shores of Light*. Farrar, Straus & Young, 1952. His review of Alva Johnston's *The Great Goldwyn* contains his thoughts on Disney as well as the Hollywood mogul as a type.

Other Material

WALT DISNEY PRODUCTIONS. Proxy Statement, Annual Meeting of Stockholders, Feb. 2, 1965. This meeting was asked to approve the purchase of WED Enterprises by Productions, and the statement contains a lengthy section on the history of both companies as well as the proposed purchase agreement itself. Both are invaluable to the student of the corporation's history.

————. Walt Disney Productions Presentation to New York Society of Security Analysts, Mar. 18, 1966. The transcript of the remarks by Roy Disney, by treasurer Laurence Tryon and vice presidents Donn B. Tatum and E. Cardon Walker is the most detailed statement of the company's recent history, its worth and its prospects available anywhere—a treasure trove for the researcher.

————. *The Disney World*, Vols. 3, 4, 5, 1966–67. The firm's six-times-a-year house organ is a handsomely produced, well-written and—naturally enough—somewhat narrowly focused record of life in The Magic Kingdom. It is, however, full of the most fascinating tidbits.

Index

INDEX

376

INDEX

INDEX

INDEX

Little Nemo, 99
Living Desert, The (film), 287–89, 309
Lloyds Film Storage Company, 96
Lost in Space (television series), 303
Low, David, on Disney, 190
Lullaby Land (cartoon), 153
Lumière brothers, 98–99

McCay, Winsor, 99, 100
Macdonald, Dwight, 210
MacDonald, John, 32
MacDowall, Roddy, 34
McLaren, Norman, 204
McLuhan, Marshall, 13, 194, 210
MacMurray, Fred, 299–300, 302–5
Mad Hatter, 296
Mad Love (film), 89
Main Street, U.S.A. (Disneyland), 48, 322–24
Make Mine Music (film), 276
Mannes, Marya, 210
Marlow, David, on Disney, 382
Martin, Pete, 146
Marty (film), 26
Marx Brothers, 302, 306
Mary, Queen of England, 159, 166
Mary Poppins (film), 136, 156, 283, 299, 304, 305, 345, 351, 356–57
    Disney's financial interest in, 31
Mason, James, 300
Mass communication, problem of, 43
Matterhorn ride (Disneyland), 324
Maurois, André, 68
Mayer, Louis B., 88, 251–52
Mellers, Wilfrid, 306
Melody Time (film), 277
Menen, Aubrey, on Disneyland, 23, 323–24, 342
Menjou, Adolphe, 252–53
Menninger, Karl, 47, 52
Merchandising program, Disney's, 162–165
Metro-Goldwyn-Mayer, 88, 138, 415
Mickey Mouse, 53, 60, 115–35, 189, 202, 211
    Academy Award for, 149
    audience for, 158–59, 166–68
    The Band Concert, 132, 223–24
    changes in, 132, 139–42
    designing of, 34, 115–18
    Disney unable to draw, 33–34
    in *Fantasia*, 239, 240, 242
    foreign market and, 159, 165–70

merchandising of, 162–65
    Plane Crazy, 50, 118, 126, 128–29
    Steamboat Willie, 50, 120–24, 130–132, 143
Mickey Mouse comic strip, 163
Mickey Mouse clubs, 20, 167
Mickey Mouse watches, 163
Mickey's Nightmare (cartoon), 166
Mickey's Revue (cartoon), 140
Midwest, the, nature of, 70, 72–75
Military insignia in World War II, 272
Miller, Diane Disney (daughter), 30, 36, 58, 80, 165
    on *Snow White*, 220
Miller, Fred, 133
Miller, Jonathan, 225, 226
Miller, Ronald W. (son-in-law), 30
Mills, Hayley, 307
Milotte, Al, 284–87
Milotte, Elma, 284
Mineral King (recreation area), 16–17, 24, 52, 340, 359
Minnie Mouse, 118, 128–29, 130, 142
Minter, Mary Miles, 91
Mintz, Charles, 103, 106, 110–12
Mr. Terrific (television program), 303
Model train, Disney's, 35, 61, 282
Monstro, 232
Montalvo, García Ordóñez de, 89
Montgomery, Robert, 251, 252
Moonspinners, The (film), 89, 307
Morey, Larry, 217
Morgan Stanley & Company, 412, 414
Morgenstern, Joseph, on Disney, 30
Morgenthau, Henry J., Jr., 270
Mother Pluto (cartoon), 224
Moving sidewalk, Disney's, 32
Multiplane camera, 195–201, 231–32
Mumford, Lewis, 73
Murphy, George, 35, 157, 253
Music
    classical, Disney's use of, 127–28, 212–13, 239–47
    in early sound films, 120–23, 131–32
Mussolini, Benito, 159, 167
Mutiny on the Bounty (film), 126
Mutt and Jeff (cartoon series), 100
Mutt and Jeff (comic strip), 96
My Three Sons (television series), 302

Nash, Clarence, 141, 416

INDEX

INDEX

RKO Radio, 214, 309
Rob Roy (film), 292, 293
Robin Hood (Disney's film), 292
Robin Hood (Douglas Fairbanks' film), 90
Rockefeller, Nelson, 93, 220, 263
Roger Ramjet, 205
Roosevelt, Franklin D., 154, 159, 166–167, 251
Roosevelt, Theodore, 99
Rorty, James, 137
Rosenberg, Joseph, 214–15
Rosita (film), 90
Rothafel, S. L., 124
Rotoscope, 218
Rouse, James, on Disneyland, 23
Rules of the Nautical Road . . ., 270
Russia, Mickey Mouse in, 166

Sabu, 267
Saludos Amigos (film), 272–73
Saturday Evening Post, The, 59, 146
Savage Sam (film), 307
Sayers, Frances Clarke, criticism of Disney by, 349–52, 355, 356
Schlesinger, Arthur M., Jr., 17
Screen Actors Guild, 251–52
Screen Cartoonists Guild, 251, 253–60
Seal Island (short subject), 285
Sears, Ted, 152
Seldes, Gilbert
 on Disney's work, 223–24
 on Mickey Mouse, 139
Sennett, Mack, 88
 on D. W. Griffith, 185
Seversky, Maj. Alexander de, 273–75
Shaggy Dog, The (film), 299
Silly Symphonies (cartoon series), 127, 134, 141, 148–50, 153, 156
Singin' in the Rain (film), 278
Sixth Symphony (Beethoven) in *Fantasia*, 240, 241
Skeleton Dance, The (cartoon), 127, 132–33, 213, 242
"Slapstick" comedy, 94
Sleeping Beauty (animated film), 28, 178, 234, 297, 299
Smith, Webb, invention of storyboard by, 147–48
Smuts, Jan Christiaan, 167

Snow White and the Seven Dwarfs (Disney's film), 132, 156, 176, 177, 207, 211, 235
 Academy Award for, 231
 credits for, 190–91
 fearful scenes in, 220–22
 finances of, 151, 213–15, 229–30
 production of, 142, 170–71, 175, 184, 195, 197, 206, 215–18
Snow White and the Seven Dwarfs (Marguerite White's film), 60
"Some Day My Prince Will Come" (song), 197, 217
Son of Flubber (film), 299
Song of the South (film), 276–77
"Sorcerer's Apprentice, The" (Dukas) in *Fantasia*, 239, 240, 242
Sorrell, Herb, 257, 260, 261
Sound, early use in films of, 118–24, 131–32
Sound of Music, The (film), 357
South America, Disney's goodwill tour of, 263–64, 272
Southern California, U. of., Disney's honorary degree from, 231
Speedy Gonzales, 202
State's-rights distributors, 125
Stampfer, Simon Ritter von, 98
Stanford Research Institute, 310–11
State Department, Disney's goodwill tour for, 263–64, 272
Steamboat Willie (cartoon), 50, 120–124, 130–32, 143
Steele, Tommy, 304
Stockholm, Disney's cartoons in, 169–170
Stokowski, Leopold, work on *Fantasia* by, 238–40, 246
Storyboarding, invention of, 147–48
Strange Interlude (film), 149
Stravinsky, Igor, 241, 244–45
Strike by Disney's employees, 134, 249–262
Stroboscope, 98
Sturges, Preston, 302
"Style and Medium in the Motion Pictures" (Panofsky), 130
Submarine ride (Disneyland), 324–25, 331
Sullivan, Pat, 96
Sweden, Mickey Mouse in, 167–68, 169–70
Sword and the Rose, The (film), 292
Sword and the Stone, The (animated film), 234

382

INDEX

Richard Schickel has been a film critic for
Time magazine since 1973 and is also a writer-
producer of television documentaries about the
movies and Hollywood. His many books include
*D. W. Griffith: An American Life, His Picture in the
Papers, The Men Who Made the Movies,* and *Intimate
Strangers.* He lives and works in Los Angeles.

ELEPHANT PAPERBACKS

American History and American Studies
Stephen Vincent Benét, *John Brown's Body,* EL10
Henry W. Berger, ed., *A William Appleman Williams Reader,* EL126
Andrew Bergman, *We're in the Money,* EL124
Paul Boyer, ed., *Reagan as President,* EL117
Robert V. Bruce, *1877: Year of Violence,* EL102
Philip Callow, *From Noon to Starry Night,* EL37
David Cowan and John Kuenster, *To Sleep with the Angels,* EL139
George Dangerfield, *The Era of Good Feelings,* EL110
Clarence Darrow, *Verdicts Out of Court,* EL2
Floyd Dell, *Intellectual Vagabondage,* EL13
Elisha P. Douglass, *Rebels and Democrats,* EL108
Theodore Draper, *The Roots of American Communism,* EL105
Joseph Epstein, *Ambition,* EL7
Lloyd C. Gardner, *Pay Any Price,* EL136
Lloyd C. Gardner, *Spheres of Influence,* EL131
Paul W. Glad, *McKinley, Bryan, and the People,* EL119
Sarah H. Gordon, *Passage to Union,* EL138
Daniel Horowitz, *The Morality of Spending,* EL122
Kenneth T. Jackson, *The Ku Klux Klan in the City, 1915–1930,* EL123
Edward Chase Kirkland, *Dream and Thought in the Business Community,
    1860–1900,* EL114
Herbert S Klein, *Slavery in the Americas,* EL103
Aileen S. Kraditor, *Means and Ends in American Abolitionism,* EL111
Irving Kristol, *Neoconservatism,* EL304
Leonard W. Levy, *Jefferson and Civil Liberties: The Darker Side,* EL107
Thomas J. McCormick, *China Market,* EL115
Walter Millis, *The Martial Spirit,* EL104
Nicolaus Mills, ed., *Culture in an Age of Money,* EL302
Nicolaus Mills, *Like a Holy Crusade,* EL129
Roderick Nash, *The Nervous Generation,* EL113
William L. O'Neill, ed., *Echoes of Revolt: The Masses, 1911–1917,* EL5
Gilbert Osofsky, *Harlem: The Making of a Ghetto,* EL133
Edward Pessen, *Losing Our Souls,* EL132
Glenn Porter and Harold C. Livesay, *Merchants and Manufacturers,* EL106
John Prados, *The Hidden History of the Vietnam War,* EL137
John Prados, *Presidents' Secret Wars,* EL134
Edward Reynolds, *Stand the Storm,* EL128
Richard Schickel, *The Disney Version,* EL135
Edward A. Shils, *The Torment of Secrecy,* EL303
Geoffrey S. Smith, *To Save a Nation,* EL125
Bernard Sternsher, ed., *Hitting Home: The Great Depression in Town and
    Country,* EL109
Bernard Sternsher, ed., *Hope Restored: How the New Deal Worked in Town
    and Country,* EL140
Athan Theoharis, *From the Secret Files of J. Edgar Hoover,* EL127
Nicholas von Hoffman, *We Are the People Our Parents Warned Us Against,*
    EL301
Norman Ware, *The Industrial Worker, 1840–1860,* EL116
Tom Wicker, *JFK and LBJ: The Influence of Personality upon Politics,* EL120
Robert H. Wiebe, *Businessmen and Reform,* EL101
T. Harry Williams, *McClellan, Sherman and Grant,* EL121
Miles Wolff, *Lunch at the 5 & 10,* EL118
Randall B. Woods and Howard Jones, *Dawning of the Cold War,* EL130